Tracy + Ben's story ♡

OH, WHAT THE FUDGE

LOVE ON BELMONT
BOOK TWO

LORI WOLF-HEFFNER

Editing by Susan Fish and Jennifer Dinsmore

Cover design by Fresh Design

Cover photograph from Shutterstock

Author photograph by Erin Watt Photography

Print ISBN: 978-1-989465-29-5

Ebook ISBN: 978-1-989465-30-1

Head in the Ground Publishing

Waterloo, Ontario, Canada

headintheground.com

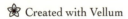 Created with Vellum

To Corey, for being the rock I needed

PROLOGUE

The *Love on Belmont* series is generally free of explicit content. This means no naked bedroom scenes and no swearing. However, on a few occasions, Ben couldn't control his language and had to swear. He asks for your forgiveness in this matter.

CHAPTER 1

Oh, fudge.

Tracy stormed into Claire's Tea Shop, the door closing off the brisk fall wind behind her. She beelined for the counter and dispensed with the niceties to her best friend, Pauline, the owner. She needed something chocolatey.

Now.

How was she going to tell Pauline what had just happened? And that was on top of everything else that had happened to Tracy this morning, which was on top of everything already happening this month.

But *this* was the cherry truffle, and Tracy absolutely despised cherry truffles.

"I need the best you've got from David's chocolate shop. And a cup of Earl Claire. Pronto."

Pauline and Todd—Pauline's employee-turned-romantic-partner—put Tracy's order together. Tracy dropped a twenty on the counter while Pauline pulled a brownie from the display case below. The instant Pauline set a fork on the plate, Tracy dug in. She closed her eyes as the layers of flavour she so savoured in David's chocolate danced in her mouth.

"Oh, Pauline, this is perfect." She took another bite and let the crumbs carry the sweetness and hints of cocoa bitterness to her tastebuds. "Get me a second piece right away. I'm going to need it." The news was that bad.

Pauline did as requested. "I'm going to assume this means you're not okay," she said. "I know it's quarter-end and that Eric's going to start as the new CFO next week, but this much chocolate is out of character even for you."

Tracy answered with a full mouth. "If only you knew."

Todd brought over Tracy's tea, a blend of black tea, lavender, bergamot, vanilla, and rose petals. The scent of the lavender alone helped relax Tracy a smidge.

But just a smidge.

"I've got the counter," Todd said to Pauline.

Tracy was grateful. Usually not one to shy away from difficult subjects—as an executive assistant, her job was to get things done, no matter how great the challenge—she couldn't bring herself to address this one straight on. After she and Pauline had lost touch with each other for the better part of twenty-some-odd years, they had rekindled their old friendship this past summer. Pauline had returned to town, where she had simultaneously taken over her mother's tea shop and helped heal the rift that had grown between Tracy and her teenaged son. Now Pauline was taking time out of her busy day to invite Tracy to talk. She truly was the embodiment of the words "best friend."

Pauline carried Tracy's tea and second brownie to a table in a quiet corner of the café half of the cozy tea shop. Tracy followed. After they sat down, Tracy pulled out her phone to check that Austin was still in school. Good. If his medication was going to send him home, it would've done so by now. She put the phone away and continued chowing down on the brownie.

"Talk to me," Pauline said. "When you come over lunch hour, you usually start with lunch. That's a super-rich brownie, and you're..."

Tracy scooped up the last crumbs with her finger.

"Okay, you're done the first one."

Tracy sighed. "It's not only work. David's caught pneumonia and can't do the rest of the marketing for the Belmont Village Autumn Festival."

Pauline nodded. "Mom called this morning to let me know. I didn't want to start your Monday morning off by telling you."

"Cecilia called me from the hospital to tell me hubby wasn't doing so well. But to top off my Monday morning..." Here came the big news. "My car's in the garage because of a—wait for it—peregrine falcon."

Pauline's final full-time mascot job had been as Perry the Peregrine for the Toronto Peregrines, a major league men's hockey team.

"I'd laugh if your story didn't involve a car accident," Pauline said. "Not to mention everything else going on in your life."

The rest of the car story got stuck in Tracy's throat. She needed more chocolate. She dove into the second brownie. "Tell me about it!" she said, her mouth full.

"Are you okay? Was anyone else involved? Are they okay?"

Tracy nodded as she took another sip of tea. *Tell her now in case he comes here.*

He being Pauline's former manager, a control freak who'd forced her to sign a million-dollar non-disclosure agreement to play Perry. Pauline had signed—it had been her dream job. But when she'd had to quit after only three years, she never wanted to see him again. Her last day had only been a few weeks ago. Pauline's anger was still fresh.

Tracy had to break it to her. Chocolate coursing through her veins, she blurted it out. "I was driving by the TV station on King Street where that peregrine family lives, and I guess one was diving for food or something. Anyway, it spooked me. I got disoriented for a moment because of all the new light-rail tracks, and I slammed on the brakes. But the car behind me was going too fast to stop and he nicked me as he swerved to avoid hitting me. Then he hit the LRT platform, causing a bunch of damage to his oh-so-beautiful red Porsche, which is now also being repaired at the Belmont garage."

There. She'd said *red Porsche* with a drip of sarcasm. That should give Pauline a hint.

Instead, Pauline wrapped an arm around Tracy's shoulder and softly squeezed. Despite being a ball of energy and a six-foot-tall wall of muscle from weightlifting, Pauline could also be incredibly quiet and gentle. All those years in costume had taught her to listen. David's chocolate had been comforting Tracy for most of her forty-eight years, but Pauline's friendship was even more soothing.

"No wonder you're diving straight into the chocolate and tea. The accident, no marketing coordinator on the committee you're chairing, *and* you're going to have to work with your ex-husband. But you're sure you're okay? Do you need anything? Now I feel bad for charging you." Pauline stood up. "Let me get you a refund."

Tracy pulled her back down onto her chair. "I'd never expect a refund for something like this. And yes, I'm fine. My car's just getting inspected to make sure it's safe to drive, and Mayumi has to do a quick touch-up on the bumper." She took another bite of chocolate. "It's almost been a year since the separation but I still hear Eric in my head: 'You don't want to take any risks.' This time, though, he'd be right."

"Then what's worrying you? Are you concerned the other driver is going to sue you?"

Tracy almost choked. She *had* to tell her. Although Pauline wasn't the type to kill the messenger, with this kind of message, she couldn't be too sure. "How many people do you know who drive a red Porsche?"

Pauline's eyes popped open and darted in the direction of the garage. "He's not across the street, is he?"

A LAUGH CAME out of his phone. "Of course that would happen to you! Just watch your language when you go in there. This isn't the Toronto Peregrines' locker room."

Just his luck. The moment Ben wanted to cross the street, cars of myriad makes and models crawled past. Kitchener drivers. But where had all this traffic come from?

He pressed his phone closer to his ear so he could better hear his younger sister as he continued down the sidewalk. "This is a post-industrial, stick-in-the-mud town. Besides, Pauline doesn't run a hoity-toity tea shop. It's near some old factory. So, it's not like I'm in an upscale Toronto neighbourhood or anything."

"Ben! I hope you're not planning on saying that when you walk in there!" Susie cautioned.

"It's been a rough day already. I'm so f—"

"Benjamin!"

Ben groaned. "Don't call me that. You know I hate it."

"Someone has to since Mom and Dad passed away. You keep telling me about how important context is in business, so let me offer you some: you'll be in Pauline's business. Watch your language."

More cars? The world was rubbing in the fact that he'd have no wheels for at least a week. Because apparently life wasn't bad enough already.

"Things were rocky between me and Pauline but they ended on a good note."

"Things were rocky between you for *three years*. Just because they ended well doesn't mean she's going to put in a good word for you with her best friend, *who you were tailgating*!"

Ben groaned. "I didn't know it was her until after. I mean, what are the chances? Besides. It wasn't *exactly* tailgating. I was just kind of close. Tracy was going too slow."

"Too slow? Or the speed limit?"

"You can go ten over without getting a ticket."

Susie let out a sigh of frustration. "Change your attitude before you go in there. Based on everything you've told me, I'm pretty sure Pauline's not going to be happy to see you."

Ben pushed up his sunglasses as he rubbed his eyes. He'd had a job to do, so he did it. It wasn't his fault that Pauline's contract obligated her to never tell her family and friends that she played Perry. A video of the previous actor completely drunk with Perry's mask off had gone viral. *Perry the Pissed Peregrine*. Ben had kept his job by having the team's lawyers create an ironclad contract to ensure the incident wouldn't repeat itself.

Besides, he was certain he and Pauline had patched things up at the end. She'd told him he'd given her the best job of her ten-year career as a sports mascot. Why wouldn't she help him this once and convince Tracy to be his reference for the chief marketing officer position at her company? That idea had also seemed ironclad—or it had until Tracy slammed on her brakes.

He looked both ways along Belmont Avenue. "Does

everyone in Kitchener drive this road on their lunch?" He shifted his laptop bag to his other shoulder.

"Isn't there a crosswalk?"

"Sure. Ten steps back or so."

"Ben! Sometimes you're impossible." But Susie was laughing. "I still think you should take a break for a bit and think things over."

"I need a job, Suse. I can't do nothing."

Susie sighed. "I know." But there was doubt in her voice. "That's why we decided on your drive to New Hamburg that this was probably your strongest first step on your job hunt. But are you sure you don't want to just ask Tracy directly? Might not rock the boat as much."

Ben was sure. Back in the summer, Tracy had convinced him to publicly unmask Pauline at a major hospital fundraiser to show that a woman was underneath all that fleece. It had been a tremendous success. Only later that night did Ben understand he'd been tricked: the publicity stunt had essentially released Pauline from her non-disclosure agreement.

If things had stopped there, then yes, it would've made sense to ask Tracy first.

Except very few people could outsmart Ben. When that quality appeared in a woman in business attire...he found that very attractive. He wouldn't have acted on his attraction—he was a professional. But...he remembered it now with a smile... as he approached Pauline's change room that night, he had passed Tracy, and a gear shifted between them. Before he knew it, he was pinned against a wall as she murmured something about his hazel eyes. His smile grew as he recalled that intense kiss.

He had been less happy when he drove all the way to Kitchener only for her to turn down his offer to work under him—professionally!—after his promotion to marketing director.

She'd said something about the drive being too much. He had been disappointed: she would've made the perfect PR manager with her administrative background, understanding of public sentiment, attention to detail, knowledge of messaging, and ability to outsmart even him. Not that they would have worked together for that long, as it turned out.

A Maserati drove by, as if to add insult to injury that his beloved Porsche Panamera was being repaired. He dragged his feet back to push the crosswalk button. "Pauline smiled when she shook my hand on her last day. We're fine."

"Probably because she was looking forward to moving on."

Ben groaned. "You've been my rock for so long, Suse, and I appreciate it, but the last thing I need today is more honesty."

Her voice softened. "I'm sorry. You've got a good heart, but it doesn't help if I'm the only person who sees it. Just don't be…harsh."

The crosswalk signals flashed, and traffic finally stopped. Ben crossed the street, feeling again Tracy's soft, curvy body pressed against him that night. And her enticing lips desiring his.

But he'd stood next to her as the garage shop owner wrote down her contact info. Her silence toward him had told Ben where he stood now: in the mud.

No. She was Pauline's best friend. Tracy probably envisioned him more in a quicksand pit while she cursed him with a slow death.

Susie was right. He needed to prepare himself for the eventuality that Pauline wouldn't be too welcoming.

After working in marketing and public relations for a major league franchise for several years, Ben knew a lot of people in high places but he wasn't about to approach them for help: word of his firing would travel faster than a Formula 1 race car.

That left him with no other connections to help him than Tracy and Pauline.

He just hoped that Tracy hadn't gone to Claire's Tea Shop: that would thwart his plans even more. She'd probably taken a cab back to work, anyway.

As he passed the cars parked in front of the plaza and the store façades that covered the plaza's original red brick, he looked around him at the Belmont neighbourhood with a few brown-bricked apartment buildings and a mixture of small houses built long before cookie-cutter houses became the norm. The tall buildings of downtown Toronto felt like a fortress. Protective. Kitchener's much lower skyline and open neighbour-hoods left him feeling exposed. Vulnerable.

"I wish I could come home earlier so you wouldn't be alone right now," Susie said. "But Genny's mom's coming around to accepting the two of us together. We really need this time with her parents."

Ben could hear the regret in her voice. "No, no. Stay there. You're home in a few days. I'm glad things are looking up for the two of you. I can't believe I didn't know you're in Quebec City this weekend."

"You'll get through this."

He stared at the sign over Claire's Tea Shop again, the reality of his situation finally sinking in. "I'm not so sure. I worked for the Peregrines for ten years. I wasn't expecting to get fired this morning."

Ben ran his hand through his hair. Maybe his sister was right. Maybe he should continue to New Hamburg.

And do what? Mope? That wasn't what Ben Landry did. He sighed.

"I heard that," Susie said. "What is it?"

"Nothing."

"Benjamin…"

Seeing Claire's Tea Shop reminded Ben of nothing good. Only Earl Claire, lots of despair, and an attraction that had ended in rejection.

Great. His marketing mind was still working, only it was using his current situation to create sad jingles about his life.

Cue depressing music.

"Ben? Are you okay? You're going to be nice to Pauline, right? And you're not going to swear, especially in front of her customers?"

But Ben wouldn't have a chance to talk to Pauline first because Tracy was staring right at him through the front door of the tea shop.

"Oh, f—udge," he said aloud.

CHAPTER 2

$\mathcal{T}$racy had been looking for her taxi, which pulled up at the same moment as she saw Ben walking through the row of parked cars.

She was trapped.

Escaping through the back room would look terribly odd to Pauline's customers. Pauline had returned to serving—she was working hard to increase business, something her mom hadn't had the energy to do in the final years she owned the store. Tracy wouldn't do anything to hurt Pauline's efforts.

But the twenty minutes she'd spent at the garage listening to Ben curse like a hockey player were twenty minutes she'd never get back. It helped deaden the depressing discovery that desire still flickered inside her. For him. Thankfully, the flicker resembled more a match about to burn out than a bonfire lit to keep mosquitoes away.

But it was still there.

Ben had not only helped raise millions of dollars in the name of research for the children's hospital, but he'd allowed Austin his life dream of dancing alongside Todd, who had been a world-famous ballet dancer before he served tea in Belmont Village.

After the event, Tracy had gone looking for Pauline to thank her once more for her help with Austin when a voice coming up from behind her caught her attention.

"They kept saying how proud Mom would've been of me. This is probably the most incredible thing I've ever done in my life," Ben said, cutting off the conversation and hanging up the phone the moment he saw Tracy.

But Tracy hadn't become a successful executive assistant by ignoring people's tone of voice and body language. In that moment, she'd witnessed a Ben Landry she'd never suspected. That moment of vulnerability was all it took to unlock her desire.

His hazel eyes looked down at her.

She took a step closer to him.

His breathing quickened.

So did hers.

Both brought their lips closer.

Would this encounter be bittersweet? Delicious? Rich?

The temptation to find out overpowered Tracy, and she wrapped one hand around his waist and reached the other around his head. Ben enveloped her in his arms as their lips touched. Unable to hold back, Tracy pressed him against the wall and soon found herself enjoying a delicious, rich, smooth, triple-fudge-chocolate kiss.

By the time Ben had come to Kitchener in the summer to make her a job offer, Tracy had come to her senses. She acknowledged to herself how much Ben had hurt Pauline and her family with his silly contract and management practices. She reminded herself she couldn't in good conscience have a relationship with him. Maybe he'd been proud of himself for doing the good deed with the fundraiser, but he'd caused trouble to people close to her. She'd buried her attraction, wherever it had emerged from, and assumed it would dissipate with time.

Those twenty minutes in the garage had reminded her of her goal now: getting past Ben without reawakening those feelings. Tracy steeled herself and grabbed her purse. Ben froze—he'd probably seen her now, too, but his sunglasses were hiding his hazel eyes. Good thing. They were capable of drawing him into her.

Her into *him*. *Her* into *him*. As in mesmerizing her. Not as in…yeah.

"Get your head out of the gutter, Trace," she mumbled to herself.

Ben slid his phone into his jacket pocket.

Tracy felt his lips on hers that summer night, then promptly ejected the sensation from her memory by focusing on Ben's selfishness: he'd claimed credit for Tracy's idea to unmask Pauline at the fundraiser. He hadn't even sent her a thank-you *text*, let alone a card and a box of chocolates.

Maybe his chocolatey kiss was the thank you?

Ugh! Why did her thoughts keep circling back to him?

Just because Ben's kiss is a triple-fudge-chocolate kiss doesn't mean he is. Ben Landry is a cherry truffle.

Ben replaced his sunglasses with his regular glasses.

Oh, sugar. She was going to see his hazel eyes.

Tracy made her break for the door, her gaze focused on the taxi waiting for her.

Ben opened the door. "Hi, Tracy."

Tracy rushed past him, pretending surprise. "Oh. Hi, Ben." She ducked into the taxi.

Don't make eye contact. Don't make eye contact. Oh, fudge, you made eye contact.

She glanced over her shoulder as the driver pulled out of the parking area, and Ben watched as the taxi drove away.

Why do you care? He didn't even thank your son for helping raise all that money at the fundraiser. That man's heart is so cold it could freeze lava.

CARRYING out his plan was going to be harder than he thought. Tracy clearly did not want to talk to him. At all. But judging by Pauline's now-angry expression, Susie was right. He'd completely misjudged how they had ended their relationship several weeks before.

Oh, s...

Benjamin! He heard his sister's voice in his head.

...ugar.

He approached the counter and smiled at Pauline. "I was on my way to my sister's in New Hamburg. Got into an accident. That garage over there was the closest that specializes in exotic cars. They'd better do a good job."

Be nice.

Okay. Maybe that wasn't the best opening. But at least he hadn't said Kitchener was a stick-in-the-mud town. Given how his day had been going, this was acceptable, right? But context was everything. Marketing 101. Pauline didn't know his context, and Ben wasn't going to tell her. He would work with the few details he intended to share, which meant he needed to change his tune.

"Mayumi will do an excellent job on your car, Ben. What can I get you?"

Okay. She was at least going to keep things professional and not pull a mascot-level prank on him in front of her customers. A step in the right direction.

He'd been deemed at fault for the accident, which meant

he'd be paying through the nose for repairs, so he couldn't risk spending money unnecessarily. But he needed to stay focused on his goal: convince Pauline to convince Tracy to be his reference.

"Nice to see you. How's your mom doing?" The tea shop was named after Pauline's mom. It wouldn't hurt to ask about her.

"She's out of town until Thanksgiving so she'll have to miss the pleasure of your company," Pauline said. "Now what would you like, Ben?"

Ouch. "I'll have a tea. What do you recommend?" Get the other person talking to relax them. Public Relations 101.

"What do you like?"

He didn't remember her staring at him with quiet contempt like she was now. Or had she done it all the time from under Perry's mask?

All the teas were stored in jars on shelves behind her. Wasn't that so the person behind the counter would recommend the perfect tea? That was the shop's reputation, so far as he recalled.

"I'm not entirely sure. I don't know my teas well."

Todd came up behind Pauline.

"Hey, Todd. How are things? How's your family?" Ben had helped his father's national chain, DIY Home, secure a major sponsorship with the Peregrines. That should produce a conversation.

Todd nodded in acknowledgement. "They're doing fine, thanks."

Or not.

Ben really needed to rethink his strategy. He stared at the wall of hundreds of teas. He was health conscious, so he'd order what all health nuts ordered. "I'll take a green tea, then."

"Sencha, genmaicha, matcha, jasmine…" Pauline rambled off another ten teas.

Ben's eyes glazed over. Green tea came in so many flavours? Of course, it would help if Pauline advised him a little. Or was this her treatment for former managers she didn't like?

"I guess I'll take the first one."

Ben paid and found a table along the wall opposite the counter. This would obviously take longer than ten minutes. He might not even get Pauline's support in one day.

He turned on his laptop, but after staring at his résumé for five minutes, he sighed. A new strategy it was. Ben returned to the counter and ordered a turkey sandwich. After he paid, he noticed the tip jar. What was the point? Weren't all employee costs already included in the price of the food? Pauline put the sandwich in front of him.

"People miss you at the Peregrines," he said. The statement pierced his chest. But he needed this reference and complimenting often worked.

"How's Derek?" Pauline had her shoulder turned to him as she wiped down the counter.

"He and the new actor you helped select are getting along well."

"Glad to hear. Anything else I can get you?"

Ben took the hint. "No, that's it."

Back at his table after his second failed attempt, Ben bit off a huge mouthful of the small sandwich. He'd had the perfect job with the Peregrines. What had happened? The new GM must have been involved.

No point on focusing on that now, Landry, he thought. *A door closed. Look for the open window. You need a new job. ASAP.*

He studied the CMO job description while he ate. This needed to work. Getting fired from a company you worked for after ten years left a stain on your résumé when you wanted to apply to the C-suite. But he had the skills. And, since Tracy worked for the CEO, having her reference would boost his chances for sure.

CHAPTER 3

*T*racy smiled at the CEO as she stepped off the elevator at work. He responded in his usual professional fashion. Good. He didn't notice that anything was wrong.

She put her purse in the cupboard and sat at her desk, ready for the afternoon, when a box of chocolates caught her eye. She opened the attached note.

> *Sorry I missed you, Trace. Hope everything's okay. I'll talk to you tomorrow.*
> *Eric.*

Tomorrow? When? Where? At work? After work? Tomorrow evening at her front door? Eric wasn't supposed to start until next week.

Should she call him now to discuss what he wanted? No. Anytime she'd spoken with him over the past few weeks to arrange everything, too many memories—some sweet, but the most vivid bitter—came grinding into her mind. So long as they communicated by email, she could keep things professional, cool, distant.

Now, the big question: did Eric send the chocolates because he remembered that the Belmont Village Chocolate House was her favourite chocolatier? Or because chocolate was a generic gift that was easy to purchase? At work, Eric was always on top of everything. As a risk assessment officer, he protected any company he worked for from unnecessary financial risk as much as possible, and those companies thrived. It made sense to hire him as the CFO of an aggressively growing tech company.

But at home? He kicked off his shoes and didn't lift a finger. Not because he expected Tracy to serve him, but because he expected Tracy to agree to hiring help to take care of the chores. He wanted to order out all the time or hire a private cook. He had good intentions, to free up time for friends and family. But Tracy wanted privacy at home. Family and close friends, yes, but strangers? Colleagues? No. And once Austin had his sights set on a ballet career, she had been quicker to reject Eric's plans so that Austin could have the space he needed to focus on his ballet and schooling. Plus, caring for your home as a family and cooking together counted as family time in her books, and it didn't waste money you could otherwise save for emergencies.

Like divorce and raising your child by yourself.

Yes, Eric paid child support. But if Tracy hadn't listened to advice Claire had given her when she'd been a teen working in the tea shop part-time—always keep a separate bank account, no matter how much you love and trust your husband—she'd be struggling today.

Tracy popped open the lid of the box of chocolates and compared the chocolates to the guide. No cherry truffles. Impressive. So he hadn't forgotten everything from their nineteen years of marriage, and this wasn't a generic gift of chocolate.

But she couldn't dwell on that. She needed to get the Belmont Village Autumn Festival committee organized ASAP or she wouldn't have time for Austin. Yes, she could quit the committee, but what kind of example would that set for her son? Plus, Belmont Village and the surrounding neighbourhoods of Belmont and Westmount were home to Tracy. She wanted to ensure that Austin had a home there, too, where he'd feel safe, no matter what. It was one reason she'd turned down Ben's job offer at the Peregrines.

After she messaged the committee through their collaboration app to ask if everyone was available that evening at eight, she ordered get-well flowers for David. Cecily would appreciate them, too. Tracy remembered her grandfather taking her to the Belmont Village Chocolate House for a treat after a shift at the tire factory in the neighbourhood. Although David and Cecily weren't family friends like Pauline's family, Tracy did know them well and they had owned their shop even before Claire opened her tea shop.

Tracy tackled her email and to-do list. Before she knew it, it was time to meet Austin at Claire's, where he was working in exchange for ballet training from Todd.

She'd talk to him about his father as they walked home. She'd thought she'd had another week to prepare her son for his father's return, but Eric had forced her hand yet again.

It didn't escape Ben that Pauline and Todd had kept Austin away from him all afternoon, even though Austin kept looking in his direction as if he recognized Ben but couldn't place his face. Although they hadn't actually met at the fundraiser, Ben had been on stage as the MC the entire evening. It'd only been a few months since the event.

Pauline assigned Austin a few tasks in the back room and approached Ben. Should he say something about Austin? Probably not. Best to leave family topics alone. After all, Ben was only here for professional reasons.

"We're closing in a few minutes," Pauline said. "You can stay while we clean up, but we're leaving in about a half hour. Do you want anything before we close the cash?"

There it was: her compassion. Clearly, something had changed her mind about him this afternoon or she wouldn't have allowed him to stay past closing.

It was now or never.

Ben stood up to be at eye level with her. "Listen, I need your help. I left my job at the Peregrines and I'd like to move out of Toronto."

Pauline's eyes narrowed.

She didn't believe him. Crap.

"That would explain why you're here during the season. I thought you loved your job."

"It was getting demanding. Anyway, I saw an opening for the chief marketing officer at Tracy's company... I was hoping that since I gave you your dream job, you might help me get mine now and put a good word in for me with Tracy."

Pauline's lips tightened and she crossed her arms.

He had his answer.

She kept her voice low. "Ben, I will be forever grateful to you for giving me the best job I could ever have to finish my career with. But I would never in a million years support anyone working for you. So, no, I will not put in a good word for you with Tracy. If you've been waiting here all day to use me to get to Tracy..." She glanced around. Ben was certain she was making sure Austin was out of earshot. "You can leave now. The garage has a waiting room, and the drugstore has snacks."

~

TRACY ORDERED a taxi and grabbed her things. Her phone beeped the distinctive tone she'd set for Pauline.

Heads-up. Ben wants the CMO job at your company. He's hoping you'll be a reference.

Tracy's heart fluttered, but anger soon squashed that. Ben was trying to weasel his way into a company that snubbed its nose at his take-no-prisoners style of management. The CEO, for example, allowed her some flexibility in her schedule to take care of Austin so long as she made up the hours. Plus, the last thing Tracy needed was to work for her ex-husband *and* her one-time secret kisser. She texted back: *You must be joking!!!*

Nope. Said I wouldn't help him.

What a difference being your own boss made. Tracy knew about several of Pauline and Ben's spats when Pauline worked for him, but so far as Tracy was aware, Pauline would've never dared refuse any request as Ben's employee.

She texted back: *You're the best.*

BTW kept Austin away from him.

That wasn't necessary. As much as Tracy disliked Ben, she knew he wouldn't have said anything mean to Austin. After all, without Ben's approval of the two shows Austin performed in over the summer, Austin might not have returned to the talkative boy he'd been at ballet school. But she understood her best friend's disdain for Ben.

Thanks

Not sure Austin recognized him though. Meds?

It was possible. The Prime Minister of Canada had picked up tea at Claire's Tea Shop several weeks before, and Austin hadn't recognized *him*.

Will make note. Thanks for telling me.

np

It had been just over a year before that Austin had received his diagnosis of absence seizures, a form of epilepsy unfamiliar to most. Instead of collapsing to the floor and suffering through painful and energy-draining muscle spasms—the type of seizure usually associated with epilepsy—Austin would freeze and stare for up to ten seconds, often appearing to those who didn't understand like he was daydreaming. Without medication, this happened at least dozens of times a day. Tracy and Eric had been shocked to learn that Austin had probably lived with these seizures most of his life.

Her phone dinged again, notifying her that her taxi was nearby.

As she took the elevator downstairs, Tracy planned out how the evening would unfold, because if she told Austin at the wrong time, it would affect his sleep, which would exacerbate the side effects of the medication, and then he would be late for school the following day.

If Eric had cared about Austin's epilepsy, he wouldn't have barged back into Tracy and Austin's lives like this. And if Ben had cared about her at all, he wouldn't be trying to weasel his way into her company. Whoever said when it rained it poured was right. But when would the pouring stop?

Or could Tracy at least get an umbrella?

CHAPTER 4

*A*ustin practically *jetéd* out of the tea shop when he saw his mom arrive. As they walked, he instantly launched into his play-by-play retelling of every second of the past few hours at Claire's Tea Shop.

Tracy loved it.

"...and then Todd told me about the time he danced Romeo in Spain, but the ballerina he danced opposite hated his guts—I mean, how could anyone hate Todd?—and she made no effort whatsoever to make lifting her easy!" Austin talked like this every time he spent time with Todd: his eyes alight with joy, his mind storing every detail of whatever new knowledge his childhood idol had shared with him.

Todd had also come into their lives in the summer—the summer of fairy tales—and Austin's hero worship of the international star had still to dissipate. But it had taken fairy tales to heal the rift between Tracy and her son. Did she have to tell Austin about Eric? His diagnosis, followed a few months later by Eric leaving them, had deprived her of beautiful moments like these for a year. Each was now precious, and she didn't want to lose a single one.

"He said I'm really coming along, but I have to keep practising. He's wondering if it might be too soon for me to…"

No, Tracy needed to interrupt him because Austin wouldn't stop otherwise. She didn't know what Eric meant by "we'll talk tomorrow," but she feared that if she waited, the consequences would be worse than if she told him now.

"…but I think I'll be ready for it. It's in March. I just have to keep—"

"Austin, we need to talk."

"So? Do you think I'll win the Youth American Grand Prix this year? I've been working so hard. I think I'll catch up on my training after losing an entire year."

Tracy's hands tightened on her purse. Naturally he was focused on one of the most prestigious ballet competitions in the world, and she preferred to spend this time supporting his dreams. But they were almost home.

"We need to talk. It's serious."

Austin turned to her and twirled. Not even sneakers on pavement prevented him from dancing. "What now? I took my meds this morning and at the shop, I was in school all day, I know my English marks aren't the best—"

"It's not any of that; it's your father."

"Are you finally divorced so I don't have to hear about him again?" He walked up to the porch of their two-storey house and leaned on the door, turning his back to her and signalling he didn't want to talk about Eric any further.

Tracy took a deep breath. "No. Our year separation isn't quite over, and we can't legally divorce until it is. I have to tell you that he's moved back to Kitchener…and he'll be my second boss starting next week."

Austin straightened up. "What? How long have you —"

He stopped talking and stared, his eyes unfocused. Tracy began counting. *One one thousand, two one thousand, three one thousand, four one thousand, five one thousand, six one thousand.*

Austin leaned on the door again. He wasn't always aware of his seizures. But apparently this time he was.

"I still don't know if this is better than no medication," he said. "Fewer seizures, but bigger ones. And then there are the side effects. I get called on in class, and I can't always remember the words even when I know what I want to say. I look stupid even when I don't have a seizure. What's the point?"

"It's only been a few months. Have you tried connecting with the epilepsy community online to see if others experience this?"

"I talk with the support group I started at school. After those videos went viral over the summer...the last place I want to air my problems is online."

Tracy remembered. They had had to make all his social media accounts private. Too many kids with severe problems reached out to him. Online trolls sent flashing GIFs to induce seizures. Others sent hateful slurs about who Austin loved. Having epilepsy on top of being a gay teen boy with a passion for ballet wasn't exactly welcome by some. She couldn't sleep some nights because she feared for Austin's safety.

Todd had used his fame to defend Austin and send out messages of support for anyone facing similar cyberbullying. Pauline did the same on the Peregrines' and Perry's accounts, which Ben—according to Pauline—fully supported. Both also continued to send out resources for those in serious trouble.

But Austin was the only one with his seizure type in his group at school. It meant he felt like even more of an outcast. He'd also faced bullying at school during that horrible year.

Who in their right mind thought it was funny to punch someone frozen in a seizure?

"Now Dad thinks he can waltz back into my life?" Austin said. "How long have you known?"

He needed the truth. That was her Austin. Truth was in his performances, too. Dancing at the anti-bullying rally and hospital fundraiser had reignited his love of dance, but he hadn't been afraid to show his pain and loneliness to the audience either. However, he also demanded that emotional fearlessness in those close to him. He struggled to comprehend that adults didn't work that way.

"A few weeks. I just couldn't bring myself to tell you."

"Makes no difference, I guess. I have nothing to say to him." The resentment in Austin's voice sent a chill down her spine. "Dad left because of my seizures."

Tracy tried to keep her voice calm. "What makes you say that?"

"Dad left right after I was diagnosed. It was pretty obvious."

Was Austin right? Now that Tracy thought about it, when the pediatric neurologist in London had discussed risks with anti-seizure medication, Eric had zoned out. He also never paid attention to Austin's medication schedule. Tracy had always been sure it had been only their crumbling marriage. Eric must love Austin deep down. Otherwise, why would he have come back?

"So? Did he? Leave because he couldn't handle having a son who'd dropped his ballet partner onstage in front of the whole ballet school because of a seizure?"

Tracy had to be honest with him. No matter what happened with Eric's sudden reappearance, the one thing she could not lose was Austin's trust. "All I know, sweetheart, is that your dad left because our marriage had been falling apart. I'm sure you remember all the yelling."

"But if that was it, then why ignore me this past year? Not a text, not even a Christmas card, birthday card, nothing. Just be honest with me. I embarrass him. That's why he hasn't contacted me, right?"

Tracy unlocked the front door. What kind of father made his child ask that kind of question? She wanted to tell Austin that wasn't true, but what if it was? To explain that his father was at least paying child support was just as cold as saying he had never contacted them.

Austin stepped into the house and headed for the kitchen before stopping. "Let me gu —"

Tracy counted ten seconds for this seizure. His emotional upheaval was too strong. She kept her voice calm to try to defuse the energy. "We'll talk about it later."

"I'm done talking about it!" He stormed upstairs.

Why had she waited this long? If she'd told him on a Saturday morning after a good night's sleep, for example, when his brain was well rested, any seizures the news might have caused would've probably been less severe and she and Austin would've had all weekend to discuss it. Instead, she'd waited until the end of the day when he was at his most tired.

You know better, Tracy Tschirhart, she admonished herself.

She grabbed the mail and carried it into the kitchen where she started heating up leftovers for dinner. She went to the basement where she found Austin, as expected, dressed in his practice clothes, searching for music on his phone.

"Listen, I've got the festival committee coming over tonight. We've got a problem because David has pneumonia."

"Is he okay?"

"He will be, but with the festival just over two weeks away, we need to redistribute his duties."

Already calmer, Austin nodded.

"If you want to talk more afterwards, though…"

"I said I'm done talking about."

"Should I make an extra appointment with your therapist?"

"I'm done talking about it."

Tracy felt guilty about the meeting but she also knew Austin would feel better and be more approachable after dancing his emotions out for an hour. Once she had the marketing problem solved, she could focus on her family again.

"Is that all you wanted to tell me?" Austin was impatiently holding his finger on his phone, ready to tap Play.

Tracy nodded and left him alone. Once upstairs, she pulled out her own phone. There was a text from Ben asking if she would see him. Her heart did its dance again. What were the chances of getting into a car accident with Ben Landry? *In Kitchener? Because of a peregrine falcon?*

"He didn't even apologize, Tracy," she said to herself. "Leave him alone."

But his drive to succeed had helped raise ten million dollars for children's health issues. And she'd seen that moment when he was on the phone. Was that a friend or relative he was speaking with? Pauline had once been certain Ben wasn't in a relationship.

But even if he was single, the last thing Tracy wanted was to date Dr. Jekyll and Mr. Hyde. Not to mention the age difference. Pauline had said once he was in his thirties. For all Tracy knew, Ben—heaven forbid—might still want children. Tracy was not going there again.

Stop thinking about him, Tracy. You don't even have to reply.

Then, as the microwave dinged, an idea occurred to Tracy. Ben was a marketing professional, and he was unemployed and stuck in town. She wouldn't have to see him every day. If she played her cards right, tonight's meeting could be over faster than she'd planned.

She just had to keep her hormones in check. If only hazel

eyes, a triple-fudge-chocolate kiss, and the energy and intensity of a man with so much drive to succeed weren't so attractive.

~

NOTE TO SELF: listen to sister when dealing with women.

Tracy would see him. The only catch was that Tracy's house was over a kilometre away. He'd just lost his job and wasn't going to waste money on a cab, but he also didn't want to arrive sweaty and smelly. Ben texted her an ETA and set out walking. With any luck, Tracy might offer him a ride back to the garage to collect his suitcase and then to a hotel. Oh wait…she didn't have a car right now either.

He had fifteen minutes to put his game plan together while he walked. He'd only have a few minutes to talk, not only because he wanted to limit her chances of saying no, but because Austin would be there. Last year had been extremely difficult for the teen. Ben understood everything had vastly improved now, but he wanted to respect their privacy. Unlike his visit in the summer, where he'd offered Tracy the job, this was ad hoc. He didn't want to intrude on their privacy longer than necessary.

The houses in Westmount, many probably at least sixty years old, were set on large properties, often with deep front yards. Ben liked neighbourhoods like these, each home custom built in its time. Some were two-storeys in a range of sizes, others small bungalows. This was one of the more well-to-do neighbourhoods in the region. Tracy's house was on the outskirts, near a golf club. It was one of the smaller two-storeys.

Ben shook his head in wonder at everything he imagined Tracy had had to juggle as a single mom this past year. It couldn't have been easy. He'd have five minutes to woo, um, *wow* her with his charm so that she'd allow him to put her name down on his application. She wasn't the type to renege on a commitment. He needed to be as cunning now as she had been in the summer with Pauline's unmasking.

But as he walked up the street, he saw several cars parked outside Tracy's house.

"Probably a women's book club," he said to himself. "Time to turn on the charm."

He rehearsed his script and several variations in his head as he walked up the driveway. He straightened his glasses and rang the doorbell.

Tracy, in a cream-and-pink blouse and dark-brown slacks, opened the door. Her tastefully made-up face was smiling at him, her brown eyes warm.

"Ben! How wonderful to see you. Thank you so much for coming!"

How was this the same woman who several hours ago had probably wished him death by quicksand?

When in shock, be professional.

"Nice to see you, Tracy. Thank you for fitting me in at the last minute. I don't want to take up too much of your time."

"Not a problem at all. And come in. No need to rush. Make yourself comfortable."

Every bone, vein, artery, intestinal twist, blood cell, and neuron in Ben's body told him something was very, very, very wrong. And it was turning him very, very, very on.

This was not a good combination.

No sooner did he step from the foyer into the family room than he noticed a small circle of people: three women and two men. No books in hand, so not a reading group. Friends? But why would Tracy allow him to interrupt a social evening?

"Everyone, this is Ben Landry, the marketing professional from Toronto I told you about."

So his reputation had preceded him. Was that good or bad? They smiled at him, so probably good.

"Ben, this is the Belmont Village Autumn Festival volunteer committee. Your timing is perfect."

Volunteer committee? Ben hadn't found himself in the midst of a book club—he was surrounded by a pack of wolves.

CHAPTER 5

Two can play this game, Ben thought. He just had to figure out the rules—and still ask for that reference.

Tracy introduced everyone by name and offered him a drink. He accepted. Not only would Susie consider it rude if he declined, but staying longer would allow him to network. No one knew anything about him other than what Tracy had already shared, and her about-face with him suggested it was positive. He could control his own narrative and keep his options open. Another bonus. Whatever game Tracy thought she was playing, Ben had the upper hand.

She brought him a cup of tea. Of course. What else would Pauline's best friend serve? It was just as well. A small burst of caffeine would improve his bedtime performance.

Evening performance. For f—udge's sake. Ben had to watch his language not only for potential innuendoes, but he had to match his language to the crowd. Tracy didn't swear, so he could assume her friends here didn't, either. He could keep himself from swearing. But Tracy looked so sexy in her work clothes tonight. And she had her hair pulled up and had already outsmarted him once this evening… Everything about her said Type A, someone who always thrusted ahead.

Oh, s—ugar.

"So, why are you in town?" asked a woman named Sabine who was the owner of a German bakery in Belmont Village.

Happy to be brought back to Earth, Ben answered eloquently. He had prepared for this question from Tracy, but he could give Sabine the same answer. "I realized it was time to leave my job in Toronto. I was on my way to my sister's in New Hamburg, but a car accident's keeping me here." Ben waited not only for the expected reactions of concern and sympathy but also to see if anyone mentioned Tracy. He didn't want to embarrass her, given that he still believed the accident was her fault, no matter what the official decision had been.

When no one mentioned her, he said, "I'm fine, thank you, but my car's in the garage for at least a week." He'd just saved Tracy from embarrassment with her friends. That should help with the reference, especially since part of the front end of his very expensive car now looked like a beginner's origami project.

He continued, ad libbing by adding the one detail he knew all small business owners desired. "But sports marketing is too cutthroat, so now I'm looking for something challenging but fulfilling, something that will reignite my passion for marketing."

Nods all around. He'd impressed them. Excellent.

But when he smiled at Tracy, he realized he'd done it again: fallen into her bed.

Um, her trap.

"We have the perfect offer for you while you're looking for something fulfilling," Tracy said smoothly. "You see, one of our committee members has come down with pneumonia and can't complete his duties as the marketing coordinator. Our festival is just over two weeks away and we're looking for a volunteer to fill his role. I thought you might be interested. It's very challenging: festival attendance has been waning for some time."

Everyone stared at him. Ben Landry *did not* volunteer. It was a dog-eat-dog world out there, his dad had always said.

"Well, I'm honoured," Ben lied. "But I'll be taking the first bus to New Hamburg in the morning. I can give you some guidance right now, though." Ben offered some advice. He pushed down the frustration he felt for giving advice for free, reminding himself that if it got him that reference and consequently that CMO position, he would consider that compensation.

He responded to questions for easily fifteen minutes. Everything looked promising again.

"So, that's what I recommend," he said, wrapping things up. "Shouldn't take you too much time. From the sounds of it, it's the engagement stage of the sales funnel you really need to focus on now. I don't think you'll have too much trouble with awareness. Everyone in Belmont and Westmount has friends and relatives. Have them help you spread the word more. Really make it a friends-and-family event."

This was going perfectly. Tracy would look silly to turn down his request for a reference.

TRACY COULDN'T HAVE BEEN MORE grateful for Ben Landry's ego in that moment. She went for the kill. "So, you have time to help us?"

Ben swallowed, clearly trying to contain his surprise. "What?"

"I've seen you in action, Ben." Always good to mention a person's name. "The fundraiser you put together this past summer for the children's hospital was fabulous." She felt guilty leaving out Pauline's name this one time, but she needed to keep stroking Ben's ego.

She addressed the group. "You should've seen the video he created—the stories he highlighted about the families being helped were touching and beautifully told, and the video itself was gorgeous." Tracy's heart skipped a beat as she remembered his work. "You designed all that, right?" Ben nodded and sipped his tea. "You just shared so many incredible ideas with us, Ben, and you said it wouldn't take much time—"

"I said it wouldn't take *you* much time. I'm busy searching for my next great fulfillment."

Tracy was certain Ben Landry was not searching for fulfillment. Money, yes. Fulfillment? Heck, no. But she had a festival to pull off in the midst of everything else.

"I'm guessing you're not searching for fulfillment in sports marketing, since it's so cutthroat?"

Ben took another sip of his tea, probably to stall for time. Checkmate again.

"So," Tracy continued. "Wouldn't it make sense to get a little experience outside your main industry? Just among the six of us are six different industries, and Belmont Village actually includes a couple dozen businesses. That's a lot of potential connections. Not to mention a lot of potential *references*."

Ben's lips tightened.

HARDLY ANYTHING FAZED Ben with all the problems he'd smoothed over in public relations. Well, except Pauline's unmasking. No one had warned him that when Perry's head came off, she looked worse than Peregrines players after three overtimes.

Tracy had planned it—with help from Derek, Pauline's handler.

Ben realized now that Pauline must've told Tracy everything. Having been so preoccupied with this meeting, Ben hadn't considered all possibilities. He really was off his game. But what other choice did he have? He'd been fired, and he hadn't worked for another company for over ten years. He had honestly thought Pauline was his best route to Tracy given his and Tracy's history.

Yet, here he was, his only option now offered to him on a dirty plate. Ben Landry did not receive opportunities on silver platters. He'd always had to convince Peregrines management that he'd deserved each promotion, even though he delivered demonstrable results every time. But this plate was dirtier than most.

Be nice, he heard Susie say in his head. Ben wasn't in charge here. He understood how that worked. But he needed to watch his spending now.

"Well, volunteering is one thing, but busing into town every day while my car's getting repaired would be expensive. Same with gas once I have my car back. Is there budget to cover my transportation?"

Sabine spoke first. "I'd actually offer you a place at my house, but I've got five kids under twelve." She laughed. "Trust me. You wouldn't last two days!"

He probably wouldn't. Ben didn't have kids of his own. What did he know about living with them?

Everyone laughed with Sabine, and Ben joined in. Similar offers and rejections were expressed around the room until all eyes landed on Tracy.

∾

HE OWNED a Porsche and wouldn't pay for gas or bus tickets?! How had Tracy not seen this coming? Now that Ben had schmoozed his way into everyone's hearts, she'd look like a snob if she exposed his true personality. But how would Austin feel having him in their home until the festival? She was certain that once Austin remembered who Ben was, he'd fight her.

And since when did everyone think she had time for a house guest?

But one glance at Ben and he obviously understood what had happened now, too.

"Actually," he said, "it's a twenty-five-minute drive each way." He looked directly at Tracy. "My car eats up a lot of gas —I don't actually drive it that much in Toronto. I can probably work virtually from my sister's."

The owner of the garden store shook his head. "You'll be doing a lot of in-person tasks with the other retailers."

"Plus, we meet in person since we're all here," said Sabine.

"Not to mention the window decorations," said the garden shop owner. "David was going to hire local artists to paint the storefront windows of any shops that wanted it. And I'm sure Tracy has a huge to-do list."

"Maybe this won't work," Sabine said. "We all understand if you don't want to commute."

Everyone nodded in agreement.

"Maybe it won't." He glanced at Tracy. All hints of competition had disappeared.

In fact, if she didn't know Ben better, she could've sworn she'd seen a hint of desperation fly across his face. Had he actually come to realize this position would help him?

But you're doing this for your son, Tracy thought. *He's been through so much. Having Ben help will let you keep everything else stable for Austin while dealing with Eric.*

She could hope for another volunteer, but this late in the

game? If she was honest with herself, she hadn't seen the peregrine falcon because she'd been preoccupied with Eric's arrival. Yes, Ben was close behind her, but if she'd been paying better attention, she might have seen the bird sooner.

Tracy capitulated. "To be honest, Ben, it's just that if you don't help, I have to take over at this point and I'm already stretched thin. Plus, it'll affect the little time I do have with Austin, now that he's back to his regular practice schedule." She glanced toward the basement door as she reconsidered one more time. No. This was her best option. Besides, it was only two and a half weeks. She could handle Ben Landry for that long.

Ben followed her gaze. "I'm sure I can make myself disappear in the evenings, since he's at school during the day."

Did Ben Landry just think about someone else? *Now's not the time to get sarcastic*, Tracy thought. *If you're going to make this work, you have to be professional.* "Unless he needs extra sleep because of his medication."

Ben smiled. In fact, it was the first honest smile she'd noticed from him all evening. "He's on meds now? Are they helping?"

She nodded. "It hasn't been a walk in the park, but there's been some improvement. He has some problems with memory, for example."

"That might explain why he didn't seem to recognize me at the tea shop today."

She glanced around the room at everyone's hopeful eyes. She had gotten them all excited about asking Ben. And whatever the reason for his sudden concern for Austin, he showed some respect for their personal space. Was there more to what she'd felt in the summer?

"Sure. Stay. I'm sure it won't be a problem." She just had to figure out how to break it to Pauline.

Ben nodded. "Great."

Tracy waited for the next words that would normally follow accepting a kind offer. But nope.

She had to extinguish that tiny flame that burned for Ben.

He didn't even say thank you.

CHAPTER 6

F resh out of the shower, Ben put on his pyjama pants. Sabine had driven him back to the garage to pick up his suitcase and laptop.

He could hear voices through the bathroom door. "Does he have to stay, Mom? You know how he treated Pauline."

Ben sighed. He'd had a job to do, he'd done it. No one was sued, and the Peregrines' popularity soared. No pun intended. Thanks to Ben, Pauline had probably been the highest paid mascot in the league.

Tracy shushed Austin. "He might hear you."

"Whatever. He wants to stay here. He can deal with it."

But Ben was used to it. "The Tin Manager," "Ice Pad Ben" —those were the mild ones. The others involved vocabulary Ben wasn't allowing himself to think now that he was in a house that didn't swear. If Tracy didn't swear, and a reference from Tracy was his only hope right now, then Ben Landry no longer swore.

Keeping his emotions inside let him make the management decisions necessary to climb the marketing ladder as fast as he could. He knew what everyone at the Peregrines had called him. He simply ignored it.

Ben dug through his things. Crap. He'd left his T-shirt in the guest room. If he hadn't been tricked into staying here, he wouldn't be in this predicament.

That's not true, he admonished himself. *If you hadn't been offered a room here, you'd be alone in a hotel right now during a time when you can't be alone.*

"Good night, sweetheart."

"Good night, Mom."

He heard two doors close. It was safe for him to sneak to his room. He put on his glasses.

But the door was only halfway open when he saw just how wrong he was: Tracy stood in the hallway, facing him, her eyes wide.

"Shirt's in the bedroom," he explained as he darted past her, his face probably as red as a cherry. "Good night."

Wow. So that was the body that belonged to those lips. She'd suspected it looked like that, but she'd had her hands pressed against the wall in the hotel, not planted on those hard pecs. Hazel eyes, lips that reminded her of that triple-fudge-chocolate kiss, and now an Aero bar for abs.

Ben Landry looked delicious.

Pauline accused Tracy of sometimes looking at men like chocolate, but when Tracy saw a fine specimen, she couldn't help but appreciate him. And if a man put effort into his physique, why shouldn't she admire it?

Pauline. Guilt overcame Tracy. Was she betraying her best friend?

Sometimes I have to make sacrifices for my son, Tracy thought.

Pauline loved children but didn't have any of her own. She always acted in the best interests of children but could relinquish that responsibility at night.

"I guess this is my way of paying back what I owe that egotistical man," Tracy said to herself. "Austin might not have performed in the summer if it weren't for him." She thought back to his genuine smile at Austin's progress. Could he really care about others?

"But that doesn't give him an excuse to treat everyone else in a way that leaves the taste of cherry truffles in my mouth."

She opened the collaboration app on her phone, created an account for Ben, and sent him the invitation. "Actually...he'll probably be faster at marketing tasks than David, and he might visit his sister for a few days here and there once he gets the major tasks rolling."

Ben accepted the invitation.

He was still awake, possibly shirtless...

Tracy! Get your mind on track! This is Ben Landry, who thinks only of himself, who has truffle-worthy kisses...who...who...who thinks only of himself...who has hazel eyes...who...

Who showed some concern for Austin when those on the festival committee suggested Ben stay at Tracy's after she'd sold them on what an amazing volunteer he'd be.

She'd fallen into her own trap.

After she assigned him tasks, she finished getting ready for bed and fell asleep to sweet images of the glimpse of the man staying in her guest room.

BELIEVING his suits would make him stand out too much, Ben dressed in jeans and a T-shirt. High-end jeans, of course, though he'd bought them at a consignment shop, like almost everything else in his wardrobe. He rarely paid full price for anything, with two exceptions: high-quality T-shirts and shoes. Guys sweat excessively in both. No, thanks.

He'd sensed some tension between Tracy and Austin the night before—not to mention the whole shirtless fiasco—so he'd left the house early. He wanted to both respect their privacy and get a sense of Belmont Village throughout the day, to see where all the festival events would take place. As much as it annoyed him to admit it, Tracy was right: he needed the experience. When Sabine had said this might not work, it had required effort to hide his panic. That a volunteer opportunity was his only chance for redemption was depressing, but he had no other way to land a job, so...

He parked himself at Claire's for the day to eavesdrop on the regulars. Hopefully Pauline would let him stay once she learned he was helping with the festival. The food wouldn't cost him too much, and Austin wouldn't see him until later this evening, since Claire's closed at eight on Thursdays.

But of course, Pauline wasn't in—Todd said she was playing a popular character out of a kids' book at a school book fair.

Ben set up shop near the front window with his cup of sencha tea to observe the street as well as the inside. Weekdays obviously differed from weekends, but he had to start some-where, and he wasn't familiar with this part of town. Today was observation day, and aside from a little social media, tomorrow he'd hit the pavement. As CMO, he'd do the same, only his observation period would last longer.

"Tracy's good at what she does," a customer at the counter said. Ben's ears perked up. Ben's Tracy? Well, not *his* Tracy. The Tracy he knew. "One of the best EAs in the country. Did you know she's won national awards of recognition for her work?" Ben did, and so did Todd, judging by his nodding. So, yes, the same Tracy. "I showed up a week early for my new position. She'll hate that."

Ben knew that about Tracy, too. Being caught unprepared embarrassed her. She took pride in her work and wanted to show that. Ben also hated surprises.

Todd barely acknowledged the customer. Pretty unprofessional, in Ben's opinion.

The customer, who fit the stereotype of a financial manager to a tee, complete with balding head and small paunch, kept talking. "Everything went according to plan so perfectly that I had all my belongings packed ahead of schedule. I couldn't wait to move back here, so I arrived early. It'll be great working with Tracy. We just need a new CMO. Do you or Pauline know of anyone? We're really looking for someone who thinks outside the box. Someone from the arts or sports might fit the bill."

As the conversation continued, Ben noticed how little Todd responded. Ben was by no means a connoisseur of ballet, but the Todd Parsons Ben had witnessed on stage in the summer was warm, entertaining, and friendly.

But now? Todd was ice-cold. *My employees —former employees —would call me Santa Claus next to him*, Ben thought.

After the man left with his order, Ben approached the counter.

"Who was that?"

"What else can I get for you, Ben?"

Ben leaned in so no one would hear. "Todd, you were so cold to him you could've reversed global warming."

Todd's jaw tightened. He looked like he wanted to say something but decided against it. He glanced over at Ben's table, and although he remained silent, his body language spoke as loudly as the speakers at the arena: Ben still wasn't welcome here.

But he also couldn't be alone right now. Losing his job was still too fresh. Ben simply had to make this work, even though his charm would have no effect on Todd. He was simply less likely to embarrass himself around people he knew, regardless of their feelings about him.

"I'll have a tuna sandwich."

"Protein for breakfast, I take it? Like Pauline."

"We workout nuts need it. And…" He stared at the teas on the wall. Another cup wouldn't hurt. Then he'd call quits on caffeine for today. He would definitely steer clear of Earl Claire. Maybe trying Pauline's tea would help him get inside her head. "Belmont Blizzard."

When Todd returned to the counter with Ben's tea a few minutes later, he stared at Ben and lowered his voice. "Why are you here? You could be hanging out at your hotel instead of bothering us again."

Word about Ben's accommodations hadn't travelled from Tracy to Pauline yet. That meant Ben had to slow down. He needed Claire's Tea Shop on his side if this marketing gig was going to succeed.

"I'm volunteering for the festival committee. I honestly don't mean to annoy anyone. This was the only place I assumed I could observe people all day without looking odd. That's all." Ben dropped a dollar into the tip jar. Susie would've told him to do that. Based on the past twenty-four hours, her rules appeared to be working better than his.

Todd raised an eyebrow. "You know, you'll find that the people of Belmont and Westmount are friendly if you extend an olive branch first. I was an outsider, too, once."

"You're also a world celebrity."

"Only in some circles. I came here because hardly anyone in Kitchener cares for ballet, remember?"

"Can't say as I paid any attention to that detail."

"As long as I avoided dance studios, I was fine." Then Todd

smiled. "Except for Austin. But that kid helped bring me out of my depression."

"You helped him a lot from what I saw. I'm guessing you're a great mentor for him."

Todd blushed. "I hope so. He loves dance, and it's nice to share that joy with someone who soaks it up like he does." Todd tapped the counter as if to say he needed to continue with his duties. "Listen. Stay as long as you need to—unless Pauline says otherwise."

Susie was right again.

Todd continued. "She'll be back after lunch. You might learn something by observing these people."

Should Ben tell Todd that, in his experience, if you extended the olive branch first, people took the olives and returned the branch? No. Let this conversation end on a pleasant note, right? He nodded his acknowledgement.

But he wasn't out of earshot when he heard Todd mutter under his breath, "He really could learn from others. Like saying thank you."

What was that supposed to mean? Didn't a tip suffice?

CHAPTER 7

*a*ustin had slept well and was attending school, and Ben had left the house before the Tschirharts had woken up. Tracy felt a little badly: he didn't need to make himself invisible, though she appreciated the effort.

But in the elevator at work, Tracy felt a pit in her stomach as she neared the seventh floor. Every time she'd deal with plans for the evening's executive dinner, she'd have to talk about Eric, type his name, send him an email. She got off the elevator and headed toward her office.

The light in Eric's office was on. Her heart skipped a beat.

It was probably just IT setting things up. His message probably meant he'd see her tonight. Her CEO just hadn't told her. Probably.

Then, out of the side of her eye, she saw an arm throw a jacket across a chair.

Eric's arm.

She hurried into her office. On autopilot, she checked her phone—Austin was still at school—tucked it away, put her purse in the cupboard, took off her jacket—

"Hey, Trace."

She whipped around.

Eric held out a mug filled with hot water and a package of chocolate-infused tea leaves. "I still can't believe Todd Parsons sold me tea. I remember when Austin had pictures of him plastered all over his room." He laughed in disbelief. "And I can't believe I'm seeing you."

As she took the mug and tea from him, she saw that Eric's hairline had receded a little more. The wrinkles on his face had sunken in a touch more, too. At fifty-one, his age was definitely showing. But he still had the cuddly physique of a man who worked excessive hours in corporate finance. She'd loved his soft hugs.

And his gentle smile was the same one she'd fallen in love with over twenty years back.

"I came early to talk," he said. "I figured you'd be in early, too."

To talk. Those words changed her sweet memories into ones coated in cheap, past-its-expiry-date Easter chocolate. *He left us last October, and "Hey, Trace" are the first words I've heard from his lips since that day.*

"Right," she said. That was the first thing she had said to him since October. But at least she'd said something. Gotten that out of the way. Now she just needed to get through the rest of the day.

Eric tapped his watch a few times.

He wasn't setting a timer, was he?

"I have a meeting scheduled at nine. We need to utilize every minute right now to sort us out, or it's going to be awkward for everyone." He closed the door and sat in one of her guest chairs.

Her heart sank even more. This was the emotional roller coaster that had become so commonplace in their marriage. She glanced at his watch. Yup. A timer was counting down. Of course. At work, efficiency was key. Repair a year's worth of soul-ripping damage in…nineteen minutes and twenty-six seconds. She was surprised he didn't have an agenda typed up.

Oh, wait. That would've been her task.

"How were the chocolates I left you yesterday?"

"Good." She dropped the tea bag into the garbage.

If Eric hadn't walked out on them, if they had discussed and agreed on the details of their separation, they actually would have made an effective team. But how was she going to get through this without the hurt he'd caused her—and especially Austin—always oozing out of her like the filling in a crushed truffle?

Eric shifted in his chair and crossed one leg over the other. He cleared his throat. "I know now's not the time to explain my actions. But I promise I will. And I swear, Tracy, there never was anyone else. Not when I left, not now, and never in between."

She believed him. He was a horrible liar. She'd even discovered the plans to her fortieth surprise party two weeks in advance. Tracy waited for him to keep talking. After a year of silence, she wasn't going to waste her breath, that was for sure.

"I just want you to know that I've been seeing a therapist for eight months. I'm really sorry—and I know a box of chocolates, a cup of hot water, a favourite tea, and twenty minutes isn't enough to convey that. But I'm hoping that, ultimately, well… The reason I didn't reach out to you earlier was because I wanted to discuss everything with you in person, and I thought it was better we first met at work, where we'd both be more comfortable, before I come home."

Tracy gripped the warm cup to ground herself. "Home?"

Eric ran his hands through his hair and stuttered. "I…didn't think it'd be wise to show up to see Austin without giving him advance notice." He recrossed his legs and opened and closed the button on a cuff. "He...knows I'm here, doesn't he?"

Tracy feared his Freudian slip about home meant something.

Eric took a deep breath. "Could I see Austin before the executive dinner tonight? I could pick you up and see him first."

The steam rose from Tracy's cup. She didn't doubt Eric's sincerity, *but it had been a year of radio silence.* She and Austin had just repaired their relationship.

"You and I need to clear things up first. Besides, I was going to head straight to the restaurant from here. Quarter-end."

Eric leaned forward, his hands hanging limp over his knees. "I know it's my fault it's been so long, but I'm so close to seeing him again." He buried his face in his hands.

His remorse filled the room. This wasn't an act. He still loved Austin.

But Austin came first and he'd made his wishes clear: he did not want to see his father.

"You're going to have to wait. Besides, we really shouldn't be discussing this here."

Eric raised his head. "I'm so sorry for everything I've done, Trace. Let me see him. Please."

Tracy's hands tightened around her cup. He obviously still didn't understand the ramifications of his actions. Given the countdown on Eric's wrist, she opted for an executive summary. "Austin's past year has been full of depression and bullying. He suffered in silence his second semester because he was so humiliated. I couldn't reach him."

"I watched the videos from the anti-bullying rally and the hospital fundraiser."

Tracy lowered her hands to her lap so that she wouldn't break the cup in her frustration. "Two five-minute excerpts of the worst year ever." She leaned back in her chair and crossed her arms. "He believes you left because of his epilepsy. *That's* how bad this is. Now do you understand why you can't just drop in on him?"

A knot formed in her stomach. Not only had she shared with Eric something deeply personal of Austin's, but the look of horror on Eric's face proved that Austin's suspicion was wrong.

Eric blinked. "He... He... That's what he thinks?"

"You left shortly after his diagnosis, so, yes."

"B-but... You told him differently, right?"

Tracy held the warm cup of chocolate tea in her hands and used its sweet aroma to calm herself. "I only found out that detail yesterday, but I didn't know what to say. Add to that your complete silence—not even a Christmas or a birthday card to your son—I couldn't honestly tell him he was wrong."

"Obviously, I wouldn't—"

"It's not obvious, Eric. I've just pointed that out. And if I said Austin was wrong, but it turned out he was right, it would've harmed our relationship, possibly forever. I wouldn't risk that and you can't expect me to."

Eric glanced at his watch, tapped off the timer, and stood up. "I should probably prepare for my meeting."

Austin's disease obviously still made his father uncomfortable.

Eric straightened his tie. "I promise I'll make this better. But please tell him that I didn't leave because of that."

Tracy agreed. If a chance for reconciliation existed, she didn't want to stand in the way. Eric just needed to understand that Austin came first.

CHAPTER 8

*B*en had spent the past two hours at a fifties diner in Belmont Village where he'd followed Todd's advice and told the owner—a Mr. Casimiro—who he was and to give him the worst seat in the establishment so he wouldn't take away a good seat from a real customer. In return, Mr. Casimiro brought Ben a dessert free of charge.

Huh.

It was now ten thirty. Ben hoped he wouldn't wake anyone up by entering the home this late, but Tracy and Austin were probably in bed by now. He'd promised to make himself scarce, and he intended to keep that promise. He appreciated privacy, too.

Once inside, he smelled chocolate and heard a quiet *hello*. Tracy was sitting at the dining room table in cotton pyjamas, her face clean of makeup, her hair brushed and touching her shoulders, her hands hugging a cup of hot chocolate.

Ben's breath caught. He rarely saw someone outside of work, unguarded like this.

Tracy glanced at the clock on the wall. "I appreciate you making yourself scarce, but you don't have to be a ghost. If you're here to save money, eating out all day won't accomplish that."

Ben took a seat at the table, only now realizing how tired he was. To avoid the tension between him and Pauline, he'd visited several of the shops before supper at the diner. He had to admit, he'd enjoyed himself. Even relaxed a little.

"I just know this is awkward as..." He couldn't do it. Even as casual as she appeared now, he couldn't swear. He was no longer mirroring her language. He'd absorbed it. "Awkward as fudge. I don't want to get in your way."

"You're not. It's just that having a house guest was the last thing on my mind." A hand flew to Tracy's mouth. "But that doesn't mean you're not welcome! I mean, you were a cherry truffle to Pauline, but I'll take whatever help I can get with this festival."

A cherry truffle? Weren't chocolate and cherries supposed to complement one another? But context was everything in communication. If Tracy referred to Pauline and him, that implied something negative. Then there was her follow-up comment, *I'll take whatever help I can get.* But Ben was too tired to start a war of words. To protect his dignity, he stood up to leave for his bedroom. "Noted."

Remorse clouded Tracy's face as she grabbed his hand. His breath caught again.

Did I just call him the most horrible insult I could have uttered? Yes, I did. It was the truth, but she wasn't trying to hurt his feelings. Honesty was important when you expected your relationship to move forward, but she just expected to tolerate him until the festival was over. Still, he was a human being.

And one she'd already kissed and dreamed about eating, but that was beside the point.

"Please, sit back down." Ben hesitated, so she tugged on his hand. "I'm sorry. Today was a very trying day and tonight's C-suite dinner drained me. But the truth is that even though you were awful to Pauline, you gave Austin opportunities that opened him up again, and you let Pauline use the Peregrines' social media to defend him when he needed it. I can at least thank you for that."

Her phone beeped, and only when she let go of Ben's hand did she realize she'd still been holding on to it. Their gazes locked for a moment before she reached for her phone and he tucked his hand into his pocket.

His posture relaxed. "I'll leave you to it."

"No, just give me a sec. I wanted to ask you about something regarding the festival in case I don't see you in the morning."

Ben took a seat while she read the message. It was an eighties meme from Eric. She laughed. "Cassette tape and a pencil. I absolutely know the connection." She looked over at Ben, a hint of mischief in her eye. "But do you?"

"To wind the tape back in." To her surprised look, he smiled and added, "My parents had a stereo system with a tape deck. I'm not *that* young."

Tracy smiled back and then returned to Eric's message. She sighed.

"Everything okay?" Ben sounded genuinely concerned.

"Yeah."

It wasn't, though.

Reminded me of the mixed tape of ballet pas de deux I gave you for our first Christmas, when your stereo ate it up. It was nice to see you smiling tonight. Can we please go out tomorrow evening? I'll explain everything.

She couldn't avoid talking with Eric, but a big part of her didn't want the excuses, wanted to just sign the divorce papers and move on. He could've called. He certainly earned enough to visit from wherever in the world he'd gone.

But he was still Austin's father.

She pushed her phone away. "I'll deal with that after. Sorry." She smiled. "Where's my Gen X etiquette? I shouldn't let text messages interrupt conversations."

"I'm a Millennial. I'm used to it."

Sugar! Why did he have to look so charming? *Pull yourself together, Tracy. You can handle two and a half weeks with a younger man in your house.* She took a sip of her hot chocolate.

Which, of course, she'd made using hazelnut milk, and Ben was staring at her with his hazel eyes.

Right. The reason she wanted to talk to him.

"We booked a Snow White and a generic prince for the festival. And it turns out they're double-booked and they've cancelled on us."

"That's what you get for hiring a generic prince," Ben said.

Tracy looked up at him to see if he was mocking her and he was smiling at her. She laughed and took a larger gulp of her hot chocolate. "When it rains, it pours."

Ben shrugged. "Or when a door closes, a window opens somewhere else."

"Is that how you work?"

"It's the only way to work." He paused for a moment. "Why not ask Austin. Would he want to play a prince? Seems like a ballet kind of thing."

Tracy laughed again. "Clearly, I'm stressed out. I didn't even think of that."

He was thinking about Austin again. But was this coming from his heart or his strategizing mind? This was what she couldn't stand about Ben: she always assumed he acted solely in his own best interests. She had fully expected the Ben she knew to ask if he could use the money from the cancelled fairy-tale actors for his gas. Yet this Ben more resembled the Ben on the phone in that corridor…

"And does it have to be a Snow White? Or could it be two generic princes Show the world that romantic roles aren't always straight. I mean, if he wants to."

Tracy's mouth gaped. *Say something.* "I'll…I'll ask him. Thank you." She took a big drink of his hazel eyes. *Hazelnut hot chocolate. Drink the hot chocolate, not the eyes, Tracy.*

"Was that what you wanted to ask me?" he asked.

She nodded.

"Great. Text me what he says. If he doesn't want to, I can start making phone calls to find a replacement company." He stood up. "Good night, Tracy."

There was no way he was putting on an act. Not over something like this. But it also didn't fit with the Ben she knew.

Tracy sighed. She also had to figure out how to respond to Eric's text and presence back in her life. She believed his sincerity, too. And she knew that despite Eric's behaviour this past year, he, too, had always supported their son's sexuality. The only relationship rules they'd had for Austin were that his boyfriend be of an appropriate age and respect him.

Yeah, but how much respect did Eric show me when he walked out on me?

However, Eric had returned humble, even asking permission to see his own son.

So for the sake of the Tschirhart family, Tracy should at least hear him out.

She texted: *Yes, let's meet.*

~

"ANY IDEA what's wrong with cherry truffles?" Ben asked the next morning as Todd served him another tuna sandwich for breakfast. He had been disappointed to learn that Pauline was again helping with a school book fair, but at least he could have a man-to-man conversation with Todd about something that had confused and troubled him since the night before.

But before Todd could answer, the man in line behind Ben said, "Funny you should ask that. My wife hates cherry truffles."

Todd became as stiff as a nutcracker, so that before he even turned, Ben knew it was the same guy from yesterday. What did Todd have against him?

"Don't cherries and chocolate go well together?" Ben asked as he dropped some money in the tip jar and picked up his food.

The repeat customer was ready with an answer. "The flavour's too sweet and artificial for my wife. Doesn't matter if it's syrup inside, marzipan, pick your option. For her, cherry truffles are the last chocolate she'll select, and only if she has to out of politeness. She loves high-quality, single-source, dark chocolate because you can taste the bitterness, and the distinct notes tell you where the chocolate's from. According to her, each of us has a side we don't like to show people, so we sweeten it a little. High-quality chocolate is like getting to know a real person. Cherry truffles remind her of people who try to hide themselves."

Ben rolled his eyes. His tea was getting cold. "Who takes chocolate that seriously?"

"You obviously haven't met my wife."

"Probably better that I don't. Chocolate's chocolate."

The man laughed. "Yeah. Never say that to her."

Ben found a seat and watched as Todd interacted stiffly with this customer. Only after the customer left did Todd relax again.

Wait a minute, Ben thought. *Does Tracy hate cherry truffles for the same reason? Is that her opinion of me? That I'm fake?*

When you have nothing, you do what's necessary to survive. But that was how Ben had learned the skill that had most helped him become successful: he mirrored like nobody's business. Fine, he occasionally slipped up, like the wishful thinking of assuming he and Pauline had parted on good terms. Getting fired did that to you. But he usually read people like a book so that nothing stood in his way.

Or so he had believed over the past ten years.

But was he the last one Tracy would pick out of a box, the one she would pick only if politeness required it? She hadn't asked him to volunteer because he was the best. She'd asked him out of convenience. He was stuck in town, had marketing experience, and she needed the help. Moreover, she'd made it clear she hadn't invited him to stay with her because she enjoyed his company.

Cherry truffles are the last chocolate she'll eat.

He pushed his tuna sandwich away.

TRACY WAS IMPRESSED. Ben was already engaging with reporters on social media and had posts scheduled for the next few days. He had drafts for press releases in the works, too. She ran one through the plagiarism checker at work, and his writing was original.

She returned to the social media and checked the numbers. Understandably, engagement hadn't skyrocketed—Ben had only begun yesterday morning. But there were a few comments and reactions under yesterday evening's posts. He really had jumped right in.

If he had accomplished this much by himself in so little time, why had he needed to take credit for others' success at the Peregrines?

Her phone dinged the special ding she'd programmed for Pauline's number. Crap. She hadn't told her anything yet.

Haven't heard from you in two days. Everything ok?

Was Pauline texting to give Tracy a chance to come clean? No. Their friendship didn't work that way.

"You're doing this for your son... You're doing this for your son..." Tracy whispered under her breath while she thought. Then another ding sounded.

Eric?

She answered. *Quarter-end stress. The usual.*

What about Eric? Everything ok there?

Survived our first meeting.

He came early?!!!!

Yeah. Long story. Time to catch up tomorrow?

Sure! Drop by anytime. Weekends still quiet.

Tracy hoped Ben wouldn't say anything until she found time to tell Pauline herself. But she couldn't tell him to say nothing. "Ben, please don't tell anyone I know you're staying at my house. They all hate you." Seriously.

She sighed. *Or maybe he knows that anyway and hasn't said anything.*

Right now, she just had to get through the last day of quarter-end and prepare for dinner with Eric. Austin still hadn't agreed to see him, but she had sensed some give when she spoke to him at breakfast. Hopefully, being at school would give him the time he needed to consider everything and at least say hello to Eric this evening.

"Back to work if you want to leave on time," she said to

herself. Although she didn't have to stay until midnight like the order entry teams, she did have to stay until seven to help with administrative tasks, resolve fulfillment and IT issues...make sure the company kept earning money. She valued her role and felt valued for it. She'd somehow make her new role as EA for the CFO work, too.

CHAPTER 9

The doorbell rang a second time, but neither Tracy nor Austin answered it. What if it was a neighbour needing help? Everyone Ben had met in Kitchener so far appeared to be extending an olive branch. Or what if it was an evening delivery?

Ben got up from his work at the dining room table and opened the door just as Tracy came running from the bathroom.

"I've got it!"

But it was too late. Staring at Ben with as much surprise as Ben probably registered on his face was the husband of the chocolate-loving wife he'd met at Claire's Tea Shop.

Immediately, both men began talking over one another.

"Who are you?"

"Who's your wife?"

"Why are you here?"

Tracy moved to stand between them. "You two, cool it."

Ben couldn't help but marvel at how beautiful she looked in her pink dress and gorgeously styled hair. "He's got a wife,

Tracy. If this is your new boyfriend, you should know he's cheating on her."

Tracy's eyes opened wide, but what she said was not what Ben expected. "You're calling me your wife, Eric? You walked out on *us* and you're calling me *your wife*? Just because we're not legally divorced yet doesn't mean I'm still your wife."

The man—Eric—stared at the ground and mumbled something.

So that was why Todd had been so cold toward him. This was Austin's father.

Eric regrouped quickly. "And who's this? Seriously, Trace? You're already living with someone?"

Not Ben's years in marketing and PR, his previous experience in sales, Nate's drunken viral video, nor Pauline's unmasking could've prepared Ben for this moment. All that came out of his mouth was…

"I'm the cherry truffle."

Eric knitted his eyebrows together. "What?"

Tracy burst out laughing. "Okay, okay. I was tired. Maybe that was a bit harsh."

Ben resisted the urge to smile. Did she mean that?

"Ben's staying here as a favour to the Belmont Village Autumn Festival committee. Trust me: when I catch you up, you'll see there's nothing between us."

Ben didn't expect his chest to tighten after hearing those words. He didn't want any confusion about his reason for staying over. He wasn't there to date her. End of story. But his reaction surprised him nonetheless.

"Ben, this is Eric. For better or for worse, he's also the CFO at my company."

Oh, sugar. Not only was this Austin's father and Tracy's… ex? soon-to-be-ex? reluctant ex?…but Eric was also a member of the C-suite at the very company Ben hoped to apply to.

Great first impression I've made...

But Eric offered his hand, and Ben shook it.

"Can I see Austin before we leave?" Eric asked.

Ben understood the effort it took to step back into the lives of people you loved after you'd stomped on that love with your poor decisions.

"I'll get him." Tracy disappeared.

Eric's chin and chest lifted with a glimmer of hope, but he soon covered it up when he remembered Ben's presence.

"So, what do you do, Ben?"

"I work in marketing and public relations. I also have a background in sales. All in sports, an extremely competitive industry. When she heard I'd left my previous position, Tracy asked if I wouldn't mind volunteering as the committee's marketing coordinator because the chocolate shop owner who was doing the marketing fell ill with pneumonia."

Concern showed on Eric's face. "David's ill? Trace hadn't mentioned that."

Trace. A nickname was a clear sign of intimacy between two people.

"So, you're between jobs?" Eric said after a pause when Tracy and Austin hadn't returned.

"When the festival's over," Ben said.

"The company's on an aggressive growth path. We're looking for someone young with a strong résumé like that to balance out us old fogeys." Eric laughed. "When I hit fifty last year, age took on a whole new meaning. By pivoting and looking to hire younger in that role, we're hoping to stay relevant with the younger crowd."

Ben's palms began to sweat. He hadn't had time to fully prepare his résumé. But he had to keep going, especially after their rocky introduction. "I worked as the marketing director for the Toronto Peregrines, and as their public relations manager before that. Fan engagement increased twenty-seven-point-six percent under me in the four years I held the latter position, season ticket sales by thirteen-point-two percent. But I worked my way up the ranks, starting at a souvenir kiosk. Engaging with fans in the front lines allowed me to hear first-hand what they liked and didn't like about the Peregrines, the merchandise, the players, everything. I tracked data, presented it to management, and delivered results."

"Impressive, Ben, very impressive. And I love the Peregrines."

Excellent. Keep focusing on what I accomplished for the team and avoid why I no longer work for them.

"So, you hired Pauline?"

"I was honoured when she applied for the job. She had an excellent reputation in the league."

"That whole unmasking stunt was stellar," Eric continued, though his eyes darted past Ben a few times.

They talked about the Peregrines for a few minutes, and then Eric let out a sigh. "Listen, man, sorry for how I came in here. I'm on edge—we're close to the one-year mark of our separation, so it's either divorce or, well, you know." He wrung his hands, seeming too scared to speak his actual hope: reconciliation.

Ben had no intention of standing in his way. "I'm only here until the festival's over. Once my car's repaired, I'll be finding a new job and spending time with my sister in New Hamburg."

Eric nodded. "Family's important."

"It certainly is."

"Eric?" Tracy called.

Both men tensed: Austin entered the family room and remained there, his face emotionless at the sight of his father, who still stood in the foyer. To Ben's knowledge, this was the first time Austin had seen his father in a year. Ben's heart beat faster than the pistons in his Porsche on the racetrack. His breathing sped up to compensate, his mouth became dry. The emptiness on Austin's face, care on Tracy's, and hope on Eric's reminded Ben of the first time he'd reunited with his parents after he'd chosen to regain control of his own life.

He excused himself. Yes, to give them privacy, but also because he didn't know if he could remain standing. Too many unwelcome memories were flooding his mind.

He dropped onto his bed and dialled Susie.

"What's up, Big Ben?"

"I… I just need to talk. I don't want to ruin your time with Genny's parents —"

Her tone changed immediately as she interrupted him. "I'll be somewhere private in thirty seconds. But tell me what's up."

He set his glasses on the nightstand and explained what had happened. "Eric is trying to make amends and I get where he's coming from but Austin's so hurt, his face was totally blank when he saw his father…"

"Everything's reminding you of those years before the Peregrines."

"Working for the Peregrines saved my life, Suse."

"No, Ben. I keep telling you, *you* saved your life. Working for the Peregrines helped keep you safe, but every day you showed up for work was a choice to stay there. But now you're facing your past without that safety net."

"Pretty much."

"We're heading home in two days. Can you work out? Or take on extra tasks for this volunteer job to keep you busy until then?"

Just having a plan for the next forty-eight hours felt like a balm. But as he and Susie confirmed how Ben would cope until

Sunday, he realized something: for the first time since his return home ten years ago, Ben believed he could truly trust the people he was with — Tracy, even Pauline and Todd, people outside his family — to keep him safe.

Even if he was the cherry truffle.

CHAPTER 10

*O*nce they were seated at a decades-old steakhouse in the south end of Kitchener, Eric's "at-home" side showed. He relaxed into his chair, folded his hands over his stomach, and the gentle smile Tracy had fallen in love with the night of their first date—a world premiere at the National Ballet of Canada in Toronto over twenty years ago—appeared.

But to Tracy's surprise, as pleasant as the memory was, it awoke no romantic feelings in her. How often had she read over the years about second chances? Seen movies and read novels about moments like this? Yet here she was, and she sensed no flutters, no tingling, no shivers.

Nothing but a few pleasant memories overshadowed by the mountain of pain from his abandonment.

Eric's smile relaxed the atmosphere, but it didn't change the circumstances. Only after their appetizers arrived did he begin to talk.

"First off, I'm sorry." He kept his eyes on his salad. "I'm so sorry for abandoning you and Austin."

Part of Tracy wanted to say "it's okay," because that's what you said after someone apologized. But it wasn't okay. Not by a long shot. So, she said the next best thing that was at least honest. "Thank you."

Eric glanced at her before staring at his plate again and finally eating a forkful. He understood the difference.

Tracy ate her scallops as she listened.

"I didn't realize it at the time, but I'd fallen into clinical depression. I honestly didn't know where I fit in the family anymore."

"You were my husband and Austin's father." What was there not to understand about that?

But Eric shook his head. "I'm talking about more than labels, Trace. I needed a therapist to help me understand this." He sighed. "This is going to sound like blaming, but I swear I don't mean it like that."

"Okay…"

"It's just that…well…you supported his ballet so much… and he had natural talent. He didn't need to practise *that* much."

Here we go again. Missing the emotional part. "Eric, remember grade school? That was when the bullying began. Austin felt so free at ballet school, where he wasn't being bullied, he couldn't help himself. He'd found heaven. Of course he was going to practise that much."

Now Eric lifted his head. "It became an obsession."

Tracy backed down. Eric wasn't wrong.

"And then he began caffeinating," he said.

"And it exacerbated his seizures, only we didn't know about his epilepsy."

"I tried to warn you that something was going on —"

"You're blaming me?"

"No, no…" He rubbed his eyes. "You know words aren't my forte. My therapist said this would be a delicate talk." He looked up again. "I just mean that I didn't see how I contributed to the family anymore aside from my paycheque. You and I hadn't had sex in years, Austin was disappearing into his world of ballet, you were occupied with your work and his schooling, and I was withdrawing more and more into myself. By the time we moved back here, I didn't recognize myself anymore."

Tracy crossed her arms. She couldn't believe what she was hearing. "You had a mid-life crisis? You left me—and more importantly, your son—because of a mid-life crisis?"

The server cautiously approached and cleared their plates, and Tracy and Eric pasted on their professional smiles as they expressed their appreciation for the food. But as soon as the server left, Tracy and Eric's true moods returned.

Eric shook his head in response to her question. "I left because..." He wiped at a drip of dressing on the table. "I left because I didn't think he deserved me as a father. If he wasn't relying on me for anything, what good was I to him?"

Never in her life would she have expected to hear Eric utter those words. Eric's income had afforded Austin that ballet school, yes, but Eric was more than a paycheque. Many male ballet dancers didn't have a father who supported their passion for the art form. Pathetically, many even feared it would "turn their son gay" or "feminize" him somehow. Todd's father had been like that, and Todd and Michael had only repaired their relationship this summer, *after* Todd's international career.

By contrast, Eric had called Kitchener Dance Academy as soon as he and Tracy had noticed Austin's love for dance. He'd welcomed Austin's first boyfriend into the home with a stern "I know where you live" protective father talk followed by a smile and a hug.

Why would Eric believe for a second that Austin had no place in his life for his father?

When Tracy shared her thoughts with Eric, he still looked sad. "It took me six months of therapy before I realized that."

The server brought their meals. Eric had ordered his favourite: the ribs. Tracy tried a goat cheese ravioli. She ate a few bites before she finally found her voice again.

"I wish you'd said something."

"I guess I thought I'd tried, but by then we were speaking past each other."

"And I guess I'd hoped the move back here would've fixed all that."

Eric nodded but ate a few more bites before speaking again. The food did them both good.

"What I don't understand, though," Tracy said, "is how you could still feel that way after Austin got his diagnosis. Are you sure it wasn't his epilepsy that drove you away?"

Eric shook his head. "His condition scared me, don't get me wrong. And I was angry with you for not getting his symptoms looked at sooner."

"I had no idea his staring was a seizure."

"We both know that now. I'm not trying to drag that back up."

"But you just did."

"I'm only trying to explain what happened. I'm not trying to get an apology from you, nor am I expecting some sort of confession…none of that, Trace. I'm just saying what I saw and felt. That's it. But maybe I'm totally wrong."

"Because you could also have called a doctor and taken him if you thought it was serious."

"I thought it was just stress. I didn't expect such a serious condition. So, you're right. I'm sorry."

"And you still can't say 'epilepsy,' can you?"

Eric shook his head. "It reminds me of the risks that come with the condition. Like SUDEP."

Sudden Unexpected Death in Epilepsy. She knew. The prevalence was low: fewer than two people with epilepsy in every thousand died suddenly and unexpectedly from the neurological disease. Chances were even lower for people with Austin's seizure type. Still, it wasn't something a parent liked to remember.

"And medication side effects, changes to his seizures, all that. I'm sorry. Calling it 'his condition' just makes it easier for me to cope with it all. For now."

Eric was turning pale from the discussion. No matter what Tracy thought about all this, she could tell Eric was struggling.

"Will he take me back into his life? I bought a condo instead of renting a place to try to prove to both of you, but especially to Austin, that I intend to stay."

Warmth expanded in Tracy's chest, but it disappeared almost as fast. She saw his pain and regret, and she couldn't erase over two decades of a deep, mostly fulfilling relationship just like that. But abandoning the family had damaged every-thing she and Eric had built over those years. And Austin's heart was so big and open...until someone punched it.

Yet Austin's heart was now healing thanks to the events of this past summer. Was he ready to take the risk of allowing it to heal more? He had agreed to say hello to his father before she and Eric left for the evening, but he also wouldn't come within ten feet of Eric. Austin might not have seen the flicker of pain on Eric's face, but Tracy most certainly had.

"Since honesty is the theme of tonight, Eric, I can only say that we have to move slowly. But we can try."

She didn't miss the flicker of pain this time either.

CHAPTER 11

The roar of the lawn mower's motor didn't compare to the five-hundred-and-fifty horsepower motor of Ben's Porsche Panamera, but it was better than nothing. He wanted to pay his way a little since he wasn't paying rent to Tracy. The last time he hadn't paid rent, he'd been kicked out. Plus, his fear of being alone had escalated. Only that morning Tracy had told him that the festival was partnering with a charity: a homeless shelter. When she passed him the homeless shelter's contact information, he'd had to fight to suppress the urge to call his sister again.

Would Sebastian remember him from that winter twelve years ago? He hoped not. But just in case, Ben planned to arrange everything via email and sign his emails with his first name only.

He turned the mower back toward the street. Although the CMO job was his best bet, property maintenance was a close second. There were always jobs available there, and no one checked your background, so far as Ben knew. But he'd still apply for the CMO job, even if it meant seeing Tracy happy with Eric. These feelings for her would diminish soon enough, wouldn't they? The festival was now exactly two weeks away. He just needed to hold out for two weeks.

He turned the mower around, adjusted his sunglasses, which had slid down his nose from sweat, and wiped his forehead. It was hot out—even though it was almost October. He'd taken his shirt off and left it on the porch by the front door.

In the two weeks, and especially if he got the job, he could bury all his uncomfortable memories and move forward again.

For now he had to focus on his plans for the morning: finish the lawn then drop by the copy centre to pick up the last-minute postcards he'd designed and distribute them to the stores and restaurants.

He also hoped Pauline was available.

Ben reached the sparsely planted flower beds and glanced up as he turned the lawnmower. His eye caught Tracy, who had apparently been looking out the window in the family room. Was she watching him? Then he saw movement on the driveway out of the corner of his eye.

It was Eric, stepping out of a Tesla. That was who Tracy must've been looking at. Ben waved, but Eric only smiled grimly in return. Ben was in marketing and he quickly realized what it must look like for Eric to see a fit, shirtless man mowing his hopefully-not-ex-wife's lawn.

Ben had missed two years with his family, two years he never got back. He wouldn't be the reason Eric's one year turned into anything longer than that. And he'd missed a lot in those two years, like his mother receiving a diagnosis of ovarian cancer, and his father, Parkinson's. Ben would do whatever was needed to earn Tracy's reference. But he'd also try to help this family get back together. If he needed to push his feelings aside to accomplish all that, well, he was good at that.

~

INSTEAD OF KEEPING an eye out for Eric, she'd been keeping an eye on Ben and gotten caught. So, that was the *whole* package. Front and back. Add sunglasses, and…sweet. But he'd looked so deep in thought. About what?

"Mom?"

Tracy spun around. "Yes, Austin?"

"Do I have to do this?"

The doorbell rang, and her heart jumped into her throat.

"Sweetheart, you know I won't force you to. But I do believe your father's intent is sincere. Can you hear him out?"

Austin considered her request for a moment before nodding.

As she led Eric into the home he'd once lived in, Tracy noticed Austin had seated himself in the armchair by the window where no one could sit next to him. Eric sat on the couch. She saw Austin's eyes darting toward the basement door —he wanted to escape to his dance.

But this was a start.

"Thank you for agreeing to see me, Austin."

Oh, no, Tracy thought. *He's starting in corporate speak. Where's the father who took his son to the ballet at every available chance? Who took him to see Todd Parsons for the first time, where Austin became so inspired he chose ballet as his dream? Where's that Eric?*

"Yeah, whatever."

"I know I didn't make the best decision last year—"

Austin snorted. "That's putting it mildly."

Tracy wanted to glare at Austin, but at the same time, if Eric was going to be honest with his son, his son had the right to be honest back. The past year had been worse than eating a year's worth of past-its-expiry-date Easter chocolate *with* cherry filling.

"And I know my course of action really impacted your life."

Austin said nothing, and it took Tracy a moment to recognize his seizure. Not all of them happened while he spoke.

"Aren't the meds helping?" Eric asked, turning to Tracy.

But Austin had heard the question. "If you were around, you'd know they've reduced them, but that they're not controlled yet."

Eric glanced at Tracy as if to express frustration. She returned his expression with one that asked, "What were you expecting?" Austin pointed and flexed his feet.

"I'm hoping," Eric continued, "you'll agree to let me visit you more often? That is, if you have the bandwidth in your schedule. And the inclination to do so."

"Sure. Are we done?"

Before waiting for an answer, Austin escaped to the basement.

To kill the uncomfortable silence that followed in Austin's wake, Tracy said, "He just needs time, that's all."

"I just don't know how much longer I can wait."

How much longer? What was he expecting? Tracy crossed her arms. "I didn't realize we were on a timer here, too. Maybe you need this in corporate speak. Then let me give it to you. As far as Austin's concerned, *you fired him as your son.*"

She'd felt badly for Eric after Austin fled the room. But where had Eric gotten the idea that this would follow some workflow with mutually agreed-upon deadlines?

Eric stared out the bay window, but his gaze didn't appear to fix on anything—or anyone. Several minutes passed before Eric finally stood to leave. "You're right. This is going to take time. At least he talked to me today, and I'm grateful for that. I really am. I just miss my boy so much." He blinked back tears. "I can't believe how stupid I was. I'm sorry."

Tracy led him to the door. "I'm sorry. I was harsh."

"But you were right. I was too hopeful." He shook his head, remorse and embarrassment obvious. But then he lingered. Was there more? Now was a good time to leave. "I've missed you," he said.

Oh, fudge. What was Tracy supposed to say? Okay, she knew what, but it wouldn't have been an honest response. Of course, she'd missed him in the early days, but once she'd accepted that he wouldn't come back, she had focused on Austin. In fact, any lingering loving feelings had turned to anger.

"Can I come back tomorrow?" Eric asked. "Or should we go out? Perhaps he doesn't want me in his house. Or do both of you want to come to my place? Was this too intrusive?"

"I'll talk to Austin."

Even the deepest part of her no longer doubted Eric's intentions regarding Austin, but he had to wait. *He* had left *them*.

She stood on the porch as she watched him get into his car and back out. A rustling sound alerted her to Ben's whereabouts in the backyard: he was collecting the grass clippings into a garden-waste bag. Property maintenance had never been part of the agreement but Austin had been so glad to get out of lawn mowing that he had accepted Ben's offer the instant Ben suggested it.

Ben had put his shirt back on, despite the warm temperature. Was that to make Eric more comfortable? As an EA, Tracy had a keen eye for ways of putting people at ease. A half-naked, fit, younger man would have given Eric the heebie-jeebies for sure. She could imagine his expression if he'd seen Ben when he pulled up.

Consideration and empathy weren't Ben's strong suits, but he was attempting to show respect. This felt like that moment she'd caught him on the phone in June, not an act to convince her to be his reference. He was surprising her, and it was leaving butterflies in her stomach.

Very inconvenient, but not unpleasant, little butterflies.

CHAPTER 12

"*A*ll that in three days?" Pauline asked.

Tracy nodded and quickly checked Austin's whereabouts on her phone — he was at home.

"That's a lot. But I also have to ask... Where does Ben fit into all of this, and why haven't you told me about him yet?"

Tracy's cheeks flushed hotter than the heat of her cup.

Pauline continued. "Not only did Todd tell me Thursday evening, but other committee members have been swarming me telling me about how *nice* he is. *Tin Manager Ben!*"

Tracy avoided Pauline's gaze. "I'm sorry."

"That's why you haven't been texting me these past few days."

Tracy nodded.

Pauline let out a dry laugh. "Did he make you sign some contract or something?"

"I just didn't want you upset with me." She ate a forkful of the cake. It didn't taste as good as she hoped it would.

"Why in heaven's name would you allow *him* to help?"

"No one else was available, and I'm stretched to the max. I

made him sound like he was this amazing marketing expert, so everyone was eager to convince him to volunteer."

Pauline sighed. "I wish I was more available to help. I've had to pick up these book fair gigs to help pay bills so whatever I might have done during quiet times here, I do at night. And Todd's great with people, which translates into great sales, but marketing is not his forte."

Tracy took a few sips of her tea and felt relieved that Pauline had accepted her explanation. The bells over the door jingled, and Ben entered, wearing jeans, an ironed, button-down shirt, and polished, brown shoes. Tracy's heart flipped inside her rib cage.

"Hey, Pauline. Tracy." He carried a small stack of postcards in his hand and he neither smiled nor looked antagonistic. He was testing the waters, cautious. If Tracy didn't know better, she could've sworn he was trying to act respectfully toward his former employee.

Pauline's eyes narrowed. "I've heard the polite version of your sudden desire to help us. What's the real one?"

Ben's shoulders stiffened, and he clenched his jaw.

Tracy placed a hand on Pauline's arm.

"You don't know him like I do," Pauline said, "and he's clearly manipulating you. Ben Landry doesn't do things for free."

Tracy removed her hand, insulted by the insinuation that she didn't know when someone was playing her. She'd been working in corporations most of her life. She was an excellent judge of character.

"Tracy made a good point," Ben said. "If I'm going to switch industries, I need experience outside of sports. She allowed me to stay at her place as a thank you for the performance opportunities and support I gave Austin in the summer."

Tracy winced inside as a dozen emotions crossed Pauline's

face, with surprise, anger, and disappointment appearing the most frequently. She should've been up front about Ben staying with her.

"Seriously, Ben? With what you earned, you couldn't have given Tracy and Austin their privacy and stayed in a hotel."

"I'm earning my keep in other ways, so you can cool it, Pauline."

Tracy stared at him in amazement.

"Tell me," Pauline continued. "When do people actually come first in your world? Or are we simply always backs you step on?"

Tracy's jaw dropped. She'd never seen Pauline like this. Yes, Pauline had fantasized about ways to exact revenge on Ben, but they'd always been mascot-inspired pranks. Never actual insults.

"Please," Ben said, "be more honest." He dropped the stack of postcards, held together by an elastic, in front of her. "I've made a commitment to Tracy and the committee, and I'm going to keep it. This festival is supposed to help everyone, including you, in this shopping district, and I'm running behind. Please give these out. Hopefully, they'll help spread the word to people who aren't online." He stopped at the door. "Give me the benefit of the doubt, Pauline."

"Wait," Tracy said, looking at the postcards. "Where did you get these?"

"I designed them and had them printed this morning."

"But we don't have the budget."

"I've got it covered." He left without saying another word.

"He'll want compensation for this," Pauline said. "Just wait for it. I'm not kidding when I say Ben Landry never does anything for free. It's his motto."

Tracy tried to see reason. As chair of the committee, she couldn't allow herself to be swindled into losing money. And

Ben *had* tried to get his transportation covered, after all. But once the committee said they had no money, he had accepted that. He was getting free accommodations, but he'd mowed her lawn, something that wasn't part of the deal. Plus, he wiped down the sink and shower every time. Austin definitely didn't do that.

Nor had her kind-of-ex-husband.

She studied the design of the postcards. It made her smile. The images emphasized community, family, and supporting local businesses. The collage of people even included two women holding hands and smiling down at their children.

"So," Pauline said. "Another reason you haven't texted me these past few days: he's staying at your house."

Ben had asked Pauline for the benefit of the doubt. Maybe it was time Tracy earnestly gave him that, too. She nodded and took another sip of tea. What more was there to say?

Pauline wouldn't let it go. "You're not being taken in by this show, are you? Don't you see all the freebies he's getting? The man drives his Porsche on a racetrack, for crying out loud."

Ben wasn't worth losing Pauline over. That much Tracy was certain of. But she needed the help. Yes, she'd tricked him into it. Yes, she'd fallen into her own trap. But maybe it was a good thing.

"I didn't tell you because I knew this is how you'd react."

Pauline sat up straight. "You mean you knew I'd look out for your best interests?"

"I knew you'd get mad fast about it all. I don't want to hurt you—" Pauline softened immediately "—But please try and see it from my point of view. Thanks to you and Todd, I've got my son back. And just when I'm close to finishing this volunteer position, I lose my marketing coordinator at the same moment my ex-husband decides it's a good time to push his way back into our lives. I know Ben showing up is painful for you, and

I'm really sorry about that, but he has been surprisingly helpful for me. Don't you think he deserves a second chance?"

Pauline slouched into her chair, and Tracy took another bite of her cake. It tasted better this time. Same with her tea.

"I'm sorry you were scared to tell me, but can you see it from my side? Having that million-dollar clause in my contract hanging over my head the entire time?"

"Of course I can," Tracy admitted.

"Until I hear an honest apology out of that man's mouth and see some kind of action that proves he's sorry," Pauline continued, "there's no second chance with me. I sacrificed a lot for him. He needs to take that first step. No, wipe that. He needs to take *several* first steps before I consider giving him a second chance."

Tracy couldn't blame Pauline. In fact, she agreed with much of what her best friend said—except for resisting second chances.

Wasn't that what Eric wanted, too? A second chance? So why was she having such a hard time reawakening feelings for someone she'd loved for over twenty years while having no problems developing feelings for someone she'd only recently met?

Both men had hurt her.

But Eric had hurt her more—far more.

Tracy shook her head. She was treating both men like a ledger sheet by comparing how much pain they'd caused her and balancing it against how much bliss they'd brought her. How did treating them like an accounting equation help?

It didn't.

"Did Ben tell you why he's no longer working for the Peregrines?" Pauline asked.

"Sure. He said it was time to leave."

Pauline laughed. "That's the best description of getting fired I've ever heard."

Tracy gasped. "Fired? After everything he accomplished for them?"

Pauline nodded. "I talked to Derek and got the truth Ben clearly didn't tell you. The Peregrines are owned by a corporation, of course. The CEO tolerated Ben all these years because Ben delivered. As much as I despise Ben, he did single-handedly raise the Peregrines' popularity long before the cup win. But along with a new PR manager and mascot actor, they also hired a new GM. I don't think it was a coincidence that Ben got fired now. According to the rumour mill, Ben was let go because he was difficult to work with. Go figure."

How the fudge was Tracy supposed to give a reference for someone who wasn't honest with her? She stabbed her cake with her fork.

CHAPTER 13

Tracy needed to get dinner on the table, help Austin with an important school assignment, and then hopefully watch a movie with him. A busy evening would help her ignore the latest text from Eric asking about when he could next visit. She'd postpone talking to Ben about the truth behind his leaving the Peregrines.

She felt relieved that she'd cleared the air with Pauline and that Pauline had forgiven her. But there was one thing she would never tell Pauline about: the kiss. That wayward kiss with Ben had been nothing more than two adults losing momentary control of themselves. The previous year had challenged Tracy like none other. She had simply not been herself that night. Nothing would happen between her and Ben again, and it was pointless to cause her best friend more pain because of a one-time uncontrollable urge.

She locked the car, ran into the house, dropped her purse by the front door and...stopped. Was that Italian food she was smelling? Austin hated cooking. Or had he messed up so badly he was trying to get on her good side before coming clean? No. Puppy dog eyes were his go-to apology gimmick, no matter how bad the transgression.

So, that left…

"Austin said you both enjoyed lasagna, so he set out the ingredients for me," Ben said as Tracy walked into the kitchen. "When everything's cooled down, I'll cut it up and freeze some for leftovers." He pointed to the two casserole dishes steaming with fresh lasagna. "That way you can grab something quick when you're in a rush. I noticed you only cook enough to eat in one meal."

Tracy tucked her hair behind her ear. "It's faster in the moment."

"This way is cheaper, though. I just need to make the garden salad. Austin also said you both like salad. So supper should be ready in about twenty minutes."

The kitchen had been cleaned, too. Either Ben was desperate for that position, or he was thankful for staying over. But how did she reconcile this Ben with the one who was coming between her and her best friend? The one with the proven reputation for brushing people aside for his own gain? Tracy had a good sense of people, but she couldn't figure out Ben's Jekyll-and-Hyde personality.

One thing she'd learned in all her years of executive administration was that you could only move forward by asking the tough questions.

So she did.

"Ben, one moment, you do thoughtful things like mow the lawn and cook this amazing food, and the next, you treat everyone with so much disdain I wonder why I don't listen to Pauline and kick you out. Why are you like this?"

∾

KICK YOU OUT. Ben knew he could stay at Susie's or even return to his condo in Toronto. But those words awoke a visceral pain inside him nonetheless. He also had money. A lot, in fact. But under the right circumstances—and he was dangerously close to those circumstances—he would blow through it fast. He had some tucked away in GICs—poor investments but difficult to quickly unlock.

He and Susie also had a backup plan, but she'd need to notice he'd slipped again. Now that he had over ten years' sales, marketing, and PR experience under his belt, he had to sadly admit to himself that he'd probably be even better at hiding it. He only needed to believe in whatever he was selling to convince people—and alcohol made him a good salesperson.

He faced the sink and began ripping lettuce. "I don't mean to be like that. It's just how I get—"

"The job done," she finished. "Ben, I'm going to call you on it. I get the job done and still treat people respectfully."

He knew why he got like that. Making his employer a success meant he'd never lose his job, so he refused to let anyone stand in his way.

Except this time he'd been fired anyhow.

"If you need a break to deal with whatever's going on," Tracy said, "take it. You don't have to cook for us, for example. I really appreciate this, don't get me wrong. But if you're rude because you're constantly under the gun... Is now the time to take a break and, I don't know, re-evaluate things?"

"I know it's an imposition that I'm staying." He didn't add that spare time to think was the last thing he needed. His life, like the lasagna, was layered, and although Ben today was far from being the tasty cheese on top, he wanted to believe he was no longer the sauce that stuck to the bottom. "I want to contribute, Tracy."

He also wanted to believe he truly was more than a cherry

truffle. *I may not be as authentic as single-source chocolate, but I hope she knows I'm not as fake as artificial cherry flavouring.*

"Well, I certainly won't say no to free help in the kitchen." Tracy pulled two wineglasses from a cupboard.

"Nothing for me, thank you," Ben said.

"Beer? Cooler?" she offered.

"Maybe another night." He didn't need to tell her everything, but given how kind she'd been to him since Wednesday, she at least deserved a partial explanation. He closed the lid on the salad spinner. By the time the lettuce was dry, his nose detected the scent of red wine. He'd been around alcohol often enough working for the Peregrines. But this time was different.

After the basket stopped, Ben began chopping a pepper and cautiously started to explain himself. "Things were really rough for a period in my twenties. My family rescued me. I've only now come to realize how strong my fear of returning to that time is. That fear helped me succeed, though it had...consequences. But I refuse to go back there."

The only sound in the kitchen was the knife slicing through the flesh of the pepper and along the board. He glanced at Tracy, who was looking at him with compassion rather than pity.

She took a sip of her wine. "Do you think..." She was trying to formulate a difficult question.

Great. What intrusive question is she going to ask? This was why I like my privacy.

She continued. "Do you think the way you treated people is...what got you fired?" Her face became serious. "Because if you want a reference from me, Ben, I need to know all the details before I put my reputation on the line. And if you plan on treating people the way you did Pauline, that won't work at my company."

Maybe it was best to ditch his entire strategy and just come clean. He cut a yellow tomato in half, removed the green part, and took a deep breath.

"I was going to tell you eventually, but it happened the same day I, well, ran into you. It was too…" He couldn't get the word *humiliating* out of his throat. "Too raw. And then I ran into your car, and the day went from bad to worse. And I misjudged things with Pauline, too. I couldn't find my footing." He paused as the day replayed in his mind. "It was one of the worst days of my life."

More silence. Was she angry at him for lying to her? Would she kick him out? He'd been kicked out before. He could handle it.

No, you can't, he told himself. The urge to drink was scratching all over him. He couldn't stay on his own, especially now.

He faced her again, watched her drink. One more night was all he needed, then Susie would be home. *Keep yourself busy, Landry.* He diced the tomato.

"I only found out Susie—my sister—was in Quebec when I got onto the 401. That's how little contact I'd had with her after the cup win." He dumped the lettuce into a salad bowl and threw the diced tomato on top.

"I see," Tracy said. "I guess it's hard to get in if you don't have a key."

"I do have one." He reached for some spring onions and sliced them all together. "But I need to be around people who know me right now, and I'm too embarrassed to show my face anywhere in Toronto because I'm too well connected thanks to my job. Once you'd agreed to let me stay here, I was relieved. When Sabine said it might not work, I was honestly scared for myself."

He felt as though he would vomit. He couldn't remember

when he had last been so open with anyone. Tracy could take these fears, mash them up, throw them at him, then drag them to Pauline and ridicule him.

Instead, all he saw was confusion on her face. "So, staying here isn't connected to your job application?"

He shook his head. "As...humiliating...as this whole situation is, I planned to tell you. But I needed to get through the weekend first in case the truth made you want me to leave."

Tracy drew her eyebrows together and tilted her head to the side, her eyes not leaving him for a second.

"If I can just stay until tomorrow, I'll be out of your hair late afternoon and will do everything virtually. I'll bus in when needed, drive in once my car's ready. I'll make it work. I did a lot virtually for the Peregrines. Susie and her partner Genny can pick me up on their way through town."

Tracy took another sip before answering. "Susie and Genny. So that's why you understand how important visibility is."

"People like you and me have it easy. I do what I can so kids like Austin can live in an accepting society. Susie's helped me with that. But you were right, too: I need an opportunity outside of sports to bolster my résumé. Right now, this volunteer position is all I have."

Ben returned to preparing the salad. He'd said as much as he wanted to. He'd been sober since the detox program—opening himself up in the public forum of a twelve-step program was definitely not his cup of tea. Even now, with someone he trusted, his palms were sweating, his heart palpitating. Once an alcoholic, always an alcoholic. That didn't mean he'd always be drinking, only that he always had to live mindfully, aware that his brain had an addiction. But now that he'd been fired, now that he had no idea if anyone would even hire him, now that he was scared for his future, the urge to drink had returned.

Tracy set her empty glass in the sink, and he wanted to inhale the dregs of the wine.

Get a grip of yourself, Landry.

"For the record," Tracy said, "this is a safe house. Always has been. If your sister and her...wife? Girlfriend?"

"Girlfriend. Two years now. I'm hoping this is the one for her. I'd finally have a quiet partner to counter Susie's, um, exuberance." Ben smiled. He reached for the salad dressing ingredients Austin had helped him assemble earlier.

"We have dressings in the fridge," she said.

A corner of his mouth lifted. "I make a mean vinaigrette."

Oh, s—ugar. Am I flirting?

Tracy raised her eyebrows. "A gourmet who cooks on the cheap. Nice." She pulled out plates and cutlery as she continued. "I don't need further details, Ben, but I assume you'll also be alone at Susie's while she's at work. At least here you're getting to know others. If they're driving through on the way home, they're welcome to stop by. Would be nice to meet them. But you don't have to leave. In fact, you're welcome to stay. I wasn't lying at the meeting when I said I needed the help. Austin's my life, and having you take care of so many tasks already has been a relief. I'd love it if you kept helping us."

She'd love it?

She looked intently at him and Ben was certain he caught a spark.

"And to be clear," she said, "I definitely no longer think you're a cherry truffle."

The corner of Ben's mouth lifted. There was most definitely something between them.

Just then Austin entered, a tray of cleaning supplies in hand. "Smells good, Ben."

"Thanks."

Austin glanced at both of them, but his gaze hung for a split second longer on Ben.

Austin had noticed Ben's attraction to his mother.

And Tracy had noticed Austin's noticing.

Oh, fudge.

CHAPTER 14

$\mathcal{T}$racy sat at the kitchen table that evening, with her laptop and papers sprawled out in front of her. A fun Saturday night. She had quotes from several places in Belmont Village for food for the festival. She'd order from all of them, of course, but she needed to figure out how much. Austin had chosen to complete his homework by himself.

Ben came out of his room, his laptop in hand. "Mind if I join you?"

Tracy nodded. "Not at all."

He sat on the opposite side of the table. Good. After hearing his story before supper, it only drew out more feelings in her. Not pity. But that he'd trusted her enough to share so much astounded her beyond words. No wonder the impenetrable outer shell. Whatever the full story was, and it certainly wasn't any of her business, it had clearly caused him a world of pain, something he likely only shared with a select few. Like Susie, maybe? She had probably been the person Tracy caught him talking with the night of the fundraiser.

But enough of Ben. She needed to decide about the food.

She sighed. Two hundred German shortbread cookies? Or five hundred? Or would little apple strudels be better? But they cost more. And from the Belmont Village Chocolate House: chocolate cake pops or truffles?

How many people would come? The businesses were donating the labour and only requesting reimbursement for the food costs, which was amazing, but Tracy didn't want to over-order on their kindness, either.

She sighed and rested her chin on her hand.

"Anything I can help with?" Ben asked.

"I've never ordered this much food for an unknown number of people before."

"Want me to look after it? I've done that lots of times. I think you have attendance numbers from previous years, right?"

"You'd do that?"

"Happy to."

Warmth travelled through her body. She collected the quotes and passed them to Ben.

"I have to admit," she said, "I'm also really distracted. Eric wants to meet tomorrow. I held him off today, but...he needs to give us space."

"He's just eager to see you both. It's understandable."

"But if he pushes Austin too much, Austin will pull back completely. I still don't think Eric gets all that happened last year." She laughed wryly. "I could try more corporate lingo, explain that he doesn't appear to comprehend all the ramifications of the permanent paradigm shift he's demanding in his relationship with his son if he doesn't desist in this persuasive approach."

"That almost sounds more like the legal department instead of finance."

"I've worked in several departments over the years. Apparently, I'm becoming multilingual."

"But I get it," Ben said. "Family is important, especially now that Susie's all I have. Maybe he's just trying to find his footing again."

What was with him? Earlier in the kitchen, she could've sworn he was flirting with her. Here, he was supporting Eric's attempts to reconcile with them.

This was not the Ben Landry Tracy knew.

THE NEXT DAY, Ben had to restrain himself from grinning like a child as Genny and Susie pulled up to the Tschirhart house. He hadn't seen his younger sister in over a year, and he felt like a preschooler in a candy store. Before Genny had even turned off the engine, Susie jumped out of the passenger side of Genny's white Honda and threw herself at her older brother.

"How's my Big Ben?"

Okay. There went part of his cover.

Austin burst out laughing. "Big Ben? Seriously? Do you chime on the hour?" He began the London clock's famous song that was annoyingly also the chime of every second doorbell in the country.

Ben rolled his eyes. "Because I haven't heard that one before."

Susie and Austin imitated the song together. Ben loved seeing Austin this happy with his sister. Her laughter was indeed infectious.

"Well?" Susie measured the top of her head from where it just reached Ben's shoulder. "What would you call him if you were my height?"

She introduced herself and Genny—short for Geneviève.

Susie definitely didn't need Ben to look after her. Not anymore, anyway.

They went inside, where Tracy took drink orders.

"I can help," Ben offered.

"Nope," Tracy said. "You haven't seen your sister in a while. Besides, that's what children are for."

Austin sulked, but Tracy grabbed his wrist and pulled, eventually whispering something in his ear to convince him. Genny followed them, asking to use the washroom, and Tracy gave her directions.

"So?" Susie said when they were alone. "How are you holding up?"

Ben kept his voice low. "Overall, okay. But I did have the urge to drink last night when Tracy had a glass of wine."

Susie wrapped him in her skinny arms, and Ben hugged her back. His muscles relaxed, and he didn't want to let go. He entrusted very few people in his life with his deepest fears, and to embrace one of them was precious. But after a minute, Susie mumbled into his chest.

"It's hard to talk to you while I'm squished into your pectoral major."

Ben chuckled as he released her.

She kept her voice down, too. "You can come back with us."

He shook his head. "I am thrilled to see you, but Tracy made a good point Wednesday when she tricked me into accepting this volunteer position."

Susie raised an eyebrow. "Tricked you? Again?"

Ben's cheeks heated up, and he scratched the back of his neck. "Yeah. She's good at that." He filled her in.

"Then why the urge to drink?"

Ben took a deep breath and let it out. "Pauline laid into me hard yesterday. I really messed up with her."

"Did you apologize?"

His hesitation was enough of an answer. Susie whacked him in the arm.

"I had a job to do."

"And you did it to protect yourself, yada yada yada. Benjamin, you're dealing with human beings. When are you going to learn?"

He pinched his nose and squeezed his eyes shut. "I know."

Tracy shouted from the kitchen, "Drinks and snacks coming up!"

For the next half hour, Austin poked good-natured fun at Ben and even at Susie. Tracy took jibes at her son, and Ben could see where Austin got his teasing from. Susie was all too happy to shoot back at Austin, and Ben gladly gave Austin a taste of his own medicine. Genny laughed along. Ben felt joy at the love between his sister and her girlfriend. Even when Austin had a seizure or two, Susie and Genny rolled with it and soon Austin was completely at ease with them.

When Susie and Genny headed out, Ben realized that for the first time in…years?…he'd relaxed without worrying about social media and PR fallout. He'd actually kicked back and enjoyed the company. He hadn't been surrounded by so much happiness in ages.

"Can I drop by next weekend for a visit?" Susie asked. "I work and volunteer all week."

Tracy's eyes lit up.

What I wouldn't do to return the favour from the summer and press her against a wall. She looks so alive and full of energy. She's pulling me straight to her.

"Why don't you come Oktoberfesting with us?" Tracy asked.

Ben's jaw clenched and he shot his sister a look she would understand as hidden panic. Oktoberfest was essentially a celebration of beer. He'd seen the advertisements all over town.

"Well, my car should be finished by then," he said quickly. "I can come visit you, Susie, and give the Tschirharts a weekend of privacy."

"We're going Friday night," Tracy continued. "Ben's already covered. The committee can't pay for your two tickets, but you're obviously welcome to come, too. It's tons of polka and beer. I mean, I'll just have a beer or two since I'll be driving. But they've got schnitzel dinners, sauerkraut, all the typical German food. And did I mention polka music?" She winked at Ben, and shivers flashed down his spine. "I'm even going to pull out my dirndl."

He tilted his head to the side. "A what?"

Austin rolled his eyes. "Oh my god, Mom, no, not that thing."

"So?" Tracy asked, not deterred by her son. "It'll be tons of fun. I know you've been under a lot of stress, Ben. It'll be a really great way to relax."

Unless you were a recovering alcoholic who'd just gotten fired from his job. But Tracy didn't know about Ben's drinking history, and she never would because then she definitely wouldn't give him that reference.

"You know what?" Susie said. "Despite living so close, I've never been. I'd love to join you, and I think Ben could really use some fun. He's been working so hard for so long." She wrapped her arm around Ben as if to say she'd protect him.

"I'm in, too," Genny said.

"Me, three," Ben added, attempting to sound enthusiastic.

"Great!" Tracy exchanged phone numbers with Susie so they could arrange details later.

~

LATER THAT EVENING, Tracy headed into the basement, hoping to find Austin reviewing whatever steps Todd had practised with him at the tea shop that morning. But she hadn't heard any music for over a half hour, so she checked on him.

Instead of finding her son sweating it out on the dance floor they'd recently installed, he was listening to music, barely moving.

"Sweetheart, what's up? Medication side effects? Has bullying started at the studio? Homework? Are you upset that you're not driving?"

Austin rolled his eyes. "Mom, quit worrying about me." Easier said than done, of course. "Yes, I've got some brain fog, but that doesn't mean you have to monitor my every move like I'm in prison." Tracy bit her tongue to avoid upsetting him. "It's just Dad." He stared off into space. Another seizure.

The neurologist had said there were five options for medication. They were on number three. Number one, an older drug, now had documented liver damage in many patients. Number two they'd tried last time, and it had made Austin a zombie. This one affected his cognition, which might make it difficult for him to learn choreography at higher doses, but they wouldn't know that until they got to that level. Another drug could lower his metabolism, which would leave him sluggish. Or not. They wouldn't know until they tried. The last drug was known for aggressive mood swings, but that didn't mean Austin would have them.

"Why is Dad back?" Austin had come out of his seizure.

Tracy gave her answer careful consideration. Anything she said would reflect on Eric and affect his attempts at reconnecting with Austin. "He's trying to fix his mistakes."

Austin leaned his chin on one hand. "But why does he think he can show up and pretend everything's okay?"

It relieved her to see Austin wanting to discuss this, but she didn't want to put words into Eric's mouth.

"I think you're seeing his hope but it's coming across as expectations."

"It's just that I feel like Ben's nicer than Dad, and that feels wrong somehow."

"What do you mean?"

Austin's eyes darted from side to side as he thought. He eventually hit the heel of his hand to his temple. "Stupid medication. I can't figure out how to say what I mean."

Tracy pulled his hand away. "You're going to hurt yourself. Take your time."

Austin stood and paced the floor. Did movement help clear the cobwebs? Or was he just letting out his frustration? Tracy couldn't tell.

"It's like… Ben's helping around the house without you even asking. Dad hated doing that kind of stuff."

"But your dad always supported you. You know that."

Austin nodded. "As far as boyfriends and ballet go, yeah. But…" Austin paced some more, the frustration at not being able to find the words he needed visible. "Ben was a jerk to Pauline, but the way his sister today—what's her name?"

"Susie."

"The way Susie treated him, and the way he was when we were all just talking. I swear to god, Mom, if I hadn't known Ben before today, I'd have thought he was the most popular guy around." He knitted his eyebrows together, and Tracy waited. "Is he, I don't know, changing? Can people really change like that? And if Ben can change like that, can Dad?" He absent-mindedly fully pointed his foot forward and pulled it back several times.

Tracy wanted her son to have a father in his life who loved him and cared for him. One he could have a stable relationship with. Anger toward Eric rose in her, but when she remembered what had happened to Eric this past year, compassion replaced at least some of her anger. Mental illness was neither easy nor straightforward. You couldn't just wrap your brain in a cast, let it heal, attend a few months of physio, and then continue with your life as though nothing had happened.

"People can change," Tracy finally said. "But we have to be careful around them, because they can easily fall back into old…less helpful…behaviours…if the right triggers present themselves. Does that make sense?"

Austin switched feet, the *tendu* exercise perhaps helping him digest what she was saying. "Kind of like how I wanted to run out of the family room while Dad was talking?"

Tracy nodded and her heart burst with pride at how her boy was maturing. Maybe now was a good time to ask?

"Are you ready to see your father again?"

Austin pointed his foot forward, stared at it, and nodded.

Tracy understood the road to reconciliation was long, and Austin's willingness to meet with Eric again covered at least a mile. But he was still a teenager, capable of producing emotion by the bucketful, but uncomfortable receiving as much. Inside her, though, a little party was celebrating the possibility that Austin's heart might become whole again.

So, where did that leave hers?

CHAPTER 15

School started at eight-fifteen on Monday morning, but Austin didn't emerge from his bedroom until eight o'clock. Sitting at the kitchen table, Ben saw a spike of concern from Tracy at the bags under Austin's eyes and his sluggish energy. He was the complete opposite of the boy who had joked and jibed with Ben's sister yesterday.

Tracy ruffled Austin's hair, but Austin pulled away.

"Mom, I'm fine. Just had—" Austin's gaze froze.

"One one thousand, two one thousand…" Tracy counted to eleven before Austin came out of the seizure. "I should really stay home with you, but I have to help clean up quarter-end. Here. It's time for your meds, too." She offered him a glass of water and his medication, which Austin promptly took.

Ben made a mental note: *medication at eight in the morning. Three pills.*

Austin walked around her to the kitchen. "I'm fine. I just had a brutal night." He paused when he saw the oatmeal, freshly cut strawberries, and pan of fried eggs. He glanced at Ben. "Did you co—"

Tracy pulled out her phone. "I'm going to call in sick."

Ben touched her hand. "I can stay with him."

"I don't know... I'm his mother."

"Who has a lot of responsibilities to juggle."

Austin helped himself to food with no hint that he'd been aware of his last seizure.

"No," Tracy said. "I'll stay home."

"Mom, I'm going to eat and go back to sleep. I'm old enough to manage this by myself. There's absolutely nothing you can do about it. Just call the school."

Ben was torn. He didn't have children, so he didn't want to presume to tell Tracy how to parent her son. On the other hand, nothing was worse in his initial months of recovery than his parents hovering all the time. It would also be healthier for Tracy to focus on something else instead of worrying while Austin slept.

"You can text or call me at any time," Ben said.

"You don't have to hang around here either," Austin said to him. "I'm fi—" He stared for at least three or four seconds.

"From what he's told me," Tracy said, "he can feel his brain fighting against the medication. So far, he's learned that problems with eating or sleeping can worsen side effects, and the seizures, though usually less frequent, are more intense. This morning is really bad."

Austin's shoulders slumped as he sat at the kitchen table, his back to them.

Tracy hurried to serve herself next. "Are you sure?" she asked Ben.

Ben reassured her he was.

Tracy stood as she wolfed down her oatmeal. The sign of a woman who didn't take time for herself. She gave Austin a quick kiss on the top of his head, said she loved him—to which he didn't respond—and ran out the door.

Ben served himself and sat opposite Austin.

"She needs to leave me a—" Austin stared. Ben counted, but the seizure only lasted two seconds. He assumed that was an improvement. "—alone. I hate this so much. Mom's being over-bearing again, like she was all last year. She never lets up. It's like a final exam every time she asks me about my seizures. I actually thought she had stopped in the summer, but it came back after the first visit to the neuro." His phone beeped, and he sighed as he unlocked and checked it. "It's her already. Yes, I'm going back to bed." He turned his phone down without reply-ing. "I just want to eat first."

"Shouldn't you answer her?"

Austin shot Ben a look, picked up his phone, and texted his mother. Ben understood Austin's frustration, but Tracy might not even back out of the driveway if Austin didn't answer imme-diately.

"Is there...anything I should know about your seizures?" Ben asked.

"Like what? That everyone in my grade is learning how to drive and I'm not? Or that it's humiliating to come out of a seizure and suddenly have someone's hand waving in front of your face while everyone else is laughing at you? Or how embarrassing it is when you can't answer a simple math ques-tion because your brain's suddenly locked away that informa-tion and that you look like a complete idiot in front of a guy you have a crush on?"

No teen should have that kind of life. "I don't know what that's like." It was a half-truth. He understood what happened when your brain hijacked your body, but addiction was a different kind of hijacking, and not one he was going to talk to Austin about. "I'm sorry you're going through this. Is there any first aid I should know?"

Ben rarely spoke to sick kids. That department had always

belonged to Pauline and Susie. He'd had a heart-to-heart about disability with his parents years before. But disability in old age was expected. Disability in the teen years was not.

"Do I fall on the floor and shake? No. It's just...it's... Crap. I can't think straight like this. Stupid meds."

It was like the medication was giving Austin a hangover.

"Brick for a brain, I'm guessing?" Ben asked cautiously.

Austin nodded. "The meds slow my brain down, and when I don't sleep, it's ten times worse."

When Austin finished eating, Ben suggested Austin head straight to bed, which he did. Ben cleaned up the dishes before returning to his volunteer duties.

He could ask Susie about Austin since she was a nurse practitioner, but given that she worked at a clinic in tiny New Hamburg, he figured she might not have too much experience with his form of epilepsy. Pauline, however, knew Austin much better. Plus, helping sick and disabled kids had always been her passion. If Ben could talk to Pauline about Austin, he could avoid hurting Austin or Tracy's feelings by asking the wrong questions.

TRACY CHECKED HER PHONE. Austin was still at home. Good. She texted Ben to ask if Austin had gone back to bed yet, and he confirmed he had. Talk about mother's guilt. Part of her still wanted to turn around.

As she stepped into the elevator at work, her heart began beating faster than she could type, which was one hundred and twenty words per minute. Was this her body's way of anticipating Eric every morning now? She hoped to avoid him until she got settled in her office, but the elevator stopped on the third floor and —

"Hi, Trace."

Great. Now she was stuck in an elevator with him.

"You really didn't have time for me this weekend?"

"I don't know what you expect of us."

"Time with you so we can sort all this."

Finally the doors opened and she stepped out and headed toward her office before stopping and turning to him. "I said this was going to take time."

She kept walking. Once in her office, Tracy hung up her fall coat, the one she used for warmer fall weather, and the sweater she wore in case of cooler fall mornings. But she wasn't sure if she'd need either after work because the temperatures were still expected to reach the low twenties today...

"Trace—" He had followed her.

She clipped him off. "You can't disappear except for a monthly bank transfer and then expect us to just welcome you back!" Her hands flew to her mouth. Yes, she'd thought that. But she didn't mean to say it so harshly or loudly. He was trying. So was she.

One of Tracy's colleagues walked by and glanced in. Eric closed the door.

"That's not fair," he said. "I told you why I left, that I got help, that I'm still getting help...all of it."

Compassion for Eric...protect Austin...compassion for Eric...protect Austin...

Tracy lowered her voice. "But you didn't give us time to get help."

"'Us.' Both of you need help dealing with me?"

"Austin is seeing a therapist, and yes, I could use a little help. I needed more time to wrap my head around your about-face. Why are you starting this here again?" Tracy turned her computer on, trying to signal that she wanted to begin her work.

"If you won't take the time to meet outside work, what other choice do I have?" To prove his point, Eric sat down in one of the guest chairs. "I've chosen to return to my family, and my family keeps pushing me away."

"You shoved us off a cliff a year ago! You have to scale the cliff to get us."

"This can't all be on me. Our marriage failed because of you, too."

"I am *not* doing this here. That you're even putting me in this position—"

"What position is that? Reconciliation?"

"You're my boss, Eric, and you're misusing that power! Now that I'm supporting both you and the CEO, my workload has increased. So, please, let me get to work so I can figure this out, and leave our personal lives out of it."

Eric leaned forward. "I've been waiting for months for this. How can you not see that?"

Tracy countered his posture. She didn't want to have the conversation here, but he wasn't leaving her much choice. "Then where were the phone calls? Skype calls? Occasional visits? Those first steps to ease into something more?"

Eric twisted his hands. "I was afraid I'd be turned away. Looks like I was right."

Tracy raised an eyebrow. "That was the strength of your resolve? You were worried about rejection, so you didn't try? No, I know what happened. You didn't calculate Austin's epilepsy into all this, did you? Now that he's trying medication, he barely has the bandwidth for anything else, and it's driving you bonkers. It was a risk factor you didn't anticipate."

He sighed. "That sounds like a horrible person."

Tracy opened her inbox and forty emails immediately loaded. She needed to get on with things. "I'm going to say it again. You have to wait. He's been so upset by your pushing that he didn't sleep last night, so he's missing his morning classes."

Eric's hands stopped. "Wait, what? You mean he's home alone?"

"Ben's with him." As soon as she spoke, Tracy realized her mistake.

"And you didn't tell me? I'm heading home to look after our son."

He was gone before she could say another word. How had she lasted so many years with someone so emotionally clueless? She picked up her phone to text Ben that Eric was on his way when the CEO knocked on her door, looking concerned.

She responded with professional concern of her own. "Is everything okay?"

"I was wondering the same about you," he said.

"I'm fine, thank you. Why?"

He pressed his lips together and took a breath. "I'm getting the sense that maybe having you support Eric might be too hard on you."

Tracy gave her usual relaxed, professional smile. "We're just ironing out a few things. We'll be fine."

He crossed his arms and nodded, appearing to think. "I just wanted to reach out to you and give you a heads-up: Leslie, who supported the CMO, has chosen to transfer to R&D. So that position's open if you want it. The company would still benefit from your expertise, and you would have all the perks of supporting one C-suite exec again."

Tracy knew the pay scales, and supporting the CEO was the highest-paying EA position in the company. In fact, she was collecting supporting material to request a pay raise come evaluation time. The company had opted to save money by not hiring a replacement for the CFO's EA, so why shouldn't she receive a raise? But she had to prove herself capable of handling the extra work first. That would be easier if Eric would wait until after work to deal with their personal issues.

"I'm good. But thanks for thinking of me!"

He tapped on the doorframe. "No problem. Also, I'm going to need you right now in my office. We're interviewing for the CMO position, and the rep from HR sprained her wrist this morning playing tennis. Bring two coffees. One with cream and sugar, and one with only sugar."

He left before she could answer. She disconnected her laptop from its docking station and folded it under her arm. As she headed to the kitchenette for the coffees, something hit her.

The CEO had just clarified that she was expendable. Eric wasn't.

CHAPTER 16

*H*ad Tracy forgotten her keys? Who else would knock so hard at the door? Ben rushed to open it before the noise disturbed Austin. He had barely stepped out of the door's way when an angry Eric stormed in.

"Where is he?"

Ben's PR experience kicked in and he composed himself. "In his bedroom, asleep."

Eric closed the door as though this was his house and spoke as though Ben hadn't said a word. "Do you know the risks involved with his condition? You both should've called me if Tracy wasn't going to be able to stay home." He headed into the kitchen.

Ben took a breath and followed. "I don't have your number." Eric was going to ruin whatever progress he'd made with Austin if he continued in this manner. Ben tried to offer an olive branch. "I've read up a little on the subject of epilepsy, but I wanted to talk to Pauline so I don't burden Tracy with ignorant questions."

Eric whipped around. "Pauline's a neurologist now?"

When someone hurt too much, they didn't see the olive branch at all. Ben could relate. How often had he refused help? He took another breath and focused on his goal: this family's reunification. "No, but in her thirty years of working as a mascot, she's spoken to a lot of sick and disabled kids—"

"First off, he's neither sick nor disabled. At most, his brain just isn't working the way it should."

Ah. Denial. Clear as day. Eric still hadn't accepted that he had a disabled son.

"Secondly," Eric continued, "I know what the doctors said because I attended the appointments. You didn't. Neither did Pauline."

So far as Ben could piece together, Eric had only been to the initial appointments after Austin's accident, certainly not the recent ones. It was clear Eric loved his son. But Eric would need to accept Austin's disease if his family was going to accept him back.

"Eric, I just mean the best for your family. I want to ensure I'm helping your family, not hindering all of you. About Pauline? She has a gift for listening to people, and I know she's learned a lot through that. Me, I'm better at talking than listening."

Eric leaned against the counter in the kitchen, stuck his hands in his pockets, and sighed. "Sorry, man. I am so on edge. I hate myself for this problem I've caused the people I love."

Ben could relate to that, too.

"I just wish I knew how I could fix things faster. It's a brutal situation to be in."

Ben wanted to share his story with Eric, to say, *Hey, I get it. I know what happens when you mess up really badly*. But telling Eric that his wife and son were living with a former alcoholic whose addiction had landed him on the streets for two years would only cause Eric more worry. Ben had a good grasp of what the general public thought of people like him. The younger crowd was, thankfully, more accepting. Eric's generation? Less so. Exceptions existed, but Ben wasn't about to test the waters.

Eric walked to the other side of the kitchen and stared at the cupboards. "I actually forget where the glasses are. I didn't live in this house long before I left."

Ben passed Eric a glass but let him serve himself so Eric didn't feel like a guest in what had been his family home. For some reason, watching Eric reminded Ben of hearing his father cry when Ben called from Montreal to say he was ready to come home. He buried the memory before his eyes teared up.

Eric took a sip of water. "Why are you here and I'm not?"

This was awkward. But Ben had to answer. "I'm just a guest, helping with the festival."

Eric eyed Ben up and down. "So...there's nothing between you and Tracy?"

"No."

Ben was surprised at how fast that flew out. In fact, he felt relieved. Yes, maybe Austin had noticed his attraction to Tracy the other night, but it had been an accident, like their kiss in the summer, and did not reflect Ben's true intentions.

"For what it's worth, Eric, I really hope everything works out for the three of you."

Eric let out a breath and nodded.

"Mind if I return to my work?" Ben asked.

"Go for it. I've got stuff to take care of, too."

The men worked in silence—Ben at the dining room table, Eric at the kitchen table.

Ben checked Belmont Village's social media and saw a DM from a local radio station. *Would an interview with Claire of Claire's Tea Shop be possible?*

Pauline had said her mother would be out of town until Thanksgiving, hadn't she? Ben replied, asking for a time to accommodate Claire's travel plans. The radio personality wrote back and they hashed out details. Ben just didn't mention that neither Claire nor Pauline was talking to him. Well, he assumed Claire wouldn't talk to him. Pauline definitely wasn't. But he had a week to figure this out. He settled on other tasks to let his subconscious come up with a plan. Sometimes it worked.

Two hours later, when he and Eric heard recorded piano music coming out of Austin's room, Ben hadn't come up with a plan for how to let Austin know his father was in the house.

"I'll tell Austin you're here."

Eric stood up. "I'm his father. I don't need an introduction."

Every muscle in Ben's body wanted to tackle Eric to the floor. What was he thinking? Communication needed to happen carefully. But Austin was at the bottom of the stairs before Ben could say anything more.

"What are *you* doing here?" Austin pushed past Eric and glared at Ben. "And why did you let him in?"

The blood drained from Ben's face. He should've stood up for Austin. Todd would've done it, wouldn't he have?

"Your mom said you were home—" Eric said.

"And you freaked out because Ben's here. I can take care of myself."

Ben stared at the floor. As important as honesty was, blatant honesty was sometimes not the best course of action.

Austin stormed into the kitchen, grabbed a banana, and returned to his room.

Neither Ben nor Eric spoke.

A few minutes later, Austin emerged, dressed, a backpack over one shoulder. "I'm heading to school."

"What about lunch?" Eric asked.

"There's a cafeteria."

"I can drive you."

"A taxi is on its way. *I don't need your help.*"

Austin slid into his sneakers and slammed the door behind him, the lingering silence underscoring his anger.

Eric slouched into a kitchen chair. "Will I ever be able to do anything right?"

"You came back. That's already a step in the right direction."

But as Ben watched the cab pull into the driveway, he wondered how he could make things right with Austin. Eric had the rest of his life to work things out with him. Ben only had two weeks, and he was done burning bridges.

BEN'S first impression of the Belmont Chocolate House was one of confusion. He had seen it before in stores in cities that were too big for small-town charm and not big enough to have cosmopolitan confidence. To put it in marketing speak, they didn't have a clear brand identity.

Was David's a vintage Parisian café? A Swiss chocolatier? A Seattle coffee shop? Between the checkered table cloths draped over wooden tables, mounds of chocolate goodness displayed in past-their-prime brass-framed display cases, and LED blue-tinged light bulbs, Ben couldn't tell. The décor in Claire's Tea Shop was up to date—now that Ben thought about it, Pauline had requested time off from the Peregrines in the summer to help with renovations—but David clearly had added to the dated look of the shop without renovating or doing a full update.

That brass, for instance, had stayed so long it was actually back in style. Only it was nicked, scratched, and dull.

But maybe only a marketing expert or interior designer would notice. Anyone as addicted to chocolate as Tracy probably wouldn't care: the scent of chocolate that had welcomed

Ben the moment he'd opened the door would surely draw her in, and it was for her that Ben had come.

"Can I help you?" A young woman wearing a white apron stood behind the counter.

Ben introduced himself and asked about the owner.

"David's doing better, but it'll be a while before he can work again. That's why we're closing in two weeks."

"Two weeks? Before Halloween?"

"David had us cancel our last order of beans as soon as he got sick." She bit her lower lip as she rubbed her hands on her apron.

"Beans? You make coffee, too?"

The employee knit her eyebrows together. "We're a cacao bean-to-bar operation. David bought all the equipment...yeah, seventeen years ago. After you run the liquor through a conche, you have to let it rest for thirty days. Our final batch is resting now but we'll be out in two weeks."

Ben didn't have a clue what she was talking about. "Speaking of closing, you were closed when I made the rounds Saturday. Here." He handed the woman a stack of postcards, and she smiled as she inspected them.

"These look great. People are getting their orders in early for Halloween, so traffic's high right now. We won't have a problem handing these out." The woman tucked the elastic band into her pants pocket and placed the postcards next to the till. "We just don't have the staff to stay open longer. Without David here, we can't keep running the shop."

Ben's instincts told him something wasn't right. The committee had said that David was over eighty years old. Surely he wasn't still working fifty hours a week to keep this kind of operation running?

Or did he love his work so much he couldn't bring himself to make a contingency plan, the way Pauline had avoided planning her transition out of full-time acting?

Be honest. I would've stayed in sports marketing my entire life if I'd had the choice. Ben hoped to return down the road, but the road back to sports marketing was long and he only stood at its entrance.

"I'm really sorry to hear that. I'll at least take some chocolate off your hands."

"The order for the committee meeting this evening?"

"Yes, but I'm also looking for something special." *Oh, crap. Have I said too much? How active is the rumour mill here?* "I mean, it's just for a friend. Tracy's been letting me stay at her house while I help out with the committee."

The woman smiled but didn't let on that she believed Ben's motive was anything other than what he'd said.

"Tracy loves almost everything here," she said.

"Is there anything in particular she likes?" Then he remembered what Eric had said at Claire's. "Do you have just dark chocolate?"

The woman surveyed her wares. "I was just going to suggest that." A corner of her mouth lifted. "It's her true love." Ben blushed. *Terrific. She knows for sure now.* "Would you like to try some samples? I'm sure it'll mean more if you select the ones you enjoy."

"Sure, okay." Wasn't dark chocolate, well, dark chocolate?

The employee presented him with samples from the Dominican Republic and different cacao farms from Peru.

"Just a moment." She poured a small glass of water. "Rinse out the flavour between samples. You should be able to pick up the distinct notes from the cacao from different farms."

"Cacao? Not cocoa?"

"The plant's name. Cocoa is the processed product. We also

don't add vanilla to our pure dark chocolate bars, so you can taste every flavour."

To Ben's surprise, he could indeed taste minor differences. One tasted slightly more acidic but had floral notes. Another had touches of blueberry and fig. In the third sample, Ben detected hints of apricot and pecan. The variations were slight, but Ben could taste them.

"I didn't know chocolate had nuances in flavour like this." One simple product—chocolate—and so much subtle variety. What else had Ben missed because he'd been—to use tired corporate jargon—so laser-focused on his career?

"It is remarkable," the woman agreed.

"But what do I pick?"

"Sometimes people look for a connection between an interest and the flavours."

An idea hit him like barrel full of wine. Tracy would never understand the true meaning behind it, but that was okay. She had accepted the small piece of his story he'd shared with her, and that meant more to him than she'd ever know. He wouldn't buy her alcohol-filled chocolate, but some alcohols were made from fruit.

Ben asked for four bars with notes of fruits in them, and the woman wrapped them up.

"I'm a bit of a health nut," he explained. "Hence the fruit."

She smiled, and he realized she'd believed all along that he liked Tracy. Crap, crap, crap.

Two weeks, Landry. You can handle two weeks.

"Anything else?"

"Yes, actually. Something for Austin and also Pauline."

The employee laughed in a way that suggested familiarity and family. Ben missed that sense of community. "Austin's not quite as discerning. Pauline likes anything sweet that goes well with a strong tea, or a chocolate backed by a social program."

As Ben calculated the totals in his head, he began to worry about spending all this extra money.

Ever since Ben had started selling stuffed Perry the Peregrines and foam fingers at the souvenir kiosk, he'd hoarded his money in case he ever fell off the deep end again. Although it meant he'd have access to more money for more alcohol, he'd hoped instead it would mean he'd have an easier time climbing out of whatever financial hole he'd have dug himself into. When Susie offered to act as his backup, he'd agreed. As his wealth grew, it became an additional motivation to not drink.

But he needed to spend this money. Olive branches often cost money, but these ones were worth it.

Within twenty minutes, Ben had everything selected and paid for.

Now it was time to walk over to Claire's Tea Shop and hope Pauline would talk to him.

CHAPTER 17

"*W*ill she let me talk to her?"

"Probably not."

Just before it had been Ben's turn at the counter, Pauline had disappeared to the back room, and so Todd served him. Ben pulled out the chocolate bar he'd selected for Pauline: something small to show he was trying, not something larger that suggested a bribe.

"This is my olive branch to her. The employee at David's said the beans are sourced from a fair-trade program that's trying to raise funds for a kids' health program for the community. I thought she might like that."

Todd read the packaging and nodded. "I have to admit, you're surprising me, Ben. I'll ask her, but no guarantees."

You had a job to do, Ben told himself. *That's why you made her sign that contract. You paid her appropriately.* He sighed. He always had a job to do, didn't he? But it had kept him sober. He'd only ever envisioned two futures: one as a homeless drunk, and one working in sports marketing. Fired but still able to work had never occurred to him.

But he no longer wanted to get on Pauline's good side just because of work. He was on another journey with her. Clearly not a buyer's journey. *Who's the marketer?* he asked himself facetiously.

A friendship journey? Would Pauline ever become his friend? She had a big heart, but would she make space for him?

Todd returned and told Ben Pauline would see him in the back room of the store. He wasn't surprised to see pictures of Pauline as Perry hanging on the walls, including one from the children's hospital fundraiser, with Todd, Austin, and Todd's family.

But he tried to ignore them.

Pauline had already downed the chocolate bar he'd bought her—the empty wrapper lay on the desk—and stood at her full six feet with her arms crossed as though she was ready to crush him.

"What do you want?"

He turned to his PR experience to stay calm. "To clear the air."

The muscles in Pauline's arms tightened. "There's no air to clear. Your tactics are underhanded. Using my best friend to get to your next job is malicious at best."

"I'm still volunteering—"

"*To get the job!* Not because you really want to help us. You may have schmoozed your way into everyone's hearts here, but if I'd been at that meeting, I'd have made sure everyone understood the real you."

Remaining professional wasn't working. Pauline wanted to fight. Ben had to accept the challenge.

"And force your best friend to take on the extra work, Pauline? With how busy she is?"

Pauline sighed and averted her gaze.

Ben didn't dare take a seat. The only thing giving him

strength right now was his extra inch of height. "I help around the house, I'm trying to advertise an inclusive festival—"

"Marketing yourself to perfection, Ben. But I know you. They don't. This Mr. Nice Guy disguise won't work on me."

Ben threw his hands in the air. "What else do you want from me, Pauline? There's more to me than what you saw at the Peregrines."

Pauline planted her hands on her hips. "Really? In three years, you couldn't once show this authentic self?"

"Like you could? Why is this the first time I'm seeing all this anger toward me?"

"Because otherwise you'd have fired me!"

"And I was scared I'd have gotten fired if I'd acted otherwise."

Pauline burst out laughing. "You honestly thought you'd get fired for acting respectful and professional?"

For the first time in his working life, Ben realized how ridiculous that sounded. He slouched against the wall. "It's more complicated that than."

"I don't have time for complicated, and I need to get back to work. Unlike you, I'm not sitting on loads of cash." She threw the chocolate wrapper in the garbage. "That was a good chocolate bar. Thanks for the thought."

Had she tossed that to keep the back room clean or to underscore her hate for him? He needed Claire's Tea Shop on board with him in pretty much every area of his life now: marketing the festival, continuing his friendship with Tracy, and better understanding Austin. Ben would start with the last area.

"Then before you throw me out again, help me understand Austin."

"So you can reach Tracy through her son? You always went for low blows, Ben, but I didn't think you punched that low."

Ben clenched his fist. What was the point of fighting? But

for reasons he didn't understand right now, Pauline was Tracy's best friend.

Plus, Ben had to admit he'd come to care for Tracy and Austin, and he hadn't lied to Eric when he said he wanted to help the family reconnect.

Pauline took a step toward the door. "I take it we're done now?"

Ben planned to build his first bridge—with the Tschirharts—before he left town. He could see that what had gotten him fired was walking all over people. Pauline's anger was proving that.

"Not yet," he said quietly.

He'd been fired before, for not meeting his sales quotas in his first job. Soon afterwards came the first comfort drink. He had told himself he was drinking away his sorrows, that it would just be a few days, but he hadn't realized how enticing drinking would become.

"I swear, Pauline, I'm not trying to get to Tracy through her son. But I can see her anxiety building, especially with Eric back in town. I was just hoping you could help me understand Austin's condition better so I don't have to ask them questions that might cause more worry."

Pauline sat down.

Ben took that as a sign that the fight was over. He continued, "I may not even have a chance at this CMO position anymore. I stayed with Austin this morning—he'd had a bad night—so Tracy could go to work. Eric wasn't pleased I was there and he wasn't."

Pauline grimaced. "And he's the CFO."

"Exactly," Ben continued. "I know how this looks. I'm sixteen years younger than him, in a lot better shape—"

Pauline waved to interrupt him. "I get it. Just because you look like you've walked off the set of a soap commercial for men doesn't mean you have to get so high on yourself. What do you need from me?"

"I'm just trying to give you the context. My presence isn't helping."

"There's a hotel."

"Not paying for that."

"Because you're too cheap."

Okay. So the fight hadn't ended. He wasn't going to get past this wall unless he spoke in her language of empathy, was he? It was an admittedly uncomfortable language for him. Another reason his past remained hidden was that he wanted to be judged by his own merits and not by pity, or worse.

Each of the first seven job interviews—it had been exactly seven—after he'd gotten sober had ended moments after he'd honestly explained his two-year gap in employment. Only after his parents had agreed to be his alibi—they'd received their life-altering diagnoses during Ben's troubled years and Ben could say he'd stayed home to take care of them—did the interviews go any further.

But Pauline was different. What if his secrecy was *causing* the distrust? What if it was time to offer the real olive branch?

"It's just that you're good at listening and I'm...not so much. And before you get sarcastic with me, this isn't a tactic. We both know that listening isn't my strong suit." He took a breath. That she wasn't making this easy on him showed how much pain he'd caused her. Maybe it was time to admit he'd pushed her too far. But the only way to do that would be to explain why.

"I haven't told Tracy about this yet, but you and I worked together for three years. It's time I...I owed you an explanation."

"If you expect me to keep this from Tracy, then forget it."

Ben shook his head. "I promise I'll tell her, just not right now. Things between Eric and her are messy, and this morning made it worse."

Pauline shifted her position and nodded. "If telling me will help you help them, then fine. What is it?"

Ben rubbed the back of his neck. He'd never told anyone outside his parents, sister, and the people at the rehab centre his full story. Pauline's gaze was so intent, he stared at the floor.

"I...back in my early twenties...I spent two years...drunk and homeless. I came to Kitchener from Toronto so my family wouldn't know..." He took a breath and glanced up. Pauline's eyes and mouth were wide open. "I used the Out of the Cold program here and overnighted in churches and at the shelter the festival's raising funds for. I eventually ended up in Montreal and drank myself into financial oblivion."

"I...wow...I didn't expect that. I had no idea, Ben."

Ben took in another deep breath and let it out. "That's good. I keep it as hidden as possible. But that's why I'm staying with Tracy—first, because I can save as much money as possible in case I start down that path again, and more importantly, so I'm not alone. The fear of embarrassing myself in front of people I know keeps me away from the bottle a little longer...which is a real temptation right now because I got fired and have no idea what to do next."

A hundred expressions flashed across Pauline's face, but none of them struck Ben as disbelief.

"Derek told me how you'd lost your job." She shook her head. "But I really wouldn't have guessed the rest of your story. Not in a million years. I'm sorry you went through that."

He extended his hand, relieved. "Are we good?"

She tilted her head. "I still don't understand why you felt it was acceptable to treat everyone like you did, especially after living on the streets."

Ben let his hand drop. "Being homeless doesn't automatically turn you into a nice person. I've always been so terrified of landing back there again that I only thought of moving forward and delivering results."

"At the expense of others."

"Unfortunately." He held out his hand again. "So?"

"Aren't you going to actually apologize?"

"Didn't I just?"

Pauline stood up and headed for the door to the café. "An apology starts with, 'I'm sorry.' That you still can't utter those words tells me you still haven't fully grasped the extent of the hurt you've caused." Pauline turned and stood right in front of Ben, and his skin burned. "Until I hear those two words, no, we're not good, because it's near impossible for you to say them."

Ben had to defend himself somehow. "I—"

But Pauline wouldn't allow it. "I'm sorry you had such a rough period in your life. I really am. I've heard so many stories about homelessness while in costume. And to think I knew someone personally who had lived through that, and so early in your life. I can only imagine the pain you and your family went through. Part of me is happy you managed to pull yourself out of it." She appeared to talk as freely as the emotions that showed on her face. "And I'm glad you're finally understanding that you can't keep running over people for your own personal gain. I can see you're changing. But until you can apologize to me—and my parents—the air between us is not cleared."

"Pauline, please listen—"

"No, Ben. You're going to listen to me for once. Remember when I was breaking down right before the hospital fundraiser... What did you say when you barged into my change room and saw me crying? I thought my world had imploded. But did you show an ounce of care? You didn't even ask what was wrong or offer me a tissue. Instead, you said, 'Oh, cripes, what now?'"

Ben stared at the floor.

"And remember after the success of Austin's dance and school talk how you told me you wanted me to book 'one of those kids' every time I did the anti-bullying rally? Like they were interchangeable and all there just to help market the team."

Ben's cheeks burned like red-hot iron.

"You backed down from the idea the moment I reamed you out about it, and I can see your remorse now. But I had to deal with that Ben for three years. You even threatened to sue me when you found out I'd told Tracy and Austin that I played Perry. That would've taken me *years* to pay back. And let's not forget you were going to fire me for wanting to come home for a week to help my mom out when she needed my help. *Fire me for helping my family!* I had never taken full vacation in those three years, and still you were going to fire me." Pauline took a deep breath. "A ten-minute chat, where you can't even say you're sorry, doesn't erase Ice Pad Ben."

Ben's stomach tightened as his guilt worsened.

"You know I feel compassion for people. But there are limits. If you want to clear the air between us, I want an apology to my face, and I want you to apologize to my parents because I will *never* forget their expressions—especially Mom's —when they discovered I'd been lying to them for three years about the job that had brought me so much happiness because you'd forbidden me from sharing it with them."

Ben couldn't lift his gaze as Pauline marched past him. When he finally looked up, the Perry photos were staring back at him. A few were community photos of kids. There were several with the hockey players. A couple with the office staff.

Ben wasn't in a single one.

He caught his reflection in a mirror on the wall. He didn't understand why, but he didn't recognize the man looking back at him.

A sudden wave of disgust overcame him. He rushed out the back door to get fresh air.

CHAPTER 18

"*I*'m so sorry about your father barging in on you like that this morning." Tracy had gotten her car back before she picked Austin up from school.

"He has to stop. That was so intrusive."

"He got the message. And he loves you...he's just being somewhat awkward about it."

Austin snorted. "Awkward? How about possessive? Intrusive? Mean? Selfish? He chose not to live here. *It's our house, not his.*"

Tracy sighed. Eric hadn't make this easier, but what parent who loved their child could control their actions when they believed their child was in danger? Add in a touch of jealousy, and you had an emotionally volatile mix. But Austin still saw the world in black and white.

Best thing to do now was change the subject. "What about an early supper since you had an early lunch?"

Austin leaned on the car door and mumbled something about having too much homework and catching up from missing class this morning. "Then I'm going to practise. Besides, there's leftover lasagna."

"But Austin, Ben made that for times when we're rushed. I got lots done today at work. I'll just explain to my boss—"

"I'm fine."

Please, not a repeat of the summer. Keep him talking about ballet.

Tracy asked him about what Todd had assigned him to practise this week.

Austin did start explaining the steps, but Tracy was only half listening. She was angry at Eric for dragging the family back and for forcing her to prove to the CEO how dedicated she was to her job or he'd transfer her to another department with less pay. She could apply elsewhere, but she'd only been at this company a year. It simply wouldn't look good on her résumé if she was already jumping ship. And because she shared Eric's uncommon surname, it wouldn't take long for people to figure out she'd left a company shortly after her ex-husband had been hired.

"So, I'm working on my five-forty jumps," Austin finished as they pulled up to the house.

"Sounds like fun."

But Austin's face didn't look like he was having fun. Tracy followed Austin's sagging shoulders into the house. Ben was in the kitchen and looked like he wanted to talk, but she held up a hand and hoped he could understand now wasn't the time.

Austin closed his bedroom door, forcing Tracy to stand outside it.

"Did you want to watch that Misty Copeland documentary tomorrow night? You know tonight I have the festival committee meeting?" she asked through the door.

"Whatever."

"Or how about *First Position*? Would probably be good to study that again as you prep for the YAGP."

"Sure." But it was the teenage, non-committal *sure*.

She sighed. Best she got out of Austin's space before he chose to not dance, period. "Okay, sweetheart. We'll just play it by ear. I might head back into work for a bit. If you need anything, call me."

"Sure."

She dragged her feet back to the kitchen. How could Eric have been in counselling for so many months and not known it would take time to heal the rift between him and Austin?

Parental love, Tracy, she reminded herself.

But once she reached the foot of the stairs, she froze. Maybe she was the one not trying hard enough. Should she go back into the office? Or what if Ben ran the committee meeting and she stayed home with Austin?

"Tracy? You okay?"

She nodded, barely registering Ben's voice.

The past school year, including the emotional anguish, raced through her mind's eye like a movie on fast forward. What if it happened again? What if new bullies surfaced and Tracy was powerless to help because she needed a second job to make up for the lost income? And what if Austin's rejection hurt Eric so much that he refused to pay child support?

A gentle touch on her shoulder broke the nightmare that had begun forming in her head.

She looked up and into Ben's eyes. How could those hazel eyes contain so much pain and hope at the same time?

"I...I might have to go back into work before tonight's meeting," she said. "But Austin—"

Ben gave her shoulder a caring squeeze, sending shivers down her spine. "If you need to get back to work, go. He's safe here. I promise I'll keep an eye on Austin and let you know if anything's wrong."

She glanced toward Austin's closed door and sighed. What she wouldn't do to have full control over her own schedule.

"Thank you," she said. "Oh, and don't expect any surprise appearances from Eric. He learned his lesson today."

Ben's mouth formed into that irresistible smile. "Thanks for the heads-up."

If she kissed her thanks on that mouth, would he welcome it? But she needed to leave. If she did kiss him, there was no telling how long it would be before she returned to work, and Ben was in no position to hire her should she get fired for not completing her duties.

EVERY SCHOOL KID learned to apologize. And Ben knew the importance of apologizing, but when had he stopped saying he was sorry?

He knew he'd contributed to the problems with Eric and Austin that morning, and that Tracy was still upset about the whole situation. He'd wanted to apologize to her for his part in the matter. And to Austin for not prioritizing Austin's needs. And it was what Pauline was asking of him, that he apologize to her and her parents.

It was that olive branch thing Todd had talked about. And it was what Susie always told him. A lot was riding on this communication skill.

But somehow it had gone dormant.

Austin passed Ben in the hallway, now dressed in dance clothes, his mood focused, like someone who needed to get something out of his system.

Or someone who'd been hurt and was ignoring the person who'd caused the pain.

"Why is this so f—lippin' hard for me?" Ben said out loud as he went into the guest room and dropped onto the bed. "I mean, seriously? I'm s...s... See? I can't even say it."

He felt like a prize idiot. Who apologized these days, anyway? He certainly hadn't apologized to fans for the Nate-the-Drunken-Mascot incident. He had promised it wouldn't happen again—and it hadn't. That was more important, wasn't it?

"Look, Ben, I'm sorry, okay? You don't have to fire me. The Pissed Perry memes will pass."

"No, they won't pass, Nate. I do have to fire you. You're not getting the hundreds of emails I'm getting from parents and grandparents saying they don't know how to explain this to their kids. Not only has your drinking shamed the franchise, but you've put my job in peril."

Now Ben was on Nate's end of the conversation. What would Pauline, Tracy, and Austin say to him if he actually apologized?

"I knew you were only ever capable of thinking of yourself!"

"You knew better than to let Eric stomp into our house like that!"

"Why didn't you keep my dad out of my home?"

Would Tracy kick him out because of this? If he didn't apologize, she might. He tried again. "I'm s...s...s..."

"You're sorry? For bringing home a seventy-six on your biology test?"

"I hate biology, Dad. I love English."

"You can do better than that, Benjamin. Besides, where will English get you?"

"Never did anything with biology," Ben said to himself dryly. His father was a good man who'd tried to keep Ben out of sports—*"Don't follow in my footsteps. The sports industry is too tough. The sciences are the future."* In fact, he'd recommended medical rehab for Ben the moment Ben expressed misgivings about sharing his difficulties in a group program, and Ben had been grateful.

What if Ben said the wrong thing when he apologized? He'd obviously heard lots of apologies at work, but he'd also heard the grumblings that happened afterwards: *"That wasn't fake, not at all...What a waste of time...She didn't even mean it."*

"I tried to explain things to Pauline, and what did I get? More anger."

But the more he reflected on that conversation, the more he realized he was wrong: she'd actually given him empathy in return. She'd said she was sorry about his years on the street as a way of connecting with the pain he'd experienced. Her anger stemmed from his refusal to admit he'd been wrong in how he'd managed her.

Ben always wanted to be right so his managers wouldn't fire him. That had no connection to Pauline now. True apologies either acknowledged shared pain or wrongdoing. Or sometimes both, as with Pauline and her family. By apologizing to the Robinsons, Ben would be admitting he'd been wrong to force Pauline into silence and he'd share in the pain that decision had caused them.

He closed his eyes and pictured facing Pauline.

"I'm s...s..."

"I'm sorry. It's just that it's warm by the bank machines at night."

"Not for leeches like you who choose not to work. Now, get out before I call the police."

Would Tracy kick him out? It was her house. He had no right to stay here. Ben had to make this work. He wasn't going to let history repeat itself.

"I'm s...s... Crap. I'm sor...sor..."

A voice interrupted him. "You are such a dork, you know that?" Austin had the biggest grin. "You were a jerk and now you're a dork."

Ben's face turned hot, but he regrouped fast. At least this wasn't a photo that'd show up in national media. "And *you're* sometimes a little too honest." He stood up from his bed and brushed past Austin. *I should've closed the door.*

But Austin followed. "Why is apologizing so hard for you?"

"Because it is." Being skewered once today was enough. "Shouldn't you be practising or something?"

"Can't concentrate. All I can think about is how Mom wants to talk to me more about Dad. She treats life like a task list. Getting the three of us together is her new project."

"That's got to be frustrating." Ben wondered if saying *I'm sorry* would fit here. But he was too ashamed of himself to try.

Ashamed. Root word: shame.

Apologizing became shameful to me and it's taken me years to realize it.

"So, what are you going to do now?" Ben asked.

Austin shrugged. "I guess get changed and hang out with friends."

Ben had promised Tracy he'd look after Austin, and he'd failed at it this morning. He couldn't well follow Austin, so he had to come up with another plan. "Schoolwork?"

"Can wait."

But the tone in Austin's voice was flat, like someone giving up.

"Sounds to me like you're throwing in the towel instead of simply rescheduling your afternoon."

Austin rolled his eyes. "Don't start lecturing me. It's only English. I do movement, music, and art. I suck at words."

Ben raised his eyebrows and let a playful grin creep onto his face. "Well, aren't you lucky today? I majored in communications and marketing. Grab your work. Let's go to the kitchen table."

Austin crossed his arms. "You're not seriously going to force me to do my homework."

Ben slowly nodded. "Like I said, you're in luck!"

Austin's mouth turned positively upside down.

"Do you object like this when Todd asks you to work hard?" Ben asked.

"No, but he treats people nice."

"Nicely. Adverb."

He had to keep Austin home. If that meant coercing him with a call to his mother, he would, but he'd save that as his last resort. He could simply try connecting with Austin as another human being, something he wasn't, admittedly, used to.

"Listen. I've made a lot of mistakes in my life. Jerk-worthy mistakes. I'm trying to fix them. If you're not doing well in English—"

"I'm failing it, actually."

That surprised Ben. He believed Austin to be a perfectionist. "How come?"

Austin shrugged. "I just don't like words to begin with. They're so limiting. Then there's the medication—for whatever reason, I have a harder time remembering vocabulary. But English is also in the morning."

"So you've missed a few classes."

Austin nodded. "And then just me not feeling emotion in words like I do in music and movement."

So, basically nothing to motivate the teen. Ben gave Austin's predicament a few moments' thought. Ben could spin almost anything. Just tackling Austin's most challenging concept in English for thirty minutes might make a difference. "Have you ever considered what English will do for you in the future?"

"I already speak it, so, like, no."

"You know that if you run your own dance company, knowing how to communicate with your audiences will be crucial to things like marketing, acquiring donations, and communicating with the press."

"But we're reading some Canadian author right now." Austin paused for a moment, then shook his head. "Can't even think of her name. How is knowing her name and 'how the book speaks to me' going to help me market a dance production?"

Wow. If the medication was that harsh on his memory, no wonder he felt so rough some days. But Ben would keep this upbeat. "That's okay. I imagine dance is like sports? Many athletes skip university for now and try to get a professional career first?"

"It can be like that. But I can't lift girls now so I don't know if I have a future in dance."

Ouch. But although Ben didn't know ballet, he knew two things. One: Todd Parsons believed Austin to have enough talent that he donated every Sunday morning to training him. And two: the two times Ben had seen Austin dance, he had been spellbound. The world of dance had to have a place for such a talented boy, even if he couldn't lift others because he feared a seizure could injure someone.

"Sounds like you're in the same boat as me: you don't know what your future holds."

"Lucky again?"

"Lucky again. But let's assume you're going to find your dream dance career. That means this is your education, Austin. Your résumé, website, social media, all of it relies on your ability to communicate."

"Still doesn't tell me how this'll help me learn this stupid author."

"Don't some of the biggest ballets get their story from books?"

Austin's gaze shifted. "I guess. But they're overly simplified."

"So, let's see who this mysterious author is, what themes she incorporates, and we'll talk about how each theme would change the style of a ballet you'd choreograph."

Austin's eyes lit up. Ben had done it—he'd found the idea that had connected Austin to a subject he detested.

"So?" Ben said. "Go get your books."

Austin bounded up the stairs, returning in thirty seconds. They were still studying together at the table when Tracy returned, her hand on her heart at what she saw before her.

CHAPTER 19

"*H*ad I known it would be this torturous for you to drive my little Toyota Yaris, I would've driven. It's only five minutes."

"No, really, it's okay. You looked wiped."

"If you could see your face right now." She drew her lips tight and sat up stiffly in the passenger seat. "And how you touched everything when you sat down." To demonstrate, she reached for the air-conditioning button with her index finger, as though testing whether it was burning hot.

"I'm, um, not used to Japanese makes."

Tracy burst into laughter. "*That's* your excuse? Admit it, Ben. The notion of driving my little putt-putter is so embarrassing to you that even with your PR experience, you can't hide it!"

Ben bit his bottom lip, and Tracy pointed at him. "Gotcha again!"

He slapped his leg. "I'm trying to be gentlemanly." But he was grinning. "I can't stand driving this thing. Almost cracked my head open just getting into it. They don't make these cars for tall people."

Tracy's stomach was full of flutters as Ben pulled into a parking spot in front of Claire's Tea Shop and turned off the car. The other business owners had their cars parked by their establishments. The store was already closed, but the light was on over the lounge area at the back, where the festival marketing committee would meet. Austin was dancing when they left.

Before Tracy could step out of the car, Ben handed her a paper gift bag.

"For this morning. I'm…" He rubbed his hand over his face. "I should've stopped Eric from intruding on Austin's privacy like that. I could feel the impending disaster. But all I saw was that he was Austin's father. I should've remembered that you have custody. Anyway, I hope you like it."

Tracy lifted out the tissue paper. Four thirty-five-gram dark chocolate bars, each from a different farm.

"Ben… You didn't have to. Eric acted like a clod this morning. There wasn't really anything you could do."

Ben shrugged. "I could've taken him down, so Austin could see us rolling on the floor like high school enemies?"

Tracy laughed. "That would have made things worse." She placed the chocolate bars and tissue paper back into the bag. "I can't wait to try these, thank you. To be honest, I don't know how to help Austin past this."

"Show him the benefits of opening up to his father again."

Tracy lifted an eyebrow. "Life is like a marketing campaign? Yeah, right."

"Life is a series of marketing campaigns. Every time you try to convince someone of something, you're marketing to them."

Tracy turned to face him completely. "Isn't that just a little cynical?"

Ben shook his head. "Marketing's only evil if you do it for

the wrong reason. But I want the same happiness for the three of you that my family had once I..." He shrugged off the rest of the sentence.

Tracy didn't know how that story ended and she wanted to hear it. "I won't think any differently of you, whatever it is. I promise."

Ben briefly smiled in acknowledgement and glanced away, only to see Pauline leaning in the doorway to her shop, arms crossed and frowning.

"Did she always glare at me like that from behind her mask?" Ben asked.

That look's for me, Tracy thought. But she was getting annoyed with Pauline's opinion about Ben. As much as she loved Pauline, who Tracy spent time with wasn't actually Pauline's business.

"That's her get-our-booties-inside look." Tracy glanced at her phone. They were right on time. "We're already five minutes late." Hopefully Ben didn't check his phone.

"She was always punctual," he said.

"Everyone's here," Pauline said when they exited the car, "and I'd like to lock the front door."

"Sorry," Tracy replied.

"My fault," Ben said, much to Tracy and Pauline's surprise. "I was helping Austin with his English homework. We lost track of time."

Still not a direct apology, though he'd actually shouldered the blame. *But it put him in a good light,* Tracy thought. *But it was also the truth.*

Ben tapped the roof of the car, a twinkle of mischief in his eyes. "It was fun driving this little thing."

The corner of Tracy's mouth curled up. "Call my beautiful car 'a thing' again, and you're *walking* home, Mr. Landry. You should be grateful I allowed you to drive it."

He raised an eyebrow. "Oh, should I now? Then how can I repay the privilege?"

Neither missed the innuendo, and they relieved the nervousness between them with light laughter as Ben reached into the back seat of the car to get the snacks.

Tracy held the door to the shop open for him, and he paused in the doorway to glance at her. Only last Wednesday had she brushed past him through this very entrance, not wanting so much as eye contact with him.

And now?

Now the flutters had spread all over her body.

"Thanks," he said.

"Happy to."

Tracy locked the door while Ben carried the box of baked goods to the back and greeted everyone.

"You haven't scared Ben off yet?" Sabine asked.

Ben came up behind Tracy. "Not yet. I cook a mean lasagna, though, so that might've helped."

"I shouldn't have told you about all my kids," Sabine said. "Then you would've stayed at my house."

Everyone laughed, including Ben, but the moment Pauline emerged from the back room to remind Tracy and Ben that they had to serve themselves tea, Ben's easy manner disappeared under his professional veneer, and to Tracy's sadness, remained there the rest of the evening. He presented preliminary social media statistics, explained his final marketing plan, and took on new tasks that others felt too busy to complete. He also followed up about painting the windows and confirmed he'd contact the artist.

At the end of the meeting, Tracy confirmed which committee members would be attending the Oktoberfest evening. Again she noticed Ben hesitate. *Odd.*

Tracy and Ben joined Pauline in picking up dishes after everyone else had left.

"I've got this," Pauline said. "It's just a few cups. You can head out."

"I'm happy to help," Tracy replied. "I really appreciate you letting the committee meet here."

"The other owners already do quite a bit by organizing the festival. But seriously, Trace, I can do it."

And there it was. The glance at Ben. Pauline couldn't hide her feelings at all.

BEN COULD WALK HOME and give Pauline her space again, but that'd give her an excuse to continue not liking him: he'd have left Tracy alone with the cleanup.

"With both of us helping, we'll be out in no time," he said. "Is there a mop I can use to clean up the crumbs?"

Pauline barely looked at him. "I said I'll be fine."

No matter what Ben did, he came between people, didn't he?

"Why don't you take the leftover food to the car?" Tracy asked. "I'm going to grab some cleaning supplies from the back room."

"Sure. I'll keep working out there, then." He hoped he sounded upbeat enough to hide that he guessed they were going to talk about him.

Tracy smiled and nodded. "Great. I'll be out shortly."

"CAN'T you give him a second chance?"

Pauline's eyes were on fire. "He's really cast his magic spell on you, hasn't he?"

"Excuse me?"

"That man wouldn't pay for a camel pack of water so I'd stay hydrated in that costume. Or a cooling vest so I wouldn't faint from heat stroke. He often had me work ten days in a row, rarely gave me the three days off I needed so I could come here to visit all of you—not that it would've done much good given the contract... And *you* were trying to get in touch with me, and I was too scared to respond because I hated the idea of lying to you! Because of him! And now you're defending him?"

Tracy took a deep breath. Ben had made some horrible mistakes, and she needed to remember that. "I know," Tracy said. "And I don't mean to ignore all that."

"But that's what it feels like." Pauline let out a sigh. "If you want to help, you can vacuum the cushions in the lounge."

Tracy knew it was Pauline's way of saying she accepted Tracy's words. When Tracy was finished, Pauline asked, "Did I hear right? He wants my mom to do an interview with one of the local radio stations?"

Tracy nodded. "With hopefully more to come."

"When was he going to discuss this with me?"

"He thought it best to ask her directly."

"To avoid me...because my mother will think differently about him?"

Tracy whipped around. "Cut him *some* slack, will you? What did you expect me to do? Take on David's duties?"

Pauline said nothing.

Tracy dropped the hand vac on the chair. "You did, didn't you? You expected me to take on the responsibilities myself instead of asking him to help us out. Ben's spending easily four or five hours a day on this." She faced her best friend. "So tell me, Pauline. Where are those five hours in my day?"

Pauline wiped down the coffee table. "No one expected you to do five hours a day. The basics would've sufficed."

"Then why couldn't you volunteer to look after 'the basics'? You had time to perform at book fairs, you've got time to perform at Oktoberfest. Why do I have a feeling that you'd only have helped me with the festival if I offered you a fleece costume?"

But the moment the accusation flew out, Tracy regretted it. She didn't have time to apologize, though. Pauline launched into her just as harshly.

"Maybe because things aren't going that great and we need the extra money. Maybe because that was my career for so long and I loved it and miss it. Maybe because I don't have kids of my own and I love interacting with them. Maybe because I'm used to performing for twenty thousand people and I still go stir-crazy once in a while in this tea shop and need an audience, even if it's only a few hundred. Would you like me to continue justifying my choices to you?"

"No, but I shouldn't have to justify every single choice to you either!"

"Fine! But if you're going to bring that much pain back into mine and my mother's lives, you can't expect us to go along for the ride!"

Tracy threw her hands up in the air. "Then why does everyone look to me to pick up after them! I don't even have a store here and I'm chairing your flippin' festival committee!"

Before she made a fool of herself—by saying she quit— Tracy stormed out. Ben was in the driver's side, which was fine by her.

"Let's go."

"Everything okay?"

Tracy stared out her window. "Just fine."

Pauline stood close enough to the storefront that Tracy could make out the sadness on her face.

Tracy felt it, too.

～

BEN HAD HEARD NOTHING, of course, but through the window he'd seen a furious discussion.

Probably about him.

A quick glance in the right-side mirror also told him Tracy was trying to hold back tears. He wanted nothing more now than to hold her and whisper that everything would somehow be fine.

He turned onto her street and approached the house.

"Austin might be trying to sleep," she said, "so can you pull into the garage? We can go in through the basement."

She pressed the button to open the garage on her phone, and Ben parked the car. Tracy locked everything and entered the basement, which had a dance floor in the middle and a seating area off to the side. Ben wondered if he should just leave her alone. Sometimes quiet time was best for people everyone needed something from.

Or should he apologize now? Maybe that would help her feel better.

"Tracy—"

"She doesn't get it! No one does!" She dropped onto a couch. "All they hear about is how Austin's doing better, so they think I'm doing fine, too. But I don't embarrass him in front of everyone and tell them about his marks, or that he hates English. I don't load on them my fears that he could die in his sleep. And yes, those chances are almost nil, but they exist because he has epilepsy, and it scares me to death!"

She ran her hands through her hair, messing it up. Ben put

his hands behind his back so he wouldn't push back the strands of hair hanging over her face.

Remember, Austin's in the house.

"I do so much for everyone, and the one time she disagrees with me, she can't let it go. You've been such a big help and have done more than any of us could've. But she... I told her you're trying to...to just be nicer, but she clearly isn't!"

Tracy balled her hands into fists. If this were Susie, Ben would give her a big-brother hug, tell her things would work out. What would Tracy find comforting and appropriate?

Ben chose the simplest language: a step. Keeping his hands clasped behind his back, he took one step toward her to see how she'd respond.

Tracy surprised him by wrapping her arms around Ben's waist. Not wanting to reject her need for comfort, he brought his arms around her, feeling her soft hair under his chin.

"It's like everyone thinks my life is like a normal mom's now, and it's so far from that."

Ben squeezed just a little harder.

CHAPTER 20

Tracy had hoped a cooler shower would wake her up. Between her fight with Pauline and the most comforting embrace she'd had in ages—with a man who upset everyone close to her—she'd tossed and turned half the night. Worst of all, though, was that she empathized with both sides: Ben had treated Pauline abysmally, but it was abundantly clear that something inside him was changing. Besides, he'd confessed to her that a terrible time in his life had caused the rough side of his personality to show through. Everyone had a rough side. Some hid it better than others.

Eric, for example.

She finished getting dressed and headed to the kitchen to prepare breakfast.

"Is Ben up?" she asked Austin, who was making himself toast and peanut butter.

"I think he's already gone."

Tracy's breath caught. "Gone?"

"Yeah. As in gone-for-the-day gone?"

She smiled. "Right, of course. Listen, do you mind if I leave early? I'm going to drop by Grandma's for an early morning visit. You can get yourself to school okay, right?"

"You're tracking my phone, Mom. You don't need to ask."

The sting in his answer hurt, and Tracy had slept poorly. "I'm your mother. I'm going to do whatever's necessary to take care of you." Her own rough side was showing.

Austin's voice tensed. "I'm sixteen. I can take care of myself."

"And you have epilepsy."

"I'm not an invalid!" He stared into space, and Tracy counted to four before he continued. "I hate this! I can't even prove my independence."

"You need help, Austin. I just—"

"But not with everything, dammit!"

Tracy's jaw dropped. "Don't you *ever* talk to me like that again!"

Austin banged the plastic jar of peanut butter on the table. "I was worse off with my seizures at the ballet school, yet you left me alone *all day*! Just because you know I have seizures now doesn't change anything!"

"It changes everything!"

"Name one—"

Tracy counted to nine before he came out of this seizure, mildly disoriented.

"What was I saying?"

If Tracy didn't tell him, she could end the fight. It was tempting. She didn't need to start her morning this way.

But that would be unfair. She rubbed her eyes. "You were yelling at me about how you don't think anything's changed just because you have a diagnosis."

Austin's eyes darted back and forth as though he was trying to retrace his train of thought. But instead of admitting that he couldn't, he said firmly, "Because it doesn't change anything."

He bit off half his toast and took the rest with him as he stormed up to his bedroom. He emerged minutes later fully dressed, his backpack over his shoulders. "I'm going to school early. Track me all you want. But it's embarrassing and stupid. Other kids my age are learning to drive and I'm being treated like some endangered species."

Before Tracy could even think of how to respond to the accusation, Austin had slammed the door behind him.

His medication!

Tracy rushed to the cupboard, poured a few tablets into a small pillbox, and ran out the door. "Austin! Your meds!"

He was already out of sight. He'd probably cut through their neighbours' properties to Glasgow Street. She pulled out her phone and confirmed his path. It meant that she'd have to drive to catch up to him.

"So much for my calm morning and healthy breakfast."

She grabbed her purse and jumped into the car. Tracy knew her son was fit, but she hadn't appreciated how fit until she found him five minutes later walking in a stream of high school students near Belmont Avenue.

"Austin!" she called through the window. "Your meds!"

A few heads turned. Austin walked over to her and snatched them out of her hand. Not even a thank you.

Seething, Tracy said, "*This* is why I worry about you. We don't know what'll happen if you miss a dose."

Austin bolted.

CLAIRE'S TEA Shop was just around the corner. She might as well stop and pick up breakfast brownies for herself and her mother. (Breakfast brownies were simply what Tracy called regular brownies she ate for breakfast.) She didn't want to admit it, but she was also hoping she'd run into Ben. She wanted to share the frustration of the morning with him. He wasn't there and she felt disappointed. She reminded herself he didn't have kids, anyway. As compassionate as he had become, Ben probably wouldn't fully understand what Tracy was going through.

Besides, he was part of the problem. Pauline had served Tracy with hardly a word.

She drove to her parents' new apartment, brownies in the passenger seat.

"Tracy, sweetheart?" Jan took her brownie out of her daughter's hand. "Oh, no. You don't look good at all." Jan's hair was still in rollers, but she was already dressed in an ankle-length, flowing floral skirt, and a loose, ruffled blouse. Jan was a gracefully aging hippie with a touch of class. "I need to finish getting ready, but I'm all ears."

Tracy followed her seventy-three-year-old mother to the master bedroom and sat on the bed while her mother finished styling her hair.

Jan unrolled the Velcro rollers. "Tell me what's wrong."

Tracy didn't need any prodding. She immediately unloaded everything about her fights with Pauline and Austin. "It's like, no matter who I care about, I hurt someone."

Jan picked up a can of hair spray and sprayed her hair into place before turning around. The floral smell of the spray tickled Tracy's nose, and she sneezed.

"I just can't make anyone happy."

Jan beckoned Tracy to follow her into the kitchen. "You realize all this started when that Ben came into your life, don't you?" She poured water into two mugs and placed them in the microwave. Tracy tried not to grimace: how could Claire's best friend microwave water for tea?

"I needed his help."

Jan shook her head. "You're capable of more than you know."

"Mom, I couldn't have handled the committee, plus work, plus Austin, without someone to step in."

Jan offered Tracy a chair at the small, round breakfast table, then filled two tea baskets with a simple Darjeeling from Claire's.

Tracy missed the kitchen of her parents' old house. By no means as large as the Robinsons' home, Jan and Sedrick had joyfully hosted all their children and grandchildren every Christmas. This coming Christmas would take place at Tracy's. Although she was happy to take the workload off her parents' hands, it was another case of her stepping in to help.

I get to save the day again. What else is new?

The microwave beeped, and Jan brought out the mugs. She placed the tea baskets in each and carried the mugs to the table.

"Being a mother means sacrificing yourself once in a while," Jan said. "I know you aren't able to stay home to raise Austin like I could to raise the three of you. But you have your father and me to help. We could've stepped in, taken over some of the driving, for example. I'm certain Pauline and Todd would've stepped up, too."

Tracy shook her head. "Pauline's so busy, Mom. She's taking on extra work playing storybook characters at schools right now. I guess Claire had, well, let things go a little."

Tracy didn't like speaking ill of such an old family friend. Claire certainly "had all her wits about her," as the older generation liked to say. But she'd grown tired, like David had in his chocolate store.

"She couldn't bear to sell it to anyone but her daughter," Jan said. "I, on the other hand, was more practical. Let fate play out for me, and *whoosh*! The perfect owner bought my hair salon off me. Now your father and I live comfortably in this apartment and I can work a little, chatting away with my favourite customers while I cut their hair. I have time to help you, sweetheart. You didn't need to invite that devil of a man into your life."

Tracy's back immediately went up. "He's not a devil! You don't know him like I do."

Jan looked at her daughter as though she were twelve again. "You always go after the bleeding-heart cases. You know that, don't you? You've got a kind heart, Tracy. But Ben's causing you trouble, and no one likes him. Your son's even angry at you."

"But not because of Ben."

"Because you couldn't pay enough attention to him. Because of Ben."

Was her mother right? Tracy wouldn't have fought with Pauline last night nor embraced Ben were he not living with her. She wouldn't have been emotionally exhausted this morning and spoken to her son like that.

"Plus," Jan continued, "if Eric is trying to make amends, having Ben there will make that more difficult. That must be confusing for Austin, too, to have a man who's interested in you in the house."

Tracy's cheeks immediately blushed. "He's not —"

"It sounds like he is." Jan took her first sip. "End this now, Tracy, before he reels you in. I've cut the hair of too many women in similar situations. This will only end in hurt. Your quarter-end is pretty much over now —"

"But now everything's ramping up for the festival."

Jan gave Tracy the reassuring smile that had helped her through so many trials and tribulations as a kid. "You can do it, Trace. It's only two weeks. One day, Austin will be thirty, and you won't even remember this time. I promise. You're not a single mother. You have your extended family and friends."

Although what Jan said made sense, it also made Tracy uneasy. She'd wanted advice from her mother, but it wasn't helping. She changed the topic to discuss Jan's circle of friends.

But soon Tracy looked at her watch. "I'd better get going. Have to be at work in fifteen."

On her way to work, Tracy tried to figure out what about her mother's comments had bothered her and she soon realized what it was: she was indeed a single mother. She was solely responsible for Austin, and therefore the only adult who knew everything about him. She provided him shelter, tracked his medications, watched over his schooling, fed him, and booked his doctor's appointments. Yes, others stepped in, but only when Tracy called.

The hurt of that realization grew as she took the elevator to her office.

When she stepped out onto the seventh floor, though, she understood why the hurt had become so strong. It wasn't just because her mother didn't grasp the responsibilities on Tracy's shoulders as a single mom. In fact, it wasn't only hurt Tracy felt. It was neglect.

To ask Ben to leave to make everyone else happy meant to neglect her own heart.

Quickly she checked her phone. Austin had made it to school. Excellent. Should she text Pauline and ask if she was okay? This morning in the tea shop had felt like ice. Tracy wouldn't apologize for asking Ben to help her. That much she'd settled on.

She smiled in spite of herself.

"I'm sounding like him," she said to no one in particular.

"Sounding like who?"

She jerked her head up and saw the CEO standing in her doorway.

"Sorry. Just talking to myself. How can I help?"

He entered and sat down.

"I've sent you a job description from HR. It's for the one I'd mentioned yesterday. You'd be EA to just one person again, and you wouldn't have to report to Eric."

The warmth drained from Tracy's face.

"We're also still looking for a CMO. Turns out the last applicant lied about a position they'd held. So, if you know of anyone, pass on their résumé." He laughed as he stood up. "You'd be able to hire your own boss."

As soon as he left, Tracy found the email and double-checked the pay for the other job.

Ten thousand dollars less than what she was earning now. If Eric intended on participating in Austin's life again, would he pay the difference? She'd first run the calculations at home and see what this difference meant to her budget.

If they hired Ben for the CMO position, though, could she work under him?

Her cheeks warmed as her mind immediately offered another interpretation of that question. But that pleasant thought soon gave way to anger at the CEO, and her cheeks turned red-hot. Maybe it was time she joined Ben on the job hunt.

Just then Eric entered her office, a spring in his step and the biggest smile she'd seen on his face since his return to town. "Guess what? Austin just texted me that he'll join us for supper after his shift at the tea shop tomorrow!"

His happiness was so genuine, almost infectious, that Tracy couldn't help but be happy for him.

She smiled back at him. Maybe the day could be salvaged.

CHAPTER 21

*E*ric held open the door at the bottom of the stairs of the Greek restaurant in downtown Kitchener. It was a family favourite. Austin, dressed in khakis and a golf shirt, sauntered through.

When Tracy passed Eric, he whispered in her ear, "You look stunning."

She wore a dark plaid pencil skirt that showed off her curvy figure, black boots to her knees, and a lightweight, cream sweater. She enjoyed dressing up in a way that showed off her body. It wasn't for Eric, even though he probably assumed it was. It was for herself.

She smiled and immediately worried she appeared to be flirting with him.

Especially after he returned her smile.

"I still can't believe you're serving tea with Todd Parsons," Eric said to Austin once they'd been shown to their table.

Well, that was all Austin need to start rambling, and Tracy was relieved Eric had learned something since his failed attempt at a conversation at her house.

"...and I can do a...I don't even know what it's called. An octuple *pirouette*? I can rotate eight times now, thanks to Todd's help!"

"Really?"

"And my jumps are getting better. I'm getting more lift again."

"That's phenomenal!"

Tracy felt that the evening was off to a good start. After the server took their orders, though, Eric asked Austin about school.

Big mistake, Tracy thought. *Do the risk analysis, Eric.*

"Okay, I guess."

Eric glanced at Tracy and then back at Austin. "Why? What's going on?"

Austin shrugged.

"Is it that bad?" Eric asked. "I know you miss a bit here and there, but...you're a smart kid, Austin. It can't be that bad."

"On these meds, I'm an idiot sometimes. I have no problems remembering movement, but random facts like what we learn at school...it's brutal."

Tracy and Ben hadn't talked about their long hug from the other evening, but they had talked about Austin. That had been a safer topic. Ben liked her, too. She could sense the vibe. Her mom was right. Keeping conversation between her and Ben on safe ground also helped protect Austin, now that he was opening up to Eric again. The last thing Tracy needed was to rock the boat, and Ben made it clear that he placed the family's needs first.

Ben had suggested responding to Austin's feelings rather than refuting what he said—no matter how much his words were painful to hear. She would try that now.

"Must be hard to concentrate sometimes when medication is slowing your brain down," she said.

"You have no idea."

Eric asked, "Can't you just concentrate more or something?"

Tracy shot him a look.

Eric rubbed his nose and apologized. "Of course, all of this is still new and probably overwhelming."

"But Ben helped me with my English homework yesterday."

Tracy groaned inwardly.

"Oh?" Eric asked.

Tracy was grateful when the server came to take their orders.

But Austin kept talking about Ben after the server left. Austin's face lit up as he described Ben's idea of analyzing a novel's themes through choreography, but the moment Eric found a break in Austin's story, he asked if Austin was taking any math or business courses.

"Not until next semester."

"Oh. Well, I can help you then if you want."

Austin's "sure" was as convincing as Eric's feigned interest in Ben.

The server brought their appetizer: a platter of spanakopita. Austin grabbed a pita wedge and dipped it in hummus. His mouth half full, he blurted out, "Why did you even come back?"

"Austin!" Tracy said.

Eric placed his hand on hers. "No, it's okay. That's why we're here." He folded his hands together. "I realized I'd made a grave error, and I've come back to fix it. I'd sunken into a deep depression while you were in ballet school."

Austin didn't respond, apparently waiting for more of an answer.

Should I step in and explain things more? No, she thought. *Eric needs to explain himself. This is like work, where I have to let those responsible share what they know.*

But Eric didn't say more.

Austin said, "That's it? You got depressed?"

Confused, Eric nodded. "I'm sorry. I wasn't myself."

Nothing else? Did Eric have nothing else to offer?

Austin laid into his father. "That's why you abandoned your family? You're an adult! What would've happened to me if Mom had done the same thing?"

Eric shrugged. "I guess she's just a lot stronger than I am."

Tracy certainly didn't feel strong. Why else had she needed that embrace with Ben?

Eric dipped his pita wedge in the hummus non-stop. "I guess, just like something's wrong with your brain—"

Tracy shot Eric another look, but before she could even open her mouth, Austin retorted. "Don't even start comparing us. The neuro said I was probably born this way. You chose to have me. That means you made a commitment. You can't just abandon that commitment because chemicals in your brain aren't working."

Eric nodded as he dipped, his eyes focused on the hummus. "You're right. Sorry. I shouldn't have left."

Austin wolfed down two pita wedges.

But as Tracy listened to the discussion continue—Austin accusing Eric of not being a father, Eric accepting the accusations and repeatedly apologizing—she couldn't help but be amazed at Eric's composure. He must have finally understood that this healing would take time and that he needed to stand trial before Austin. During the main course, Eric discussed some of his therapy sessions, explained that he had been paying support this whole time—which thankfully went over well—and although Austin was a world away from jumping over the table and giving his father an all-forgiving hug, he eventually stopped with the aggressive accusations.

"I can't erase what I've done," Eric said. "I'm ashamed that it'll always be a mark on our relationship. But all I can do is say

I'm sorry until you're tired of hearing me say it, and I hope one day you'll be able to forgive me. What I'm asking for right now, though, is a second chance at being your dad."

Austin finished his meal, not saying another word. But this time, Tracy believed it was to consider everything Eric had said.

Eric, on the other hand, appeared to be force-feeding himself, probably because he hated wasting food but was too nervous to enjoy the meal anymore. She admired his courage: Eric had chosen a location that wasn't invasive (Austin's home) or threatening (Eric's home), but one that held lots of happy memories, a location that was public and would've therefore been embarrassing to Eric should Austin bolt (an emotional risk for Eric). A park across the street could've served as an outlet for Austin's energy should he have needed one.

But Austin had stayed seated.

Eric had noticed, too.

They declined when the server approached and asked about dessert. Eric paid and the family walked back up the stairs to street level.

Eric paused. "I'd like to take you to Toronto this weekend," he said. "I'd pick you up late Friday afternoon, and we'd stay at a hotel for a night? Or two? I promise we'll be back Sunday afternoon so you can do your homework and then enjoy the Robinson-Brubacher Thanksgiving Day festivities on Monday. But we could catch a ballet, maybe a contemporary show… whatever you want, depending on what's on, of course. We might find some drop-in classes you could take, as well?"

Tracy's heart rose in her chest. For a man who abhorred risk, Eric was now risking walking the emotional plank. Not only had he bared his soul to Austin in the public space of a restaurant for the past hour and a half, but he was now asking Austin to trust him enough to spend a full weekend with him.

Austin still hadn't replied by the time they reached the car.

"I'd have waited to ask you later." Eric's hand shook as he reached for his door handle. "But I don't know when your midterms start. I was thinking maybe this would be a good weekend because it's Thanksgiving and your teachers wouldn't assign you too much homework."

Eric glanced at Tracy, and she gave him a small nod of encouragement. Part of her wished he'd asked her first about this although she hadn't planned anything concrete with Austin. But he needed time to rest and to study, and she'd been hoping he could invite some friends over. Plus, Eric didn't know Austin's medication schedule, or what to do in an emergency, or...

"Sure." Austin had finally spoken.

Eric's face lit up like a Christmas tree. "Really?"

"Don't make a big deal about it. Yeah. Sounds like fun. I just need to let Todd know I won't be practising Sunday morning."

Once they all sat in the car, Tracy was certain she saw Eric blinking back tears.

She turned her head away, watching the streetlights as they drove home.

Tracy didn't want him to see that her eyes were turning red, too.

PARENTING TOGETHER. Definitely a familiar experience, as though nothing had changed. A strange sensation. If Eric hadn't wounded their family so badly, she could almost be tricked into believing that the past year hadn't happened at all.

Austin had disappeared into the house after thanking Eric for dinner, leaving his parents alone on the porch. Where Ben was, Tracy had no clue.

"I need to thank you, Trace. Feeling you there in my corner

again…I don't have words for that." Eric took hold of her hand, intertwining his fingers with hers. "I should've asked you first about the weekend, but the idea just occurred to me earlier today." He smiled. "And I'm trying to leave the personal at home.

"I didn't know if Austin would accept. But I had to take the risk."

Over twenty years of love, challenges, family, sorrows, and joy circled in her mind. Was her mother right? Was Eric the answer to her problems?

"There's another question I've been wanting to ask this whole time," he said.

Tracy wasn't ready to answer what he was about to ask.

He placed his other hand over hers. "What about us?"

Could their life—their family life—be rekindled if Tracy tried hard enough?

But since when was love reawakened through effort? Especially love destroyed by abandonment? Tracy believed his struggles with depression. But what if it happened again? Was she ready to deal with that?

Was it cruel to even think such a thing?

But Austin needed care, stability, and love. What if Eric disappeared again? That would harm their son forever. Eric was his father, not some random man. At the same time, Tracy did want Austin to reconnect with his father. Was she setting her son up for more disappointment, even without considering whether her love for Eric could be reawakened?

Eric kissed her knuckles, sending shivers through her whole body, another familiar—and very pleasant—sensation. "You don't have to answer now. I know I have to earn back your love."

Your love. He was expecting her to love him again.

He let go of her hand. "Would anyone mind if I joined the

family on Thanksgiving? It would be nice to see everyone again."

Unable to think rationally, she said, "I'm sure Mom and Claire will be fine with it."

"Excellent. Well, I'll see you tomorrow morning at work." He gave her a quick peck on the cheek, giving the evening a seal that promised a future.

Too distracted to do anything but make herself a hot chocolate, she headed for the kitchen. Austin was in his bedroom, and she noticed the light was on in the guest room where Ben slept. Part of her hoped he'd come out so they could talk about the festival and get her mind off the evening with Eric. Part of her hoped he'd stay in there so she wouldn't have to talk to him at all.

As she pulled out ingredients—hazelnut milk, one of the dark chocolate bars Ben had bought her, and sugar—and began heating everything in a saucepan, her mind debated with her heart about what to do.

BEN WAS THIRSTY, but after Austin had entered the house and left the front door open, Ben could see Tracy and Eric talking through the screen door. Although he'd immediately retreated to his bedroom, he'd seen enough after five seconds to know what was going on: Eric wanted to get back together while Tracy was uncertain.

Which meant Ben's attempt at ignoring that long hug on Monday evening had been the right decision.

But Ben had just finished a bodyweight workout in his bedroom and needed a protein drink before bed. Plus, he was parched. He listened for any noise that suggested that Eric was gone and it was safe to go briefly into the kitchen without running into Tracy. He'd grab some water to mix with his powder, then read in bed or check social media.

He hopped down the stairs and crossed the dining room.

"Hi, Ben." Tracy was sitting at the kitchen table, enjoying a hot chocolate.

"Hi, Tracy." He kept going, got a glass, and headed back toward the stairs. "Good night, Tracy."

"Good night, Ben."

And he was back in his room. Easy peasy!

"You've got to be kidding me." He stared at his empty glass of water.

A moment later, someone knocked at his door. He opened it, and Tracy was smiling, a filled glass of water in her hand.

"Is this what you wanted?"

She'd noticed. "Thanks."

He took it from her, careful not to touch her fingers. He'd melt if he did.

Tracy stood still after he took the glass.

"Did supper go okay?" he asked.

She nodded, then swallowed. He didn't miss it, her eyes darting to his lips.

He looked back at her lips. "But we can't." He took a long drink of water to occupy his mouth.

She kept her voice low. "This isn't what I bargained for. Not in the summer, not now."

"Should we at least talk about it?"

"And say what? We know this can't work. I have to stay focused on my son."

Ben wanted to wrap his arms around her again and comfort her. But everything had become complicated in the past forty-eight hours. Eric wanted her back, but Ben didn't know what she wanted, and he didn't want to stand in this family's way.

This hug wouldn't be the same hug as the one on Monday.

But not only because of what Ben had seen at the door. It was because every moment of affectionate touch between him and Tracy had become a treasure he'd begun collecting, and as each such moment became increasingly scarce, it became more valuable.

"Then...have a good night, Tracy."

She nodded and left without a word.

CHAPTER 22

"Oh my god, Austin!" one of his ballet friends said. "Did you see Jasmine look at you this week? That little girl is so adorable."

Tracy still couldn't believe the change in Austin since the summer. When he stopped having friends over last year once the bullying had begun, it had broken her heart.

Tracy carried out a tray of fresh vegetables to the table. "Who's Jasmine?"

Austin smiled. "Just this girl from one of the younger classes. She'll make it big one day, I'm certain of it."

"And she has a crush on you?"

Austin laughed. "Maybe? I think she's, like, twelve or something. Too young and, well, a girl."

His friends laughed with him, but not in a mean way toward the girl, just at the comedy of the situation.

Tracy set the water on the stove for whole-grain pasta while the students gossiped about studio happenings and the professional world of ballet and grilled Austin about what it was like to know Todd Parsons. Austin didn't share that Todd was tutoring him privately, but he and Todd agreed that it was okay to share ballet tips Todd might have passed along during Austin's shifts at the tea shop. Tracy's heart warmed: even though Austin had lost a year of dedicated practice, he believed he could pass his ballet exam this year thanks to Todd's help.

Her phone beeped as she added the pasta to the water.

Tent supplier isn't responding. Have tents have been confirmed? It was Sabine.

Great. The last thing they needed was to not have any tents.

Let me check.

She scrolled through her emails.

"Tracy! Watch out!"

Ben reached past her to grab the pot as it boiled over. Water sizzled as it hit the burner. He turned off the stove and grabbed tea towels to wipe off the white foam.

"This is what happens when you multitask," Tracy said. "Thanks, Ben. I've got this now."

But he didn't move. "It's okay. Finish your message. I can clean up here. I know you've got a lot on your plate."

"Mom? Everything okay?"

Austin stood in the entrance to the kitchen, his eyes darting between her and Ben. He definitely suspected something between them, but whether he liked it...she couldn't tell.

Oh, fudge.

TRACY RETURNED HOME after dropping Austin off and was stunned to find the kitchen spotless.

Ben nodded to her from the dining room table, his laptop in front of him.

She hung her purse on a hook by the front door and slipped

out of her shoes. "You didn't have to clean all this up, but thank you."

"It was the least I could do." He looked back at the screen in front of him.

"I didn't mean for this volunteer thing to be a twenty-four-hour-a-day position," Tracy said. "The last thing I'd want is for you to resent it like I do now." Ben looked up, concerned, but she waved it away. "Never mind. Another week, and it's over. I'd probably be more motivated at this point if I worked in the Village. Anything I can help with?"

Ben shook his head. "Actually, I'm tackling my résumé."

"Oh! I'd love to do something different. I've seen thousands of them over my career. I don't mind helping."

Ben hesitated. "Well... there's not much to it. I worked two jobs before the Peregrines, helped my parents for two years, and then spent ten years with the team."

Tracy pulled up a chair and sat next to him. He was right: his résumé was sparse. He was still relatively young, probably only thirty-five, judging by the year he graduated high school.

What would Austin think if Tracy dated someone...she did the math...who was only nineteen years older than him? And what happened if this relationship lasted? When Tracy hit retirement, Ben would still have thirteen years left to work. She didn't want to wait till she was seventy-eight to start travelling and enjoying the retired life.

And *did* Ben want kids of his own? Because she certainly wasn't starting from scratch again.

Tracy, you haven't even gone on a date yet!

"I mean," Ben continued, "you've been really helpful to me already. Don't you have a hobby or something you'd rather be doing?"

Tracy playfully scoffed at his suggestion. "A hobby? With what time? Besides, helping you would make me feel useful.

I've been feeling more use*less* lately." As soon as she spoke, she wished she hadn't said anything. The last thing she wanted was to dive into her fights and explain her conversation with the CEO. "So, let's get to it. What's up?"

Ben followed her lead. "I just can't figure out the angle on my story. I always believed I could spin anything, but I'm stuck. I know I have to explain at some point what happened at the Peregrines, but how? Disclosing it right away isn't exactly a powerful hook."

She scanned through his full résumé, which included a degree in communications and marketing, part-time work as a model (she wasn't surprised), and experience in sales and marketing.

"Why your parents?"

Ben scratched the back of his neck. "Dad had Parkinson's. Mom had ovarian cancer. I know it's not exactly relevant to a marketing career, but if I don't include it, I'll have a gap in my résumé. A no-no."

Tracy had to agree. He could go for a functional résumé instead of the standard chronological one, but not every hiring manager liked that format.

She reviewed his years at the Peregrines. "You started in the souvenir booth? With the sales experience you had before you helped your parents?"

Ben scratched the back of his neck again. What was with the nervous mannerisms? "If my basic questions are making you this uneasy, how are you going to deal with a job interview?"

Ben shrugged. "Just not used to it, I guess. And how do I handle the fact that I got fired?"

No time like the present to get Ben to consider his approach to that question in his application. "Do you mind talking about it? It might help you start thinking about how to address it in your cover letter and interview." She hoped he didn't feel threatened by her question.

Ben leaned back in his chair and placed his hands in his lap. "They never tell you everything because they worry about retaliation, so the best I can gather is that it had to do with how I treated people." He swallowed hard. "The next thing I knew, I was canned. The CEO said he was sorry to let me go. How can you say you're sorry for firing someone?"

Tracy's cheeks burned. She'd probably said that a few times in her career, never really thinking about how empty it sounded. "I guess it's just what people say. But perhaps, in his case, he actually felt that way because you'd been with the company for a decade…"

He pinched the bridge of his nose and squeezed his eyes shut. Another one of his habits, she'd noticed. "I suppose. Either way, being fired after ten years looks horrible on a résumé." He set his glasses on the table and rubbed his eyes.

Tracy inwardly smiled at the tan lines along the sides of his face where the arms of his glasses sat. They were cute.

"It had to be the way I treated everyone. The results I delivered were documented. I guess I really can't blame him," Ben said.

His comment surprised Tracy.

"I'm still connected on Facebook with some guys from my early days with the Peregrines. We never unfriended each other, just stopped commenting on each other's posts." He stared into his lap. "Turns out, there was a 'We're Glad He's Gone' party."

Tracy's hand flew to her heart. Although she understood how Ben's management style had affected others, the Ben before her was a human being realizing the mistakes he'd made and experiencing the extreme discomfort of understanding he'd hurt people. It was when people avoided that realization that they kept hurting others. And whatever happened in his twenties had led to this extreme behaviour. He was finally acknowledging it.

"Sounds like you could use a drink."

Ben gave a dry laugh. "Tell me about it."

Tracy stood up. "Red? White? Beer? Vodka? Rum? Cooler?"

To her surprise, Ben shook his head. "No, I'll be fine, thanks."

He needed something to comfort him. She moved behind him and placed her hands on his shoulders. "May I?" He nodded, and she began kneading his tight muscles. With every breath he released, her fingers pressed in deeper. She was only helping a friend, right? She could bury the tingling sensations racing over her body. Wouldn't be the first time she had set aside her own feelings to help someone else.

"To be honest," Ben said, "I don't know if I'll get any job right now. I won't get a reference from the Peregrines, and my previous place of relevant employment was so long ago, they wouldn't remember me."

Tracy continued massaging Ben's shoulders. "No other volunteer work?" She tried to keep her voice casual.

"If it didn't bring in money, I didn't do it."

The regret in his voice tugged at her heart. She pulled her arms around his in comfort, her hands clasping each other across his chest, her chin resting on his shoulder. He leaned his cheek against hers.

"And if this turns into anything," he said, his voice low, "you can't be my reference either."

Tracy hadn't thought of that. She tried to drop her arms and stand up, but Ben grasped one of her hands.

"Can we enjoy this for just a few more moments?" He continued holding her hand as he turned in his chair and stood up.

Tracy couldn't imagine anything else but being with Ben, no matter the age difference. Why did he have to come into her life now?

I should pull away.

Oh, what the fudge? Nothing wrong with another hug.

But to avoid kissing him—because she knew she wouldn't be able to stop—she tucked her head into his shoulder and wrapped her arms around him tight.

He stroked her hair. "Thank you," he whispered in her ear as he leaned into her body.

His whisper flowed all over her skin.

"I'M MESSING up so bad, it's not even funny," Ben told Susie. Tracy had left to pick up Austin, so he had about twenty minutes to fill his sister in on everything that had happened.

It tumbled out in three.

"Has it ever occurred to you that she wants you and not him?"

"Of course, it has. But Eric's a good guy."

"Who walked out on his family."

"I walked out on mine *and* got drunk *and* wasted all my money. He cares for them, and he wants to come back into their lives."

Some clanging in the background suggested Susie was emptying her dishwasher. "And that's fine, but why does that mean that Tracy has to fall back in love with him instead of falling for someone new?"

Ben couldn't answer her. All he knew was that Austin needed a father, and his father had returned.

"My car's ready tomorrow. Maybe I won't go—"

"You're going to Oktoberfest. Genny and I have already

bought our tickets, so we'll be there with you. You'll be safe. For once in your life, Benjamin, you're going to go out and have fun."

"I don't know…it's all about alcohol."

"You were around alcohol your entire career with the Peregrines, and unless you were lying to me, you didn't have a drop. Cut to the chase, Benjamin. What's really bothering you?"

Ben sighed. He could drum up a million excuses or he could save themselves the time.

"I'm falling for her hard, Suse, and her husband's taking Austin away for the weekend."

"Good! It's about time you opened your heart to someone else."

"But—"

"I'll help you hide that you're not drinking, but you need to throw caution to the wind for once, and not while you're protected in your car driving alone around a racetrack or locked away at the gym. Genny and I can protect you from the alcohol, but there's no way I'm letting you protect your heart."

"But Austin…"

"Has taken a liking to you if I'm right. You're not stepping in to be his father, just another mentor. Do you think Todd's trying to be his father?"

"Todd's not dating his mother."

"Details."

"Important details."

Sizzling. Susie had begun cooking. "You've never been afraid of asking direct questions. You'll have the weekend alone, so ask her how she's feeling about everything."

"I've already tried talking to her about it. She said she didn't want to."

"Which was before five minutes ago. Things have clearly changed between the two of you. *Ask her again.*" More sizzling.

"I hear stories like this at the clinic all the time, and I always want to scream at patients, 'Just ask!' But I can say it to you: just ask!"

Ben really had no way out of this, and his sister was right. Tracy's feelings for him were growing, too, he was certain. They needed to talk things out, and this weekend would be the perfect time to do that.

"Okay."

Susie squealed in his ear, which made Ben laugh. It would be good to have fun with her tomorrow. His insistence on climbing the corporate ladder had prevented him from spending time with his family.

Just like I prevented Pauline from having time with hers, he thought.

Had he been taking out his frustrations on her and his other employees? That would make him a horrible human. Horrible enough that he wanted to drown that realization in alcohol.

"Susie?"

"Yeah, Big Ben?"

"Can we keep talking?"

CHAPTER 23

"Good morning, Tracy." Eric waved as he walked by her office early Friday morning.

He didn't stop to chat.

She mumbled to herself, "Pigs can fly."

She sighed. Why couldn't he make her so angry that she'd have no choice but to emotionally shove him off a cliff again and cut all ties with him? But apart from his badgering to spend more time with his family and his sometimes heavy-handed attempts at communication, he wasn't really doing anything wrong. He was even answering all Austin's questions, and Austin would surely ask more this weekend.

Austin! She texted her son: *Did you take your meds?*

A minute later came his reply. *Yes!!!*

Are you feeling ok?

You'll get a call from the hospital if there's a problem.

That crossed a line. How did he not understand what she went through as a mother?

Not funny, Austin.

Wasn't meant to be. Leave me alone. Let me pay attention to class.

She tossed her phone into her purse. Austin most certainly texted with his friends during class. But she had her information. After the festival was over, she planned to investigate patient registries where Austin could track his medication and symptoms daily, and his neurologist could access the information. If Austin consented, his data would be used in approved research, too. It wasn't exactly social media, but it would be a safe space for him to meet others with epilepsy without the exposure of social media. The viral videos had been wonderful, and the number of tweens and teens who'd messaged Austin that they'd come out or had gone to their doctor to investigate odd neurological symptoms had made Austin realize just how far his message had reached. But the sheer need of those who'd reached out to him had overwhelmed him.

"Would've been nice to have his father around to help him navigate through that mess," she said to herself. "Instead, Todd, Pauline, and even indirectly Ben helped us deal with it."

A moment later, an email from Eric landed in her inbox. *Please proofread.* Attached was a PowerPoint presentation. Okay. He was really going for professional in the office. Good. That'd make life easier here for them both. Would especially help her keep her job.

She opened the file and scanned it to get an overview. It didn't take long for her to realize it was an overview of the changes he planned to implement. Her heart sank when she realized that his plan for new process automation software would lead to layoffs. Many would lose their jobs. She couldn't say anything, of course. Confidentiality was one of the most important aspects of an EA. But judging by the timeline, the layoffs would happen not long before Christmas.

That was her husband. Jettison what caused the most risk: people.

She proofread the slides and sent them back to him. *Here you go.*

Thanks.

No problem.

I'll be in meetings most of the day. Can you get me the following reports…

Was he sending her a list of tasks so he had reason to contact her all day? Or did he actually need these tasks taken care of? But if she was going to remain professional, she had to follow his instructions.

At lunchtime, Eric jumped into the elevator with her. "Heading to Claire's?"

Seriously?

"Yes." She stared at the panel of buttons.

"Can I join you?"

"Sure."

"I'll drive."

She followed him out the elevator and to his Tesla, which was charging at one of the company's charging stations.

"I get free charging as part of my compensation package," he said.

"How nice."

When Eric parked in front of Claire's Tea Shop ten minutes later, Tracy didn't wait for him to get out of the car. Hoping Pauline was inside, she rushed right in.

Instead of Pauline behind the counter, though, she found Claire herself and Todd.

In her white cotton dress, light makeup, and white hair blow-dried into soft curls just above her shoulders, Claire was the epitome of a fine tea drinker.

So long as you stayed on her good side, of course.

Claire's knee surgery in the summer had affected her walking, and she now used a cane. That didn't make her any less cheerful, though. Claire immediately made her way around the counter to greet Tracy with a hug. Over Claire's shoulder, Tracy saw Todd give a cool nod to Eric, who'd come in behind her.

"How was Niagara?" Tracy asked Claire.

The women pulled apart. "It was magnificent, Tracy. Just wonderful. I have to admit, I haven't seen Richard that tipsy in a long time." The two women laughed.

But to Tracy's dismay, Claire turned to Eric and extended her hand. "It's so nice to see you again, Eric. Jan told me you were back in town."

Eric, ever the gentleman, said, "It's wonderful to see you, too, Claire." He topped off his charm with the best-friend-son-in-law peck on the cheek.

Todd, still behind the counter, cringed, but it was how Eric had greeted Claire all the years he and Tracy had been married. Todd wouldn't have known that.

"Is Pauline in?" Tracy asked. "I was hoping to speak with her."

Claire shook her head. "She's playing Onkel Hans at an Oktoberfest event this afternoon. You know her: she can't stay away from those costumes for long. I'm just glad she's playing someone who doesn't do backflips or jump through fire."

Eric laughed. "I'm having a hard time imagining Onkel Hans doing a backflip. She was amazing to watch, though. I'm sorry I don't get to see her perform like that live anymore."

"She's amazing to watch—unless you're her mother! The heart attacks I was at risk for! I needed to drink pure lavender tea. But *three years* she was acting so close to us and was forbidden from telling us. And now Jan tells me *that man* is staying at your house? Tracy, I'm surprised."

Tracy took a deep breath before speaking. She owed who she was to Claire. Without the part-time work in the tea shop all those years before, she would've never kept her own bank account while married, never learned how to organize supplies, count cash, or order stock.

I probably wouldn't have become an independent woman if it hadn't been for Claire, she thought. Tracy wanted to defend Ben, but without insulting Claire or upsetting Eric. "He's proving to be very helpful, and he is paying his way at home. He cooks, for example, and he's helping Austin with his English homework. I hope you can...tolerate him for just a little?"

Claire's lips tightened. Tracy was certain her own shoulders rose three inches, as though they might hide her head like a turtle.

"I'll try," Claire said coldly. "At least he's helping you a smidge. Now, what can Todd get you?" Just like that, her joy of life returned.

Tracy and Eric took their order to a table. To avoid discussing any future for their own relationship, Tracy jumped right into discussing what Eric would need to know about Austin for the weekend, beginning with his medication.

"He might seem a little forgetful, so be patient with him."

"I will be, I promise. He'll have enough medication packed with him?"

"Yes. Three pills each time. Eight o'clock."

"Morning and evening."

"Right."

"Understood. Adds up to sixteen, his age."

Tracy had never thought of that.

"And no tonic-clonic seizures?"

"Thankfully, no. But the neuro said that was still a possibility."

"What are the chances?"

"Minimal."

"That's good."

Tracy couldn't stand this about Eric. So long as the risk was low, something was *good*, even if Austin's well-being was still in danger. "Eric, there's nothing good about that. He can still develop the big ones. Or absence status epilepticus."

"Get stuck in an absence seizure?"

"For half an hour or longer."

Eric rolled his eyes. "Tracy, really. The chances of that happening are so slim, they're almost negligible."

"But they're there! We need to watch out for them." How could he not grasp the importance of this? Should she allow this trip to happen?

When Ben walked in the door, Eric's face fell. "I can't go anywhere without running into him, can I?"

Judging by the expression on Ben's face, he was none too pleased to see Eric, either.

ASKING Claire during lunch hour to be his go-to for media interviews was risky. She already despised him, and asking her during one of her rush hours might annoy her even more. However, being surrounded by so many happy customers might mean she'd be in a good mood.

Just so long as she didn't make him drink Earl Claire. He'd hated the smell of lavender since the last time they'd spoken, all because she'd set a cup of Earl Claire in front of him. Ben would simply do his best to remain professional and to forget the tiny detail that he'd forced her daughter to lie to her for three years.

"Good afternoon, Mrs. Robinson."

"Ben."

Okay. Introductions weren't needed. Ben had assumed that would be the case, but he was prepared to reintroduce himself if required.

"I don't know if Pauline or Todd has told you —"

"They have."

Check. His purpose for being here was out of the way, too.

"Would you mind doing the media interviews for the festival?"

"I'd be delighted."

"Thank you."

"But not as a favour to you."

Here we go. Ben had prepared for this, too. "I understand."

"That doesn't bother you, does it?"

Ben took a breath. "I can't change the past, Mrs. Robinson."

"I see."

"How should I get in touch with you?"

"Let Pauline know."

"I will. Thank you, again."

She looked at him expectantly.

"I'll take a tuna sandwich to go, please."

She asked Todd to retrieve a sandwich from the display case, and Todd obliged. Ben left a generous tip in the jar, and Todd gave him a quiet, approving smile from behind Claire.

How could an elderly woman Ben hardly knew intimidate him so much? Good thing he wasn't going to that Thanksgiving event Monday. Pauline's sister was flying in from Vancouver with her family. Three children, apparently. The sister and brother-in-law would probably intimidate him, too. So would the kids.

But as he passed Eric and Tracy, he sensed a different kind of intimidation from Eric, the "stay away from my wife" kind.

The only problem was…Ben was getting the distinct impression Tracy didn't see herself as Eric's wife.

So where did that leave him?

The ache in his heart was growing, and the one thing that could kill it was a few shots of liquor.

Which would never happen. Not with his sister—and now Tracy—in his corner.

He smiled and waved to Tracy and Eric as he left. Eric would pick up Austin later this afternoon, and that would leave Ben all weekend to do what he'd promised Susie: ask Tracy what she felt for him.

Ben headed to the garage to pick up his car.

CHAPTER 24

*H*ad he been transported without his knowledge to another planet? Had no one else noticed the horrendous cacophony of accordion music blaring—not in unison—out of *two* halls at the top of the main staircase? Would it be rude if he covered his ears?

"So?" Tracy asked. "What do you think?"

Ben tried to keep his eyes focused on her face. Not because anything on her face was repelling his gaze. But because this dirndl was truly designed for a woman's body and drawing his gaze...downward. The bodice of the navy-blue knee-length dress was form-fitting, like a soft corset, and had a zipper down the middle that Ben so desired to open...and a plunging neckline. Under the bodice was a white, puffy blouse but it didn't cover everything. Whatever man designed it—it must have been a man!—Ben wanted to thank him. Ben had savoured those lips in the summer when Tracy's enticing body had pressed him against a wall. He'd also embraced her twice. Now she'd given him a glimpse of more and yet he was supposed to spend the next four or five hours listening to *that* kind of music while her house was empty?

Life was so unfair.

"I know, I know, it's not your thing. But a few drinks and you'll find this music fun. I promise. At least, that's how I think most newbies get used to it."

Now he was a newbie. His parents used to talk like that when he was a kid. He'd tell her later the word was *noob*.

Rhymed with…never mind. He forced his eyes to focus on her beautiful face.

You're thirty-five, not fifteen.

Thinking of teenagers, what would Austin think if his mom dated someone so much younger than her. Ben's age was probably halfway between Austin's and Eric's. Was that…weird?

Todd and Pauline offered to buy the first two pitchers while the group found tables. Ben still sensed tension between Pauline and Tracy, and he wished he could mend the fence between them.

The planning committee found two long tables with chairs packed together in the brightly lit hall. Everyone—*Tracy*—could easily see that Ben wasn't drinking alcohol. Crap. Susie waved to get his attention over the music blaring from the tiny bandstand in the middle of the room, then mimed to ask if he wanted to sit between her and Genny.

And feel like he was sitting between his parents? He shook his head.

She signalled that she was going to the bar. He nodded.

Ben had wanted to drive his Porsche here, but leaving his newly (and expensively) repaired car in the parking lot of a drink fest was inviting bad luck. Tracy said she'd enjoy only a beer or two at the beginning and stick to pop and mineral water the rest of the evening since she was driving.

So, unless he wanted to spend more money on a cab, he was stuck.

Todd and Pauline returned with a stack of plastic cups branded with the big orange head of the Oktoberfest mascot. Pauline skipped Ben when she handed out the cups, but Todd shot her a look of annoyance and placed a cup in front of Ben. So Pauline hadn't told Ben's story to Todd. And apparently Todd's opinion of Ben was improving.

When Todd poured beer into Ben's cup a moment later, the sweetness of the fermented hops reached his nose and cravings began their crawl all over his body.

One sip. It would just be one sip. It would quell his cravings and he'd look like one of them, right?

No, Landry. Your problems started with one sip. The difference between here and the Peregrines is that everyone there knew I didn't drink, so no one poured me anything.

When Todd reached Genny, though, he asked if she wanted anything rather than just pouring. Why did women get asked and men get automatically served? Women who didn't drink got a free pass.

Susie returned to the table with a cup filled with ginger ale and discreetly switched cups with Ben. He drank immediately, trying to erase the memory of the beer that had stood in its place, enticing him like a cup of liquid gold.

Genny squealed and showed her phone to Susie, who hugged and kissed her partner.

"*Both* my parents want to celebrate Thanksgiving with *both* me and Susie!" Genny yelled over the music.

Ben's eyes opened wide. "Seriously?"

"*Vraiment!*"

Ben put an arm around Susie and grabbed one of Genny's hands and squeezed.

"Do you mind?" Susie asked in Ben's ear.

"Don't worry about it," he shouted over the music. "I'll make myself scarce."

"Oh, no! I didn't mean that! Still come!"

He didn't want to be the fifth wheel. Plus, Genny's parents spoke little English. Susie had been working on her French for at least a year, but Ben had bad memories of trying to get by with grade nine French during his worst year in Montreal.

Tracy asked what the good news was. Ben filled her in.

"That's wonderful!" she shouted over the music.

"But now Ben thinks he can't stay with us!" Susie shouted back.

"Oh, he can join us!"

Ben couldn't hide his terror at the thought of joining the Robinson-Brubacher Thanksgiving event. All the families—including Todd's—would be there.

All. Of. Them.

Including the parents, the siblings, and their kids.

And Eric.

Todd's family would probably be friendly enough since Ben had helped arrange DIY Home's first national sponsorship. But that wasn't enough to balance out the hate from everyone else.

Tracy joked and slapped him on the back. "It's just like here. A few drinks and you'll be fine." She looked at his drink. "Oh. Ginger ale?"

Ben shrugged. "It smelled good. I'll have beer later."

The band leader announced something called the "Wedding March." Tracy's eyes lit up. "You have to join me! Come on!"

Before Ben knew what was happening, Tracy had whisked him away to the dance floor.

∾

TRACY HADN'T BEEN OKTOBERFESTING in the several years she'd been away for Austin's training. She wasn't going to miss out on her favourite song this time. Besides, Ben had looked so glum at the thought of spending Thanksgiving alone. This would lift his spirits.

"Loosen up!" Tracy shouted. "This is supposed to be fun!" She grabbed his hands and jiggled them to relax him as the band leader explained the dance. When the music began, the crowd galloped across the dance floor and then jumped once at the end, throwing their hands in the air, only to grab hold of each other again and repeat the sequence in the other direction. Tracy and Ben had to gallop in time with the music to avoid being trampled by the other couples: the dance floor was small.

By the time the dance was over, Ben was all smiles, something she hadn't seen in days. A polka came next.

"Have you ever polka-ed?"

He shook his head and leaned forward. "My parents insisted Susie and I learn a little ballroom when we were kids, but polka wasn't part of those lessons."

Tracy took up the traditional ballroom stance with him. "No time like the present! It's like the waltz, only you bounce."

Ben did indeed pick it up quickly, and as he led, Tracy pointed out the older couples, some who played it safe but danced as though they didn't have a care in the world, and others who twirled around the floor and would flatten you if you stood in their way. "They're probably club members and have been doing this for decades," Tracy said. "When I was younger, there were so many more of them here." Tracy wished she could dance well, but had to satisfy herself with tried-and-true Oktoberfest dances: the polka, the "Wedding March," the "Chicken Dance," and the "Mexican Hat Dance."

Ben's hazel eyes stared down at her, and she looked up at him. Bouncing from foot to foot was the only thing that prevented her from kissing him. Well, that and Pauline's presence. When the music switched to something fast but contemporary, Tracy asked if Ben wanted to sit, and to her astonishment, he said he wanted to keep dancing.

Only after several songs did they take a break.

"It's my turn for a round of beers," Tracy asked. "Help me carry?"

Ben's entire body stiffened. "Um, okay, if you need it."

What was going on? For the past hour or more, he'd been Mr. Congeniality. The moment she asked for help, he suddenly felt inconvenienced? "It's fine," Tracy said. "I was just worried I'd drop something. Don't bother."

Ben shook his head. "Of course I'll help you."

"No, really—"

He touched her by the elbow and nudged her toward the bar. "I mean it. I can help."

He ordered a ginger ale for Susie, too. "Since I stole hers." His cheeks turned red.

How sweet was that? Always thinking about his sister.

When they returned to the table, Pauline immediately took the pitcher out of Ben's hand and helped pour drinks, and Susie accepted the ginger ale. The band took a break and put on some quieter, pre-recorded music on the speaker. That meant everyone could talk at a normal volume.

Tracy noticed Ben was drinking the ginger ale and Susie the beer. Did Ben love ginger ale that much? Or was he concerned about Tracy drinking and was going to offer to drive? She'd only had two and it would be hours before she drove home. She'd be fine. But Ben never seemed to be in the mood to drink. He had refused alcohol twice at her place, and now both times here.

But wait…Pauline had taken the pitcher out of Ben's hand…

and his sister had taken his alcohol and given him pop that looked like the very drink they were drinking…. They were trying to help Ben stay away from alcohol. It had all been planned. Tracy hadn't become a successful EA without developing a keen eye for people's personal preferences, but this was more than a preference. People who didn't like something didn't plan with friends how they could avoid it. They only planned if they were allergic or…

Tracy gasped. Was Ben an alcoholic? That would explain his fear of being alone right now. Getting fired from a job you loved could drive you to drink if you had alcoholism in your history.

She looked over at Pauline. Did everyone at the Peregrines know? Impossible. Ben would've never been hired for such a major brand. But why hadn't Pauline told Tracy?

Maybe Ben asked her not to say anything because he didn't want me to know.

She leaned forward and spoke into Ben's ear. "You don't drink, do you?"

He hesitated. What was Tracy thinking, asking about something so personal?

"I can't."

And I pushed him to come to an event that's all about drinking and assumed it was Old Ben who didn't want to help me carry the beer, when he was trying to avoid it. Oh my god.

"I'm so sorry," she said.

His hair brushed against her temple as he whispered, "It's all right. Besides, I'm having tons of fun."

The physical contact was too much for Tracy to withstand. She turned her head so her lips could meet his just as the band leader announced, "Onkel Hans is in the house!"

The room erupted in cheers.

Startled, Tracy and Ben burst out laughing. But inside,

Tracy was disappointed. She no longer cared who was watching or what they thought: she was falling hard for him.

But Ben's horrified look at the giant costumed figure with the bulbous, orange head, red Oktoberfest hat, green lederhosen, and white shirt made her laugh again.

"*That's* Onkel Hans?" he asked. He picked up his cup of ginger ale and compared the drawing of the head to the real-life figure.

Pauline swatted at him from across the table. "He's a legend! And I'm playing him in the parade Monday, so don't make fun of him."

Ben pretended to zip his mouth shut.

When the band leader announced the "Chicken Dance," Ben grabbed Tracy's hand. "This one I know!"

Tracy didn't miss Susie's smile—which she interpreted as her blessing.

Nor did she miss the corners of Pauline's mouth turning up just a little, either.

CHAPTER 25

*B*en and Tracy sat beside one another on the sofa in the family room, each with a glass of water. Susie and Genny, tipsy from the night out, were already asleep on the pullout couch in the basement.

"I feel absolutely horrible about tonight," Tracy said. "I really had no idea. Had I known, I wouldn't have pressured you into coming."

It was uncomfortable talks like these that Ben wanted to avoid. He didn't want to be wrapped in bubble wrap or handled with white gloves. Oddly enough, it gave him some comfort that Pauline was still angry with him: she hadn't turned to pity after he'd shared his background.

But if anything was going to happen between him and Tracy, he had to tell her the whole truth. He'd also promised Pauline he would, and if he wanted to prove that he was changing, he needed to keep his promise.

"I don't tell people my full story for a lot of reasons, but a big one is that they'll treat me differently."

"But Pauline knows?"

"Everyone at the Peregrines knew I didn't drink, but I just told them I always needed to be ready for media. I only recently told Pauline a bit more about why."

"It's why you've been scared to be alone?"

Ben took a sip of water. His skin heated up, his throat tightened, his hand clenched the glass. He gently placed it on the coffee table and folded his hands in his lap. He watched his thumbs twiddle as he spoke.

"In my early twenties, I got fired for not reaching my sales quotas three months in a row. I know lots of people fail. But I didn't. Landrys don't fail. My sister and I were honours students, I'd been voted valedictorian, had gone to university on a scholarship, the whole nine yards. Mom had helped the children's hospital—and before you ask, yes, the same one—raise millions already, too. Dad had reached VP of sales by the time he was thirty-eight. I know overachievers sound like babies when they complain about failing, but when that fear of failure grips you, you can't see past it. You really believe your world has been destroyed. I was so humiliated, I couldn't tell anyone right away, so I figured I'd just drink a couple of days to get over it. I didn't expect it feel so good. It snowballed from there. Within a couple of months, I'd been evicted."

Still staring at his hands, he heard Tracy's gasp, but he couldn't bring himself to make eye contact with her.

"Didn't your family help you?"

Ben shrugged. "I'm sure they would've had they known, but they didn't." Ben played some more with his hands. *Are you drunk, Benjamin? No, Dad, just tired. Long day yesterday. Month-end. You know how it is.* "I'd lied my way out of explaining the first time my dad heard the drunken slur in my voice and I high-tailed it out of Toronto before they started looking for me. I actually spent that first winter in Kitchener." Ben let out a dry laugh. "Talk about the world coming three-sixty. The volunteer coordinator you have me working with at the homeless shelter? We've already met. Sebastian volunteered with the Out of the Cold program that year."

Tracy's hands flew to her cheeks. "Oh, Ben. I feel horrible. I've pretty much brought every terrible memory of your past back to you. If you want to quit and go back to Toronto or...I don't know...Prince Edward Island or somewhere nice, I'd completely understand. I am so, so sorry."

Ben finally lifted his gaze and lowered her hands from her face. "Tracy, please, don't blame yourself. It's okay. You had no idea because I didn't tell you." Could he kiss her now? The compassion in this woman was pulling him into her with as much force as chocolate lured her.

"I moved on to Montreal and lived on the streets there for another year. *As-tu de la bière?* is the only French I remember." He let go of her hands and leaned back against the couch, the unwelcome memories of that time flooding his mind.

Tracy's voice was almost a whisper. "How did you turn things around?"

Ben swallowed. This was the hardest part. "Seeing one of my friends dead from a drug overdose. I hadn't started on the hard stuff yet, but I knew it wouldn't be long before I did. I was disgusted with where I'd let alcohol take me..." His voice caught in his throat.

Alcohol had created friendships with people he cherished but could no longer be around if he was to save himself. *Damned if I do, damned if I don't.* His voice cracked. "I couldn't let myself care about anyone after that or I'd always be wondering what happened to everyone I left behind in Montreal and couldn't help." His eyes burned as he faced Tracy. "But I can never get the image of that lifeless body out of my mind, and I never want to return to that life again."

Tracy's eyes were red. "I put you right into the lion's den tonight with a healthy dose of do-gooder volunteerism for good measure."

Ben squeezed his eyes shut to push the tears of the memory away. "Susie and Genny were there. I was nervous, but I was safe. And I did have a lot of fun. Plus, I'd spent a good part of my years at the Peregrines hanging out around alcohol and I was fine. It's wonderful that you're trying to help those living without shelter. I'm just maybe not the best person to do it."

"Talk about life repeating itself." She pulled his hand onto her lap and threaded her fingers between his.

"Yeah."

They sat there in silence, the truth of Ben's past melting into their hearts. But then Ben remembered what his ultimate goal was: to help this family reunite. He pulled his hand away.

Tracy seemed to read his mind. "I know how you feel. About us, I mean. I feel it, too, Ben. God, do I ever." She crossed her arms and leaned her head back against the couch.

Ben didn't want to hear the answer he was anticipating to the next question, but he needed to ask it for their sakes. "And Eric?"

She sighed, glanced at him, and then stared at the ceiling. "I've been asking myself since he kissed my cheek the other night."

Jealousy shot through Ben, but he pushed it down and waited for her to continue.

"I felt something familiar, but it evaporated. It was a memory, not a desire. I've been trying to guilt myself into having feelings for him again, but I can't do it. No matter how hard I try, I can't reawaken my love for him. I've forgiven him.

I've tried telling myself how good it would be for Austin to have his parents back together, all of it. I can't do it."

Ben was relieved. Very relieved. But she hadn't given Ben permission to move forward.

"It's because of me, right? If we hadn't kissed in June, you wouldn't be having these problems."

Tracy let out a dry laugh. "No. As they say, it's not you, it's me. Mine and Eric's relationship was already on the rocks when he walked out. He just dealt us the final blow."

"Then why…?"

Tracy sighed. "Eric realized he'd made a big mistake."

So, their relationship was unfinished. And even if Ben wasn't preventing Tracy from falling back in love with her ex-husband, he was most definitely complicating things. If he stayed another night, he couldn't promise himself that he and Tracy wouldn't keep their hands off each other. After all, they'd hardly known each other in June, and now they were certainly falling for each other. It maybe wasn't love yet, but it was heading in that direction.

He stood up. "I should go. I'll finish the rest of my commitment virtually. I can't keep your family apart, Tracy."

She stood up with him. "Ben…" Was she going to say he should stay? Her eyes said so. "You'll head to New Hamburg, then?"

His hope deflated, he shook his head. "I'll find a hotel somewhere. Last thing I want to be is the fifth wheel, romantically, linguistically, and economically. And I'm not ready to return to Toronto. Not yet."

"But your drinking…?"

That Tracy was this concerned about him dug into his heart. He had to convince her he'd be okay, which meant sharing with her his backup plan, as humiliating as it was. Not even his parents had known about it when they were alive. But he didn't want Tracy to worry about him, and he was confident she wouldn't share it with anyone.

"Susie and I have a plan in case that happens. She'll change all my banking passwords so I can't access funds. I have one credit card that has a one-thousand-dollar limit on it, which will suffice for the weekend. Even I can't drink myself that silly." He smiled, trying to lighten the mood.

But Tracy's face was cold. "That's not funny."

He clasped his hands behind his back so he wouldn't wrap them around hers. "You have Austin to take care of, and the last thing he needs is his mother to be dating a recovering jerk."

"YOU'RE NOT A JERK, BEN."

But he was right. Austin liked Ben but he wouldn't be happy to learn he was in the running for Father Number Two. She'd received texts from both Austin and Eric, and although Austin's required a little reading between the lines, it sounded like both of them were enjoying themselves in Toronto.

Who was she to stand in the way of her family reuniting?

But before her was a man she'd come to admire. Yes, he'd made mistakes—some pretty big ones at that—but he was changing, showing remorse, trying to make amends. If she'd developed feelings for him, didn't it make sense to at least see where they could take them?

But what if they broke up? What if Austin finally accepted Ben, and Tracy then realized Ben wouldn't change, and she had to break things off?

Tracy and Ben stood in the same position they had in June, staring at each other's lips, their breathing heavy, fighting to keep their hands to themselves.

Tracy hadn't made any promises to Eric, hadn't even

responded to his uninvited kisses except with silence. Yes, she had memories of their lovemaking, but those remained in the corners of her mind like movies from long ago. What was real now was the touch of Ben's hands on the dance floor, whether they were romping back and forth during the "Wedding March," or pressed against each other during a slow dance.

She reached for his hand again and remembered the kindness he'd shown her by watching over Austin, not just the morning he stayed back until Austin was ready for school—even if that did end in chaos because of Eric—but the evening she arrived home to find them sitting at the table, focused on schoolwork.

Tracy guided Ben's hand behind her waist. He followed her cue and combed his fingers through her hair.

He touched his forehead to hers. "Are you sure?" he whispered.

"I stopped loving Eric long ago."

"But your family…"

"If Eric is in my future, we'll have to start over again. But you and I are here, now. Maybe this weekend is all we have. Maybe we're a rebound relationship for both of us for different reasons. I don't know. But I want to enjoy this weekend together if you do." She pulled her head back to stare deeply into his hazel eyes.

He gazed into her eyes with equal intensity. "You're not concerned about our…" He took a breath. "Age difference?"

Tracy entwined her fingers with his, their ages showing in their hands. "We've been trying to ignore our feelings for each other, Ben. It hasn't done us any good." She smiled. "My extra years of wisdom tell me we should take this weekend and explore them." She giggled. "Our feelings. Not the years between us."

"I would love that." A glint of mischief appeared as he raised his hand to the zipper on the bodice of her dirndl. "May I?"

Tracy rose to her tiptoes and pressed her lips to his. But in truth, she couldn't wait for Ben to undo that zipper so she could finally untuck and unbutton his shirt.

If she was to be quite honest with herself, she'd been waiting since June to do just that.

CHAPTER 26

Someone knocked on the door.

"Ben?" Susie asked in a low voice.

Ben felt his legs. His pants were on. How he had managed to get his pants back on and return to his bed was a puzzle that would forever remain unsolved.

"Yeah, come in."

"You're decent?"

"Why wouldn't I be?"

She poked her head in.

Another unsolved mystery: how Susie had fallen into bed drunk at one in the morning and look bright-eyed and cheery at...Ben checked his phone...eleven. Okay. So it was less of a mystery. Ben had easily stayed up another two hours.

With Tracy.

A sly smile slid onto his sister's face. "If she saw you now, she'd *totally* fall in love with you. Shirtless, tussled hair, morning scruff." Then she wrinkled her nose. "Or maybe not."

Sometimes it didn't matter whether Susie was thirty-two or

ten. She could still annoy him. "What do you want?" He threw on deodorant and a T-shirt.

Susie closed the door behind her and sat on the end of Ben's bed, all kidding gone. "You're certain you're not coming to my place this weekend."

Ben sat down on the wooden chair at the small desk in his room. "I'm staying here."

Susie pulled her shoulders up in gleeful anticipation. "Here? So things are looking up?"

Ben couldn't hold back a smile. "Maybe? For the weekend anyhow." He sighed. "Somehow, I feel like this is cheating on Eric. They're not officially divorced."

"She's made it clear to you she doesn't love him and that she's okay with trying something with you."

"Behind everyone's backs."

Susie nodded, acknowledging his concern. "This is probably completely new for her, Ben, and it's normal for single parents to date without telling their kids at first. Enjoy the weekend and roll with it. Just call me if you get into *any* kind of trouble."

He nodded. "I told her about our backup plan."

Susie's jaw dropped. "You've never…"

"I haven't trusted anyone like her in a long time. She didn't flinch." He ran his fingers through his hair. "It's been forever since I've met a woman that sexy and compassionate. And genuine."

Susie beamed at him.

Ben stared at his hands. "I feel uncomfortable when you smile like that at me."

"Because you don't believe you deserve this kind of happiness. Have fun with her! It's been, like, forever since you enjoyed yourself as much as you did last night."

Susie was right. Not having to worry about turning the

evening into a social media campaign or protecting players from social media pariahs meant he could just be himself.

I was myself, wasn't I?

Susie opened the door. "I love you, Big Ben, and I'll always have your back."

How lucky was Ben to have family like Susie? And a friend like Tracy?

What would life be like, though, if he had a *partner* like Tracy?

BEN BRUSHED his lips against her ear. She glowed when she faced him.

"About your suggestion to join you and everyone else on Monday..."

"You looked positively horrified. Has something changed your mind?"

Ben leaned against the kitchen counter and stuffed his hands in his pockets. "I thought maybe it would be a good time to actually own up to everything and apologize to everyone."

Tracy blinked.

Even if Claire had been curt with him, she had had the decency to tell him where he stood. Just like Pauline. For everything he did to protect the reputation of others, his own was in shambles. How did that make sense? He had to start clean somewhere, and Thanksgiving at the Robinsons seemed like the place to get a fresh start.

"Pauline said she wants me to apologize to her parents directly before she could even think of forgiving me. It's important to her, which means it's important to you." He swallowed. Doing things for others was becoming easier, but he also realized easing his deep fear was hard. "I also need to do it for myself. I keep running, and it's time I stopped. I had so much fun last night. I kept Pauline from sharing her joy as a mascot with her family—and you."

Tracy drew her finger down his temple, to his neck, over his shoulder, and along his arm, before reaching for his hand. "We're not always our best selves. We can't be." She squeezed his hand. "I know they'd appreciate it. But there'll be a lot of people there. Are you sure? We could also go over there now." Tracy reached for her phone, which was on the counter. She was never far from it. He watched her quickly check Austin's location before pulling up Claire's number.

"It's better I do it there. It scares the living daylights out of me to apologize in front of everyone but I know my actions didn't just affect Pauline and her parents. I'd rather just dive into the deep end."

"If you're sure?"

"I'm sure." Ben lifted her hand off her phone and kissed it. "Why don't we go for a drive in the countryside? Grab some groceries on the way back? I can cook."

The corners of Tracy's mouth curled up. "But which car should we take?"

Ben's smile preceded his joke. "I finally have my Porsche back. So, clearly, not your Nash Rambler."

Tracy staggered back as though she'd been run through by a rapier in a Shakespearean play. "You're equating my modern Japanese car to an American car from the fifties?"

The mischief in Ben's eyes shone. "The horsepower's the same. But don't worry. A Nash Rambler is a classic. Even stars in its own song. Ever heard 'Beep Beep'?"

Tracy crossed her arms and delivered her rebuke. "For your information, Benjamin Landry, I know that oldie. If my car's the Nash Rambler, then that makes your Porsche the..." She paused dramatically, and Ben, playing along, opened his eyes in mock, horrified anticipation. "A massive, boat-y, *American* Cadillac. *Beep, beep*!"

Ben's hands flew to his heart to cover the imaginary bullet wound, and he stumbled backwards until he hit the wall opposite the sink, sliding down it as though the wound to his car-loving heart had been fatal.

Playing dead serious, Tracy approached him, hands on her hips. "If you admit that Japanese engineering—no matter the size—is as good as your German engineering..." She kneeled down in front of him and lifted his chin with her finger. "I might breathe life back into you."

Tracy's vivacious brown eyes invited him into her soul. Years had passed since Ben had known someone this deeply, and it frightened him that it was happening again. But he wouldn't run from this fear. For once, he was going to dig in his heels and not let fear dictate his next actions. For touching him ever so gently was a courageous, fascinating, confident woman Ben didn't want to leave behind.

"I think I can make that concession, Tracy Tschirhart."

He tilted his face up, and their lips touched. At first, the kiss was tender, soft, full of longing. He raised himself to his knees, Tracy engulfed him in her embrace, and the kiss became deep, sweet, and smooth, her touch telling him she had missed intimacy as much as he had.

When they paused for air, Tracy outlined his face with her finger. "I have to confess: I've never driven a Porsche before."

Ben kissed her finger. "If you're nice to me, I might let you drive it."

Tracy kissed him on the cheek. "Nice like this?"

"Um...a little nicer."

She kissed him the nose. "Like this?"

"A little more."

She kissed him on the lips. "Like this?"

"Mmm."

But to his utter disappointment, it was only a brief kiss. A coy smile appeared on her face. Uh-oh. Was she about to outsmart him again? Because Ben was nearing the point of whisking her back to the bedroom and skipping their afternoon drive. When the woman you were melting for treated you like the most delectable piece of chocolate, your brain lost all ability to function.

She continued her kisses down his neck. *This is better than driving on a racetrack.* "If you're nice to me," she said, "I might be nice to your car."

Without warning, she jumped up and ran for his key fob in his jacket in the foyer.

Ben needed a moment to regroup, then he scrambled to his feet. "That was cheating, Tracy Tschirhart!" But he caught her in his arms before she could unlock the front door.

This time, Ben pressed Tracy against the wall and proved how passionate he was about her. He caressed her soft curves, responded to each moan and gasp, and drank in the hot desire emanating from her as she wrapped her arms around him and pulled his body tighter against hers.

Ben would no longer be able to hide his feelings for Tracy after this weekend.

CHAPTER 27

"*I*'m sorry again about the accident." Tracy turned down a country road. "Truth be told, I didn't see that peregrine falcon swooping out of the sky. And then I thought it was going to crash through the windshield."

Ben placed his hand on her leg. "And I shouldn't have driven so close to you. My truth is that I was tailgating you because you were going too slow."

Tracy flashed him a smile and returned her attention to the road. The roads outside of town were often hilly. They could come upon a cyclist or even a massive tractor taking up the whole lane and shoulder. You literally never knew what lay on the other side of a hill.

She shifted gears. "It's been ages since I've driven manual."

"You can feel the torque vectoring on winding roads, can't you?"

"Say what?"

Ben laughed. "Just a feature on performance cars. It improves handling, but it only activates under certain conditions. Does feel nice, though."

"Hey," Tracy said, "can you check my phone to see where Austin's at? I haven't checked in on him in a bit." She gave Ben her passcode.

"You don't trust Eric?"

"For the most part, I do, but he wouldn't tell me if he was at the hospital with Austin to save me worrying. I just want to make sure."

Ben eventually reported that Austin appeared to be at a dancewear store. Tracy hadn't been aware she'd been holding her shoulders near her ears until they dropped upon hearing the update.

She pointed to a sign up ahead at the end of a farm driveway. "Eggs. Fresh vegetables. Should we stop there?"

Ben agreed, and Tracy laughed as she turned his sleek Porsche down the long driveway of what would likely be an Old Order Mennonite farm. Talk about two worlds colliding.

This particular farm had a small store on-site. Ben chose a squash, some corn, apples, tomatoes—saying he'd make her a delicious squash-apple soup—before adding a bouquet of fresh flowers and paying for everything.

Eric would've never wanted to spend a Saturday afternoon like this. The youngest of six kids, he'd never learned to cook.

"A word of warning," he'd said on a date. "I hate doing anything that produces dishes."

He had come around somewhat once he'd seen that cooking had saved money, but he never stopped trying to convince Tracy to hire someone. Tracy knew that Eric wanted to hire help precisely so the family could spend more time together. They also loved seeing ballets as a family.

Tracy had a hard time believing Ben could stay awake throughout an entire ballet.

But she would enjoy cooking with him, baking chocolatey

desserts, and taking weekend road trips like this one. For Eric, travel only counted if it involved an airport shuttle and a plane.

Still, she could imagine herself spending time with Ben. Lots of time. Of course, only if Austin accepted it.

But Austin had been through so many transitions already that Tracy didn't want to ask him about another.

As they left, they saw several young Mennonite girls helping a pair of older women in the large vegetable garden. Just then, one of the girls, who was perhaps seven, tripped, spilled the contents of her bucket, and burst into tears.

Without a moment's pause, Tracy rushed over and bent down next to the child. "Are you okay?"

The girl didn't answer.

One of the older women spoke in a light German accent. "Anna will be fine, thank you."

"Are you sure? I have a first-aid kit in my purse." Tracy hadn't won best executive assistant in her national professional organization for nothing.

The woman smiled kindly. "No, thank you. She is fine."

But the girl kept crying, holding her knee.

"Honestly, I don't mind."

Ben put his arms around Tracy's shoulders. "Let's let them take care of their own family, Tracy. Kids fall down all the time." He helped her stand up.

"She might have twisted her knee or torn a ligament..." She turned to the older woman. "We could take her to the hospital if you'd like."

The woman looked annoyed. "Thank you but no. We are fine."

Ben spoke in the firm but comforting tone you used to urge someone away from a situation. *Why is he using that tone with me?* "I've seen lots of torn ligaments and twisted joints, Tracy. I spent ten years with the Peregrines, remember? Let's go. I'm certain this girl just bumped her knee, like her mother said."

"But—"

The other woman joined them now. "I am her mother. Thank you for your care. Anna will be fine."

Ben nudged Tracy to turn around. "See? She's in good care." He nodded to the women. *What was that look he gave them?* "And see? The girl's calming down."

Maybe Ben's right? And the girl's mother is with her, so maybe she'll be okay?

Tracy allowed herself to be led back to the car.

BEN SAT in the driver's seat and turned on the ignition, but something wasn't sitting right with him. Kids everywhere bumped into things and fell. He didn't need to have children of his own to know that. It happened all the time at the arena. The girl's reaction would've been much stronger had she torn or broken something. She had probably been upset by the shock of falling and for having spilled her bucket.

But Tracy's hands were shaking in her lap. When they reached the end of the driveway, Ben pulled over.

"I'm sure she'll be okay."

Tracy gave him a quick kiss on the cheek. "Really, I'm fine. Keep driving. I'm fine."

But that fall had scared her, as though it'd brought back a memory.

Ben would bet his Porsche on what memory it triggered. Ben had run away from his tough questions for over a decade. He didn't want Tracy making that same mistake.

"Tracy, I can read people easily. That fall triggered something. I'm going to ask. Did it remind you of Austin's accident?"

Tracy took a quick breath that confirmed that the answer was yes.

Tracy's hypervigilance about Austin's whereabouts and apparently with the well-being of other children, her drive to keep moving, denying her own wants while helping everyone else, her scarcity of friends… Ben had seen similar trauma responses on the streets, although those were more pronounced and usually accompanied by abuse of at least one substance.

He even recognized some of those behaviours in himself.

Tracy smiled and stared out the window.

Avoidance. Another classic symptom.

It was as clear as the sky outside now: Austin's accident two summers ago had traumatized Tracy and she'd probably never sought help to heal from it.

"No," she finally answered. Denial, yet another classic symptom. "Just a mother's instinct. Nothing worse than seeing a child potentially injured." Her voice became artificially chipper. "Let's see what the next farm has!"

Ben turned the engine back on and drove onto the road. How could he not have seen it? And all this time she'd been listening to his story, supporting him as he tried to exorcise his own demons. What support did she need to get herself help?

You're assuming she recognizes she needs help, Landry. It's pretty clear she doesn't think she does.

He placed a hand on her thigh. She smiled at him as though the past few minutes had never happened and put her hand on his.

"I never thought I'd be so happy to wreck my car," he said.

"I'm so sorry about that."

"Don't be." He hoped she'd forgive him for the next question. "But I have to ask you, Tracy. Do you think that peregrine falcon falling out of the sky reminded you of Austin's accident, too?"

Tracy yanked her hand away and faced the window again. Nothing said more clearly to him that his suspicion was correct. "Not everything's about Austin's accident."

Arguing with her would only alienate her from him. That wouldn't help. "Of course not."

But how could Ben convince her that she didn't need to live in constant fear of Austin being hurt—emotionally or otherwise —again? Epilepsy was obviously a concerning diagnosis and came with potentially severe consequences. She'd always worry about Austin. But seeing her reaction to that girl, not trusting Eric to inform her if he and Austin were in the hospital... Tracy's vigilance over Austin had as much power as his Porsche's engine with overboost engaged.

One thing Ben had learned in therapy was that the grieving process wasn't just for death. Grief was something you went through when any part of you died or any part of your identity—or the identity of someone you loved—changed. When Austin had dropped his dance partner onstage after camera flashes had set off a prolonged seizure, it had led to an epilepsy diagnosis that suggested that Austin's promising future in ballet was finished. That would have begun a grieving process for each of the Tschirharts. When Eric, who had sworn to stand by Tracy in sickness and in health, had abandoned her right then...it wasn't hard to believe that the events of the past two years in Tracy's life had traumatized her.

But to get help, you needed to admit that you needed help. It had taken Ben two years on the streets to accept he'd needed help even when the evidence was screaming in his face: he'd been begging on the streets to feed addiction, which had claimed the life of a friend. Tracy had no such external signs to tell her she wasn't thriving. She owned a house, worked a successful job, belonged to a loving family, and was raising an incredible son. And most importantly, she'd survived emotional hardship.

Austin was likely Tracy's saving grace, Ben thought. Not only was she vigilant about his health and safety because she was his mother, but because he distracted her from her own grief.

Ben had to tread carefully. If he pushed too hard, Tracy would push him away. But if he did nothing, she wouldn't get the help she needed. And judging by what he knew of Austin, she risked losing him, too, if she increased her vigilance.

Maybe Tracy wouldn't open up to Ben this weekend. But he would do whatever it took to ensure he was around when she was ready.

Even if it meant just being friends after tomorrow.

TRACY SIGHED as the credits scrolled for *Rush*, the movie Ben had chosen. Her thoughts were already racing ahead to tomorrow, when this perfect weekend alone with the perfect man would end.

Ben caressed her cheek. "So? What's the verdict? Chris Hemsworth? Or me?"

She ran a hand along his shirt, relishing his smooth, hard chest and abs. She maneuvered onto his lap as she traced his ear and drew her finger down his neck. She pressed her lips to his, and enjoyed a long, sensuous kiss before saying, "My verdict is you."

Ben kissed her several times along her neck. "I'm so glad to hear that. I'd have been jealous otherwise."

Ben's touch was tender, gentle, passionate. But unlike their first kiss back in June, his touch now contained more than physical pleasure, as did hers. Tracy hadn't enjoyed the care of a man like this in years.

She climbed off Ben's lap and sat next to him on the couch again.

"Everything okay?" he asked.

"Not really. Eric won't be happy if he notices anything between us."

"I don't think I can hide my feelings for you. I...care about you too much."

"I care about you, too."

The words had fallen out before she'd had a chance to stop them. It didn't escape her that when Eric had tried to get her to express any feelings for him, she couldn't. She no longer doubted Ben's intentions toward her or Austin. He cared for both of them. And she was certain he was not, as Jan had said, one of her "bleeding-heart cases." Yes, he'd gone through a difficult time. Yes, he'd chosen poor ways to cope with it. But now he'd made different choices. Susie had mentioned his good heart, and Tracy had seen it, too. She trusted him with her heart, and she trusted him with Austin. But would Austin trust him? Allow Ben to care for him?

"It's just that Austin comes first," Tracy said.

Ben nodded. "I get it. I don't want to make his life any more difficult. You're certain he doesn't want us together?"

"I need to take any potential changes in my life really slowly because of him. It's best if he and Eric don't know what happened this weekend."

Ben gave her hand a squeeze. "It's just been a very long time since I've felt this about anyone." He smiled that intoxicating smile of his. "It's extremely enticing."

As though acting without her permission, Tracy's body leaned into him. Everything about him—his body, his heart, his soul—was just as enticing for her.

Tracy woke up first Sunday morning, this time with Ben beside her in her bed. He looked so peaceful and imperfect with his twenty-four-hour beard, mussed-up hair, and closed eyes. She knew in her heart he was the right man for her.

Everything about Ben felt so right. But if he didn't find a job in Kitchener, would he pack up and leave again? A stable family for Austin was her priority, even if she had to give up Ben.

CHAPTER 28

*W*hen Tracy mentioned that she hadn't cleaned the gutters since Eric had moved out, he knew what his next don't-kick-me-out task would be. Although Ben doubted she'd ask him to leave at this point, the fear was so deep that it still motivated him.

When he dropped the clump of leaves into the wheelbarrow below, he glimpsed his shiny car. Mayumi Enomoto, the owner of the garage, had done a fantastic job with his beloved vehicle. She'd said he'd also taken good care of it. His Panamera had been his reward to himself for five years' sobriety, so taking care of it was a way of continuing to take care of himself.

And taking care of it meant moving it out of the way of last year's mushy leaves. As Ben climbed down the ladder to move his car, Eric's yellow Tesla pulled up next to Ben's red beauty and Austin jumped out.

"Hey, Ben!"

Ben waved back but did not miss Eric's jealous daggers. *At least I'm wearing my shirt*, Ben thought. The weather had cooled again.

Austin ran into the house.

"You both obviously had a good time," Ben said to Eric.

"My son and I had a wonderful time." Eric eyed the Porsche. "So, this is what brought you into my house."

Okay. So this was where the conversation was going. "I picked it up on Friday. I'll probably visit my sister this week now that I have wheels again."

"What's the fuel consumption on that thing?"

That thing?

"It varies. But *my Porsche* can go up to about fourteen litres per hundred kilometres."

Eric scoffed. "Such a waste of money, not to mention it's bad for the environment. Mine doesn't use any gas."

"Neither does mine when I'm in Toronto. I usually walk to work. I just use my Porsche in the summer for road trips and to burn off energy at the racetrack."

"You race?"

Ben had forgotten about Eric's aversion to risk.

"I just rent time on the track to drive two hundred and ninety-five kilometres an hour." Ben eyed Eric's car. "A 2015 Model S? I think the maximum speed is one-ninety, if I'm not mistaken."

Eric crossed his arms. "Why should I care? Last place you'll find me is on a racetrack. I don't need to risk my neck. I just need to max out at a hundred and twenty when I need to overtake someone."

Ben climbed the ladder. "Then you're right. You don't need a powerful motor." He pulled out an old bird's nest. "But mine can do zero to sixty in three-point-six seconds. If I recall my stats on your car, it's six-point-two."

"Three hundred and eighty horsepower. Three hundred and seventeen pound-feet of torque."

Ben fought not to laugh. "Five-hundred-and-fifty hp on my

Porsche. Five-hundred-and-fifty-three pound-feet of torque. Five hundred and ninety with overboost."

~

"AND IF THE ROADS GET ICY?" Ben continued. "You've only got rear-wheel drive. Not that I'd ever take my beauty out in a Canadian winter, anyway."

"Defensive driving, in case you haven't heard of it."

Tracy covered her eyes and shook her head. Austin covered his mouth to muffle his snickering. Neither Ben nor Eric had realized that the windows in the family room were open a crack to let in the scents of fall.

Tracy beckoned Austin to join her in the kitchen and pulled out ingredients for a chocolate protein shake for each of them. While the men were engaging in a twenty-first century version of jousting, now might be a good time to ask Austin how he felt about her dating again. Austin had clearly enjoyed the time with his father, so things might have settled between them. She'd talk to Eric privately afterwards.

"Why are men like that?" She laughed, wanting to keep the air relaxed.

"You're asking me? I'm not a man yet."

Tracy smiled. "Can you reach the cacao nibs? I need the extra chocolate today."

After she blended the shakes, they sat down at the kitchen table. But to her dismay, Austin began the conversation.

"Why is Dad like that? We had so much fun on the weekend. It felt like I had my dad back. But the moment he sees Ben, he freaks out."

Tracy took a deep breath. How much should she explain to him? How much did Eric want her to explain? In human resources, she'd learned that every relationship had at least two versions of "the truth." Was she actually right about everything?

Austin noticed her hesitation. "Mom, I'm not a kid anymore."

She wanted to note that he'd just admitted to not being a man, but she understood his meaning: he also wasn't that young. He was a teen: half child, half adult.

"I think he's scared that reconnecting with you might slip away because Ben's spending time with you."

"Ben's helping me with my homework."

"It's more complicated," she said. "Ben's eating with us, hanging out with us…"

"And he likes you, Mom."

Tracy's cheeks heated up.

"I get Dad's jealous, and I think he wants to get back together with you. But you don't."

Austin's observation blindsided Tracy. She wanted to talk to him about dating, not reuniting with his father. Although related topics, in her mind they were still different.

"It's complicated," was all she could think of saying.

"Stop trying to protect me! My father disappeared out of my life when I needed him most. And then showed up and expected to pick up right where he left off. Don't tell me I don't understand 'complicated'! What's going on here? I have a right to know!"

The front door opened and closed.

"Hey, Trace!"

Maybe she and Ben had been right all along with just enjoying the weekend together. As strongly attracted as they were to each other, now wasn't the time for a relationship. She had to sort things out with Eric first.

For Austin's sake.

~

GIVE YOUR HEAD A SHAKE, Landry.

What was he doing sparring against Eric? Electric versus internal combustion? Utterly pointless. And when it came right down to it, Eric possessed something Ben didn't: a good-paying job.

Done with the front of the house, he carried the ladder to the side.

Ben wanted Tracy, and she'd said in no uncertain terms that she felt the same way about him. But his guilt about interfering in this family was growing. Austin had enjoyed his time with his dad, and Tracy didn't want to tell them about her weekend with Ben. A part of him felt hurt when she'd said they should keep their time together a secret.

But he didn't regret the weekend for one moment. Ben couldn't remember when he'd last felt so alive. There were worse things in the world than getting over a broken heart.

Ben returned to push the wheelbarrow into position.

His first fresh start after homelessness had been about reuniting with his family and re-entering the workforce, but this fresh start was about promising to treat people better. He vowed to apologize to everyone at Thanksgiving before moving on.

Todd had pointed him in the right direction, shown him that people who didn't take the olives and return the branch did exist in this world. It had started with Sabine, who had driven him to get his things that first night. Then Mr. Casimiro, who had given him free dessert.

And it had snowballed. Every time he'd entered a store—except for Claire's, and he understood why—he'd been greeted with a friendly hello.

Ben climbed the ladder and inspected the gutter. More leaf

gunk. He threw it into the wheelbarrow and climbed back down, jumping over the last few rungs to the ground. After moving the ladder over several feet, he climbed up again.

It had embarrassed him to hear Pauline out, but in some puzzling way, he appreciated her honesty. It gave him a chance to try again. He understood she wasn't trying to hurt him but that she needed problems between them resolved before they could move forward.

Did that mean she saw the possibility of friendship with him?

The realization gave him goosebumps. She hadn't said she never wanted to see him again. Instead, she'd laid out the stipulations for forgiving him.

He pulled out more muck and dropped it into the wheelbarrow.

But forgiveness didn't mean friendship. Okay. So maybe they wouldn't be friends. But forgiveness had to happen if friendship was a possibility, and she appeared willing to forgive him—if he met certain conditions—despite the way he'd treated her for years.

"And despite my wanting to find more 'kids like Austin.'" He checked along the gutters to see where he should place the ladder and wheelbarrow next, saw nothing, and moved the ladder and the wheelbarrow to the back of the house. Westmount was *covered* in old trees. Fall colours were just beginning this year, so few leaves had fallen yet. But how Tracy had managed a year with clogged gutters, he didn't know. He placed the ladder near the end of the back roof and climbed up.

"Ah, and there's the damage." Her wooden deck had concentrated water stains where water had poured over the edge of the clogged gutters and pooled. With her permission, he could rent a pressure washer and sander and, depending on the weather, re-stain the deck before the weather turned cold and wet.

Unless he couldn't get that job and moved in with Susie for a while.

But what if Ben made Kitchener his new home? He didn't have to stay in Belmont Village or Westmount. Kitchener was big enough. And if he didn't like Kitchener, its twin city, Waterloo, was right next door. (He'd even heard that the border cut right through the living rooms of some houses.) If he wanted to live a little closer to Toronto and therefore his beloved racetracks, Cambridge, on the other side of Kitchener, was an option. Then he could also catch his major league sports. There were the surrounding townships, like New Hamburg, where Susie lived, but Susie had always been the country mouse, and Ben, the city mouse. But if the people he'd met in Belmont Village were any indication—and he was certain they were—this area was welcoming. He could picture himself settling here and starting a new life.

He could stay out of Tracy's way if need be. Or they could act on their feelings if they agreed it was in everyone's best interests.

But until she gave him permission, he was going to follow through on her request: do his best to pretend as though nothing had happened between them this weekend. That meant giving the family, including Eric, as much privacy as possible now.

Ben didn't realize how much time had passed until Austin opened the back sliding door to tell him supper would be ready in thirty.

Was Eric still there? His car was so quiet, Ben wouldn't have been able to hear him drive off.

CHAPTER 29

Tracy had invited Eric to join the family for supper. She was delighted that Austin continued talking about the weekend between bites, his hands gesturing in excitement, his face so animated she thought it would fall off. And hardly a seizure! The lack of stress had greatly benefited him.

But as supper continued, she saw Eric's eyes darting frequently between her and Ben, Austin talked more to Ben than Eric, although Ben tried to redirect the conversation to Eric with statements like "it's amazing how much dedication you've shown to Austin's ballet training over the years."

When it came time to clear the dishes from the main course, Ben insisted on doing it. Tracy knew that it was important to Ben to make himself useful but it stoked Eric's jealousy more: she could see he took Ben's actions to mean Ben was the better man because he helped in the house.

And to make things worse, Austin jumped up to join him. "Ben, you should've seen the show. The way they depicted death...I've never seen anything like it. I had some new thoughts about the way the protagonist dies in the novel."

When Ben threw Tracy a quick glance, Eric's scowl deepened. Eric loved the theatre, but pick up a book? Not on his life.

Same with Austin until Ben showed up.

"It sounds like you had a great time this weekend with your dad. I'm afraid I know very little about ballet. The only reason I knew Todd even existed was because of the posters of him all around Toronto and the odd article in the newspapers."

Tracy silently thanked him for his soft attempts at nudging Austin back to Eric, but Eric was no idiot. He could see what was happening. That Ben had to encourage Austin to talk to his father was a blow to Eric's ego.

Austin, oblivious to everything in his excitement, punched Ben in the arm. "You sports types. It doesn't have to be one or the other, you know. Some of the others in my ballet class like swimming or golf or whatever. And Dad likes the Peregrines, don't you, Dad?"

"Uh-huh."

Okay. That was a start.

"But there was one show I didn't like that much, eh, Dad?"

Good…

Eric shrugged. "It wasn't that bad."

Oh, for fudge's sake.

"What happened?" Tracy asked.

But Austin jumped in. "They had strobe lighting, but the theatre didn't advertise it or warn anyone other than a printed sign on the door to the theatre. Plus, you don't know when the strobe lighting will come. There's one girl in my epilepsy group at school who has tonic-clonic seizures *and* is photosensitive. If she'd been there…"

Ben looked lost. "I'm not entirely sure what you just said there. I know you can't handle flashing lights. That's what you mean by photosensitive, right? But what was the other word?"

Ben looked to Eric for an explanation of "tonic-clonic," but

Eric said nothing.

Does his jealousy run that deep that despite Ben's best attempts at making this dinner work, he won't even answer a question?

Eric had chosen to stay, fully aware that Ben would be joining them. Why was he here if he was going to make this meal so unpleasant?

When Eric didn't speak, Austin responded to Ben's question. "Tonic-clonic seizures are what people usually think of when they think of epilepsy. Mira loses consciousness, her body goes stiff—the tonic part—and then her muscles jerk—the clonic part. If she had one of those in a theatre because of strobe lighting, she'd probably lose a day or so of school while she recovered from a seizure. Plus, she'd be terrified that some idiot would've filmed it and uploaded it without her permission. All because some lighting designer thought strobing was cool. Theatre should be for as many people as possible. You don't need strobe lighting."

RECOVERY FROM A SEIZURE almost sounded like Ben's early days of drinking when he'd lose the next day to a hangover. Different cause, of course, and after he'd entered addiction therapy, his cognitive impairment had cleared. Once Ben stopped taking the medication he used to help wean him off alcohol, he had full control of himself again, while for those living with epilepsy, trying to achieve control usually meant a lifetime of drugs that often came with side effects.

"Only three percent of people with epilepsy—most don't like being called epileptic—are photosensitive. Photosensitivity is a stereotype," Austin explained.

Eric jumped in. "Consider the positive side, son. At least your seizures aren't that severe."

Tracy shot him a look. Ben agreed with her. Was Eric encouraging Austin to feel *superior* to his friends because his seizures were, in his words, less severe? Eric was not faring well in whatever was happening at the dinner table tonight.

"That doesn't make it much better, Dad. It's why I can speak up for the others. Mira is so tired from staying on top of school and managing her seizures, she barely has time for activism. She just comes to talk to others who get it. My group will be emailing the theatre and production manager this week."

Ben couldn't ignore Austin's desire to make the world a better place. "I could help if you wanted?"

Austin's eyes lit up. "That'd be amazing! It's not just for people with epilepsy. Strobe lighting can affect people with autism, seniors with advanced dementia, people who have migraines, and I think even some people with cognitive disabilities or visual impairments, but I'd have to research that some more."

Ben smiled. "See? You're already thinking like I would: broadening your scope so the people whose behaviour you want to change understand that their change would help a lot more people."

Austin jumped out of his chair. "I've got to go write this all down before I forget!"

TRACY FELT like she was sitting between the hot and cold taps at the sink: Ben's smile and happiness contrasted starkly to Eric's scowl and anger.

"It's normal to channel your anger into an email or social media post and fire it off, and then your desire for change gets ignored," Ben said to Eric, feeling like Eric expected him to apologize. "I can give his request a better chance for success."

"Train him to be a rabble-rouser like that, and he'll have a hard time finding work. Kids these days think they can send out letters, scream at organizations on social media, and force organizations to change. They have no clue about the kinds of background checks we carry out today to ensure we're hiring stable, consistent employees. Add to that his epilepsy, and he'll have a hard time finding work."

Eric jumped up to collect the dessert plates, and Tracy shot Ben an apologetic look as she followed Eric into the kitchen.

In the kitchen, she lowered her voice when she spoke. "What is with you?"

But Eric made no attempt at keeping his voice down. He also made no attempt at helping load the dishwasher. "I'm fine. But I have to ask myself what's up with my wife? Who are you letting live here?"

"Later," she whispered.

"No, now. I had HR investigate his background. Do you realize he got fired from his first job right out of university, and again from the Peregrines? And that he didn't work for two years between those two jobs? He says on his LinkedIn profile he spent them with his parents, but he's not registered as having lived there."

Tracy clenched her fists. "How dare you check his background without his permission."

"Who's living in our house, Trace?"

"First off, it's *my* house, regardless of whose name is on the deed, and I know very well who's living here. Secondly, a corporation doing a background check into someone without their knowledge is illegal."

"I was considering recommending him for the CMO position, despite what you'd mentioned to me on our date. He delivered some solid results at the Peregrines, assuming he was telling me the truth. After the last person we interviewed lied on his résumé, I wanted to save everyone time and run the check on Ben first. Where was he during those two years?"

"It's none of your business."

Ben's history was his to share. Besides, what enraged her now was that Eric, who wanted to rekindle their love, had gone behind their backs.

"You can leave now."

"This is my house, too. *My name is on the deed.*"

"This may also be your *house*, but it's *mine and Austin's home.* That you don't trust me is insulting beyond belief."

The rumble of a sports car through the front screen door interrupted them.

Oh, sugar. Ben had heard them.

A knot formed in her stomach as she rushed to the front door in time to see Ben pull out of the driveway. She checked the guest room to confirm her suspicions and yes, his suitcase was gone. She ran to the foyer and grabbed her phone out of her purse.

Eric gently touched her hand. "I just don't want anyone hurting you or Austin."

She whipped around to face him. "Ben wouldn't hurt anyone!"

Eric pulled back his hand. "How do you know?"

"Because I know him. I know where he was those two years, and it's none of your business. You expect me to trust you, but apparently, trust goes only one way!"

Eric threw his hands in the air in exasperation. "It's not like you listened to me when I tried to tell you something was wrong with Austin in the first place, and I was right about him! Sometimes, I know what I'm talking about! There's something wrong with Ben and he's manipulated you! I'm certain of it!"

"Just get out!!!" She dialled Ben and held the phone to her ear.

CHAPTER 30

You're an idiot, Landry. You never had a chance with her.

He'd complete his commitment virtually, and he'd still help Austin. But his presence in the Tschirhart household was creating a rift in the family.

Ben slammed his hand on the wheel. Why had he followed his feelings? He'd been able to suppress them for so many years! Why hadn't he kept them buried where they belonged? The last time he'd fallen in love, it had only ended in pain. He was racing down that road again.

His phone rang and announced it was Tracy. He didn't want to ignore her. He just wanted to make it easy on both of them and call it quits before...before they both fell in love.

Because he already had.

He tapped the call and put it on speaker. "Hey."

"Ben, what are you doing?"

"Finding a hotel. I'm interfering too much."

"No, you're not."

"Eric wanted me to hear everything he said. He doesn't want me anywhere near Austin."

"Don't you think my say counts, too?"

"I think Austin's say counts the most, and he deserves as little conflict as possible."

A traffic light.

"Come back, Ben. We're adults. We had fun."

And I'm in love.

"You're taken, Tracy." He turned onto Glasgow Street.

"I am not taken! It would be so nice if the two of you would let me decide my relationship status! It's not my fault the courts in this province wouldn't let me divorce him for a year!...And honestly, Ben, I didn't know I'd meet you and that...this would happen."

Her words pierced his heart as he crossed Belmont Avenue.

"We need to stop before it grows into something..." He interrupted himself before he said *beautiful*. "Something bigger. Austin's still going through a lot. And your family is still sorting itself out. I'm in the way right now."

Ben turned right onto Park Street and drove by rows of houses.

"Austin knows how I feel about you and I think he's okay with it. And we agreed to explore our feelings this weekend." She sighed. "Maybe you're right. I don't know how to have a relationship with you while I'm sorting this out. I'm sorry, Ben. If Eric hadn't shown up..."

"I'm sorry, too, Tracy." Ben paused. He'd said it. He'd apologized. Relief washed over him. If only it hadn't been at the end of their...whatever it was they had. "I didn't mean to put your family through this. But Austin has a chance at reconnecting with his father. As someone who lost two years with his parents, trust me when I say Austin and Eric need every chance they can get. Let Austin know I meant what I said at the table—I'm happy to help him with his cause. He can send me a link to his draft when he's done. Have a wonderful Thanksgiving, Tracy. I'll be in touch with festival updates."

He hung up before she could reply.

Ben turned his car onto Jubilee Drive and drove through Victoria Park, where he'd spent many days during his time on Kitchener's streets. He remembered parents pulling their kids closer to them as they passed him.

He felt sick.

A few minutes later, he parked in the downtown hotel's parking garage. He lifted his suitcase and briefcase out of the car, locked the doors, and walked to reception.

After he'd arranged and paid for his room, he paused and swallowed before speaking. He'd never said this to anyone outside his most trusted circle before. "I'm a recovering alcoholic, and I'm not in a good place right now. Is there any chance the mini-bar could be emptied before I get to my room? I'll be happy to wait."

The employee didn't ask any further questions and immediately made a respectful call to housekeeping. Ben inspected the mini-bar when he entered his room: the only bottles left were water and juice. He'd be sure to leave an extra tip and an excellent online review.

He threw his suitcase onto the suitcase rack, opened his briefcase, pulled out his laptop, and did what he always did when he was upset: worked.

BEN WAS RIGHT, and Tracy knew it. They'd both agreed the weekend was just to explore. Neither expected they'd unearth such deep feelings.

Talk about naïve. She wiped away the last tears on her cheeks. Ben had made the right move in leaving. Eric had sensed their attraction at dinner. Ben had left to kill it. So Tracy tried to do the same, drowning her feelings in chocolate.

A chocolate bar Ben had given her. Which meant she wasn't too successful.

The doorbell rang.

"That had better not be Eric."

She wiped her face, scraping away any potential signs of chocolate from the corners of her mouth, and opened the door. A moment later, she found herself engulfed in Pauline's arms.

Tracy held on tight, and the tears started again. Only a minute or two later did she pull away and let Pauline in.

"Why are you here? Especially after…well, after the night at your shop."

Pauline hung her jacket on a hook and nudged Tracy to the family room.

"Austin heard a lot of shouting, saw both Ben and Eric drive off, and heard you crying, so he texted me." Pauline pulled a bag of loose-leaf tea from her handbag. "I assumed you'd have chocolate so I brought you some Evening Sunset: black tea with a little peppermint, lavender, and lemongrass. Green Sunset might be more relaxing, but it doesn't pair well with chocolate."

Tracy smiled. "You're the best. But I still said some really mean things to you…"

Pauline gave Tracy's shoulder a squeeze. "I was hurt, but I'm not proud of what I said, either. I'm sorry."

"So am I. I'd like to think our friendship is stronger than one argument."

"Me, too."

While Pauline prepared the tea, Tracy headed to Austin's bedroom. She knocked on his door and peeked inside.

"Thank you, sweetheart."

He smiled. "It's good to have friends, Mom. You need to call them more often."

She sighed and nodded. "I'm so sorry you had to hear all that. Ben...he..." She didn't know how to finish the sentence.

Austin crossed his arms. "Mom, you need to stop worrying about me this much. My seizures are my seizures. They don't hurt, we're trying to get them under control, and I'm sorry, but Dad needs to accept that there'll be other men in your life. Away from Ben, and to be honest, away from you, he was totally normal. The moment he saw Ben..." Austin snapped his fingers. "It's not right that he expects you to give up someone who makes you happy. So, tell Dad that Ben's not going to replace him as my father."

Tracy leaned against the door. "If only it were that simple."

"It is that simple! Not talking to anyone last year was like living on a dark stage with the curtain closed. I had no one to listen to me. It was torture. You're going to end up like that if you don't do something about it."

She couldn't argue with him on that.

"Can I go back to my letter now?" he asked. "I'm going ahead with this, with or without Ben. I'll lose my ideas if I don't keep at it."

"Ben said he'll still help you with it. Just send him the link when you're done."

Austin's face brightened, and he returned to his work. Tracy closed his door. Ben had become another mentor to Austin. It comforted her like the tea she now smelled as she entered the kitchen.

Tracy accepted her cup and inhaled its beautiful aroma as she leaned against the counter. "Eric's breaking my heart. He's trying so hard to reconnect with Austin, but he's like a giant in a garden: with every step he kills everything he's trying to grow. And I know you don't like Ben, but—"

Pauline motioned to the family room, where they sat down on the couch. Pauline yelped in pain as she sat.

"Your hip?"

Pauline nodded. "Onkel Hans doesn't do aerials like Perry did, but it's still an active gig. I'm glad I can do it while running the tea shop, though."

"Owning your business gives you the flexibility."

"Not in my hip." She laughed. "You're right, though. I work stupidly long hours sometimes, but I can adjust those hours within reason, eat when I want, and between me and Todd, Austin and my mom, we actually make it work." Pauline took a sip of her tea. "But back to you and Ben. Has he gone to New Hamburg?"

"He's gone to a hotel."

Pauline set her tea down and whipped out her phone. "We should check if he's okay."

Tracy had always admired how Pauline's compassion trumped her other feelings. "I've talked to him. He's at the Valhalla, said he'll be fine. He told me everything, by the way."

Pauline hesitated as she spoke, as though worried she might give away information she wasn't supposed to share. Another hallmark of a loyal friend. "Everything?"

Tracy nodded. "His drinking, his homelessness, everything."

"Do you have his sister's number? You should let her know, too. I've heard too many stories over the years. We can hope he'll be fine, but hope isn't enough when people have addiction in their history."

"I'll contact her right now."

"I'm here to support you," Pauline said, tapping with her thumbs. "But if Ben doesn't text me back in thirty, we're going to him."

Tracy picked up her tea after she finished her message to Susie. "Have you changed your mind about him?"

Pauline took a sip of her own tea. "Not entirely. He still hasn't apologized to me. But I swear upon the grave of my

Perry costume that I never once saw Ben smile like he did when he was dancing with you at Oktoberfest. I couldn't ignore what was right in front of me: that there's a side to him I'd never seen and you're bringing it out."

Tracy and Pauline were still talking when Ben replied that he was okay and Susie texted that she was glad they'd contacted her.

Later, Ben messaged Tracy that he wished they hadn't called his sister in case he'd ruined her weekend with Genny's parents.

Tracy texted: *I care about you, and if you won't stay here, I need to make sure you're ok. Your sister's the only person you fully trust.*

Ben replied, *I fully trust you, too. Happy Thanksgiving, Tracy. Thank you for showing me what compassion means.*

CHAPTER 31

"Now I know why Pauline was a mascot and not a professional singer," a still sleepy Austin complained.

It was seven-thirty Thanksgiving morning.

But a singalong Bette Midler movie with her best friend had been the perfect antidote to her troubles. Talking through her feelings about Ben and Eric had helped, too. Now Tracy's head was clear: Ben was the perfect man for her. But how could she navigate this with Austin and Eric? Pauline had suggested she wait, but "wait" was synonymous with "procrastinate" in Tracy's mind. Tracy did not procrastinate.

Tracy checked her phone. Nothing from Ben.

"I thought more about Dad and Ben last night," Austin said as Tracy cracked eggs into a frying pan. "I realized something. You're not *not* dating Ben to protect me, are you? Because that would be stupid."

Fudge. He had to blindside her with the direct question.

"Austin, I'm your mother. It's my job to protect you."

"But you're doing it too much! It's ridiculous that you're

tracking my phone, for starters! Where am I going to go? Downtown to hang out with druggie friends? Break into a business at lunch? Skip more school?"

That was it. She'd had it with his accusations. Tracy spun around to face him. "Of course not! But if I look and find that you've stopped for longer than five minutes on the street, there's a good chance you're having a tonic-clonic seizure and no one's helping you!"

"Or that my friends and I are in line getting a slice of pizza! Do you have any idea how embarrassed I'd be if you showed up?"

"If you have kids one day, you'll understand how it feels to watch their whole world crash when you could've done something to stop it!"

Both fell silent: Tracy, because she realized what she'd just admitted, and Austin, because he appeared to be processing what she'd just said.

"You mean...you're acting like Big Brother because of my accident onstage?"

Tracy felt like she'd been caught sneaking a chocolate bar before supper. She turned around to flip the eggs.

"Seriously, Mom? That was *June of last year*. You're still hanging on to that? Grandma and Grandpa were there, too, and they don't act like this. Neither does Dad."

"They're not in charge of looking after you."

"I wish they were."

Tracy banged the pan on the stove. "What do you want, Austin? Because you can't have it both ways! Parents who love you enough to be with you no matter what happens, or parents who leave you the moment the going gets tough? At least I owned up to my mistakes and am doing my best to make sure you're not harmed again!"

Only now did Tracy notice Austin's startled face and that

he'd backed away from her. He looked like a deer in the head-
lights, but it wasn't a seizure. She'd frightened him.

"I...I'm sorry." She turned around and poked at the eggs.

She remembered what Ben had said on Saturday. Had he
been right? Impossible. An accident like that didn't leave
trauma behind. Naturally, Tracy would worry about her son.
But Tracy was a strong woman. Anyone who knew what she'd
endured since last year had said so.

He paused, almost seeming scared to ask his next question.
"What do you mean, own up to your mistakes?"

Tracy swallowed. She owed her son an answer, but she
couldn't face him. "Your father had said for several months that
he thought something was wrong with you. I ignored him. You
were free from the bullying at your grade school, you were
jumping so high—practically flying—you were giving yourself
over to the music. When you were dancing, Austin, you were
joyful and at peace. I didn't want to risk taking that away from
you. I brushed off his warnings, and he turned out to be right."
She flipped the fried eggs.

Austin dropped bread into the toaster. "So...Dad knew I
was having seizures?"

Tracy pulled out plates and cutlery. "Not exactly. He just
knew it was more than daydreaming. Had I listened to him, we
would've discovered your seizures earlier and you might still be
at ballet school."

Austin filled himself a glass with water. "And we wouldn't
have come to Kitchener, where I met Todd Parsons. And you
wouldn't have reconnected with your best friend...or met Ben.
Don't get me wrong, Mom. I'm not thankful for my seizures.
I'm just saying...it's not all bad." He pulled butter out of the
fridge.

"You also wouldn't have spent the latter half of grade ten
being bullied again."

The toast popped, and each placed their slices on their plate. Tracy let Austin butter his first while she turned off the stove and placed her eggs on her plate.

"You can't protect me from everything. So stop trying. I'm certain Ben's in love with you. And you definitely like him. Call him and invite him to the parade. He was going to come to Thanksgiving lunch, anyway. Things will be a pain with Dad, but he needs to get used to you dating other men." He passed the knife to Tracy and lifted his fried eggs out of the pan and onto each slice of toast.

"I don't think your dad expected reconciling would be this emotional."

"What was he expecting? To just *chassé* back in here?"

"I think it was supposed to be more of a *grand jeté* sequence. But in all seriousness, Austin, you're really okay if I date Ben?"

"He wasn't the nicest to Pauline. But he seems to be changing. And you wouldn't date just anyone." A twinkle of glee appeared in her son's eyes. "You do remember that I'm the one responsible for making sure Todd and Pauline got together in the end, right?"

Tracy couldn't argue with him on that one either.

So she phoned Ben after dropping Austin at Todd and Pauline's. "I'm coming to get you. You're joining us at the parade."

"I don't think that's a good idea, Tracy."

"And I don't think you should be alone. Or I could call your sister, tell her you sound groggy, and have her drive out here to get you."

Ben groaned.

"You have fifteen minutes to be in my car. I have your sister on speed dial."

Fifteen minutes later, Ben, looking sexy in khakis, polished brown shoes, a black leather jacket, and a woollen fashion scarf emerged from the hotel lobby.

He opened the car door. "I really don't want to be around your family."

Tracy reached for his hand. "It's Thanksgiving, and Austin and I are thankful you came back into our lives. *We* want you around us. Let me worry about my family." She took her hand back to make the turn out of the hotel entrance. "Austin and I talked this morning. He understands you're not trying to be his father. In fact, he fancies himself somewhat of a matchmaker after he was part of helping Pauline and Todd get together."

The light turned red as Ben placed a hand on her leg. "Smart boy, your Austin. But I'm guessing he got those smarts from someone."

Tracy blushed. "Pauline's coming around too. But Austin's the most important person in my life, and he told me it's okay if…well…if you and I try dating. If you still want to, that is."

Without hesitation, Ben leaned toward her, and Tracy did the same. But before they could kiss, a car behind them honked.

"They can wait," Ben said, and gave Tracy a quick kiss. "I have priorities."

They drove in silence to the parade viewing spot, neither daring to admit that they'd both hoped the weekend would become more than just a fling, that they'd both always wanted more but had been too afraid to take the risk.

Tracy found a parking spot, but before they got out, Ben reached for Tracy. His kiss was triple-fudge-chocolate.

"I'm ecstatic about this but still terrified of your family," he said when they broke apart. "And the Robinsons."

Tracy laughed. "We'll work through it."

They carried lawn chairs and blankets to the viewing spot.

"Hey, everyone!" Tracy called out, contentment emanating from her heart.

But it wasn't just because of Ben. Everyone she loved was there: her younger twin siblings and their families; her parents; Pauline's parents, Claire and Richard; Dawn, Pauline's sister from Vancouver and her family; Todd's father, brothers and their families, also from Vancouver; and Eric and Austin.

Ben, on the other hand, looked like someone about to get a bucket of ice water dumped on him.

"I've got you," she whispered.

Only Austin looked happy to see them together.

Until Todd smiled.

Tracy welcomed Todd's offer of friendship, and she and Ben headed in Todd's direction.

But Eric approached her, wrapped his arm around her waist, and pulled her away.

⁓

THIS WAS A BAD IDEA. I should've stayed in the hotel room. Todd's giving me pity points.

"Ben, you remember my family? My dad, Michael, and my brothers, Tim and Mark," Todd said.

Ben shook their hands. "Of course. Never forget the faces of DIY Homes. Nice to see you all again." It felt strange being thrust into his old role. "I hope the sponsorship with the Peregrines worked out?"

Michael patted Ben on the back. "You drove a hard bargain, but I have to admit, it did. Sales increased by five-point-three percent in the first month."

"Excellent to hear."

"Speaking of business," Todd said. "The Belmont business owners have been really happy with your work."

"That's great. Thank you. Hopefully the festival's a success."

Ben appreciated the compliment, but who was he kidding?

A three-week volunteer gig wasn't sufficient to cover the fact that he'd gotten fired. And now that he was dating the volunteer committee's chair, he had no reference. Yes, another committee member might suffice, but a reference from the chair was best. Withholding that personal detail? It might come out during the reference interview. When Ben had been driving through Kitchener that fateful day, he'd had a strategy. Now, he had none.

That scared the crap out of him.

Sirens sounded. Police officers on their motorcycles cruised down the street and formed a tight circle. Everyone clapped, but Ben's heart hammered in his chest.

I'm sorry, officer. It was just warmer in here. I'll leave now.

The police officers broke formation and continued down the street. Volunteers for the food bank walked along the road. Ben pulled out his wallet and dropped two twenties into a bucket.

Working with the homeless shelter on the festival had brought back memories. Sebastian had asked a few times if they could meet in person, but Ben had feared Sebastian would recognize him, and Ben didn't want to enter into any further discussions about his past. Sharing everything with Tracy and Pauline had been hard enough. It had helped him become a better person, and his talks with Susie had supported this change, but he could only handle so much.

Two people carried a sign that announced the name and origin of the first marching band, but the band itself rested as it marched past. Too bad. The more noise, the less chance for awkward silences.

Austin came over to join Ben. "Hey."

"Hey."

Next came some costumed characters, followed by a German club and its folk dancers.

"For what it's worth, Ben, my dad's an okay guy."

Ben's body went stiff. Was this Austin's way of telling Ben

he'd changed his mind and that Ben should back off? If it was, Ben might as well leave now. The walk back to the hotel would take maybe forty-five minutes.

"But I know Mom and him don't have it anymore."

Ben glanced over at Eric and Tracy in conversation. Maybe they still had a chance.

But Tracy had kissed him so willingly in the car.

"If you like Mom, go for it."

Ben's heart almost stopped. "You don't think I'm too young?"

Austin snorted, looking at Ben and Todd. "As far as I'm concerned, you're all ancient."

Todd ruffled Austin's hair, prompting a protest. "He hates it when you do that, just so you know," Todd said. "It's his one weakness."

Austin glared playfully at Ben. "You do that to me, and I'll renege on what I just said!"

"Thanks," Ben said. "That means a lot. The part about dating your mom, that is. As for your hair…" He reached for Austin's head, and Austin darted behind Todd to protect himself.

The fun had attracted Eric's attention from fifteen feet away, and Ben could taste his jealousy. He wiped the smile off his face and stuck his hands in his pockets.

CHAPTER 32

*B*en and Tracy had agreed to remain separate until she'd spoken to Eric. So once Tracy had been swept up by the brood at the Robinsons' house, Ben did what all unwelcome people did: checked things out.

He began with the two-storey home's classic layout: to the right of the foyer were the living and dining rooms, with tables laid out end to end for the guests. Behind the dining room was yet another room, which, judging by the flowery wallpaper and cabinet of tea sets, was the tearoom.

Definitely fitting.

Straight out from the foyer was the kitchen.

"Wow," Ben said to himself. The Robinsons had ordered catering, and quite the smorgasbord was on display on the kitchen island and table, with salads, bread rolls and butter, sliced turkey, cranberry sauce…the works. His gaze stopped at a small, makeshift bar where the kitchen table likely normally stood. The woman working behind the bar smiled and lifted a glass, offering him a drink. Ben took a breath. A drink would relax him…and completely embarrass him. He shook his head.

Off the kitchen, to the left, was the family room where some of the family had congregated.

"Aunt Pauline!" a young girl cried out as she rushed past Ben to where Pauline and Todd were entering.

Ben smiled as Pauline effortlessly picked up the girl. He remembered how her contract had kept Pauline from all this happiness.

Ben stayed back in the kitchen as the family crowded into the foyer, though Todd squeezed through and joined him. Todd chatted as he warmed up a heating pad in the microwave. The microwave beeped and he took out the pad. "I've got to take this to Pauline."

Ben watched Todd push his way back to Pauline, then saw Pauline press the pad to her hip. Ben winced. He obviously couldn't prevent arthritis, but had he managed with more compassion, he could've insisted she cut back her schedule a little and see a specialist.

Maybe one drink…

Tracy came up and stood beside Ben and looked where he was looking. "I envy her life now," she said. "She can do what she loves—mascotting and running the shop—because she has control of her own schedule."

"I'm pretty sure I paid her better."

Tracy sighed. "It's not always about the money, Ben."

"After these past two weeks, I can honestly say, 'I know' and mean it."

Their gazes locked.

"She hopes to create a similar mascot for Claire's Tea Shop," Tracy said. "But coming up with a character is more complex than I thought. Can't be a little tea pot, short and stout."

Ben laughed. "People would be surprised to learn what goes into designing a mascot. The short part's a problem for Pauline, and teacups and pots don't fit easily through doors.

Also needs to be something kids can hug and she can move in freely."

Eric approached, so Ben headed into the family room and sat next to the girl who'd greeted Pauline so exuberantly.

"Hi," he said. "I'm Ben."

The girl's knees were pulled into her chest and she didn't look so exuberant anymore.

"Is everything okay?"

"Mom and Dad didn't bring diabetic dessert for me. There's pumpkin pie and I can't have any!"

"That must be tough."

"It sucks." She lifted the edge of her shirt and showed Ben her insulin pump. "I have to wear this all the time, and I can't have lots of sugar like other kids in my class."

"I don't eat a lot of sugar because it's bad for building muscle. See?" He flexed his arm. "Squeeze that."

The child did and her eyes popped out.

Ben pointed to her arm. "What are yours like?"

She had sticks for arms. She laughed at the difference.

"So, you and I will eat no dessert together, okay?"

But she still looked unimpressed.

"I know it sucks," Ben said, mirroring her language. "That pumpkin pie does look fantastic. But sometimes we have to give up something so we can be better—I mean healthier—people."

Was he giving her advice? Or himself?

"What's your name?" he asked.

"Destiny," she said.

He held up his fist for a fist bump, and Destiny accepted it as Pauline entered the family room.

The girl's eyes immediately lit up. "Is that how Aunt Pauline got muscles?"

Pauline smiled at them. "What are you two talking about?"

"How good the pie looks," Ben answered, "and how it sucks that both of us can't eat it. Destiny because of her diabetes, and me because it's a no-dessert day for me. You know how important it is to follow your diet when you want to stay healthy and get muscles."

Pauline's expression told him immediately that she understood he could've eaten whatever he wanted but was giving that up to support her niece. "Absolutely. When I was Perry, I had to be careful with what I ate, too, so I was strong and had lots of energy."

"Aunt Pauline, can you do a handstand?"

Ben smiled at Pauline. The lecture on healthy eating already bored Destiny.

Pauline ensured she had enough space, and within two seconds had inverted herself. Destiny and Ben clapped as Pauline stood back up.

Destiny turned to Ben. "Can you?"

"Nope. I can do a hundred push-ups, though. Just not right now if that's okay."

Apparently in a better mood and believing the adults could no longer entertain her, Destiny jumped off the couch and raced away to find her other cousins. Pauline laughed and sat down next to Ben.

"So, there is a nicer side to you."

"I asked for a second chance. I meant it."

"Pauline, honey, I need your help with something," Claire called from the kitchen. The moment she saw Ben, her lips thinned into a straight line, sending shivers down his spine.

"She really hates me."

"You robbed her of something special, Ben."

"I know. And I'm sorry. I promise to tell her that directly today. Can you and I talk later?"

Pauline blinked. "I'll talk to Mom. And yes, you and I will

talk later. I promise." She stood up. "I'm glad you could make it today."

But by the time everyone sat down at the very long dinner table, Ben hadn't found a moment to speak to Pauline. As dinner progressed, he deliberated standing up whenever there was a pause in the conversation, but he couldn't gather the courage.

Then Claire and Richard announced they had decided to sell the house before Christmas, which was why they'd invited the Parsons to fly in: the Robinsons wanted *everyone* to participate in one last family celebration in the family home. The rest of the meal was taken up with memories, some that went back decades, of the house.

Ben felt like an intruder to a private celebration.

By the end of dessert, Ben had said nothing. But he didn't want to break the promise he'd made to Pauline and Tracy.

But most importantly, he needed to follow through for himself. What he wouldn't give for a drink right now to lessen his fears, but that was also a promise he wouldn't break.

He pushed his chair back.

CHAPTER 33

*H*e was going through with it. He'd looked like he'd wanted to say something a few times over dinner but had decided against it. Tracy wouldn't have blamed him: over twenty people, mostly strangers to him, were at the table.

"I…I'll be brief." He clasped his hands behind his back and surveyed the table, including the youngest family members. Was he adjusting what he had to say to fit his audience?

"I…" He let out a nervous laugh.

Tracy wanted to hold his hand to comfort him, but she hadn't spoken to Eric yet.

Ben looked at Destiny. "For a long time, I was a bully."

Wow. He had changed how he wanted to express himself to suit his audience.

He lifted his chin and addressed the table. "That's the only person you know me as. When I was younger, I made some very bad choices, and out of fear of repeating those choices, I began treating people poorly."

Ben took a deep breath and looked directly at Pauline's parents. "Claire, Richard. I am deeply sorry for stealing happiness from you and taking away part of your relationship with your daughter. My parents passed away a while ago, and I still miss them. What's worse, though, is that my choices led me to lose two years with them while they were alive. I know you'll never get those years back with Pauline, and I'm very sorry I was the cause." Ben swallowed.

Tracy sat on her hands to keep herself from reaching for his.

Ben faced Pauline, who was sitting across the table from him. "Pauline, I am very sorry for all the hurt—and even the physical pain—I caused you. You loved your job, and because of me, you'll never have memories that are only joyful. Not only should I have encouraged you to visit your family, but I also should have helped you find a specialist for your hip. I know you love what you do now, and your family needed you home, but I also know how I treated you played a part in ending your full-time career as a mascot."

Ben looked around the table. "I know the way I behaved toward Pauline affected all of you, too. She's an amazing woman with a compassionate heart and she couldn't share that with you. So, I apologize to all of you, her family and friends, for being a bully to someone in your family. I hope that, in time, you'll be able to forgive me."

Almost without missing a beat, Austin walked over to Ben and gave him a hug. "Thanks for the opportunities to perform in the summer and for letting Pauline use the Peregrines' social media accounts to help me out when I got overwhelmed online."

"I'm glad I could help."

Ben had really changed.

As Austin returned to his seat, Tracy saw Eric looking at her with suspicion. She needed to talk to him. It was over between them, and he would have to accept that.

Awkward silence filled the air, but then Claire spoke. "I

must say, Ben, I am quite surprised to hear you say what you've said. But thank you."

"Mind if I help with the dishes?" Ben said.

Claire smiled at him warmly. "Be my guest."

PAULINE, dressed in a giant turkey costume, was cavorting around the dining room. Ben laughed, as much relieved that his apology was over as he enjoyed Pauline's antics.

Eric came over and put an arm around Tracy's waist. Her body went stiff. Ben's heart did, too.

"Dinner at my house tonight, as planned?" Eric asked Tracy.

"Sure."

"We'll keep it small."

Ben could read between the lines: he wasn't included. He excused himself and found himself alone again in the family room, with only his phone for company.

A few minutes later, a loud slapping sound caught his attention. He looked up: the giant turkey was walking toward the family room.

"Come to take your revenge on me?" he asked in jest.

The turkey stopped and parked its wings on its hips in indignation.

Ben knew Pauline never spoke while in costume. Even when she'd worked for him, it had always driven him nuts that she wouldn't break that rule.

The turkey entered the family room and motioned for Ben to close the door. Pauline would also never undress in front of her audience: she honoured her character and the audience's desire to see a performance.

But once the doors were closed, Pauline removed the gloves and lifted off the head, a smile on her face.

"So, you knew about my plans to get you back, did you?"

"The rumour mill was pretty loud. But I'll grant you one revenge prank. I deserve it."

"It wouldn't be as satisfying as the fantasy since I discovered you can actually be nice."

Ben blushed.

"I wanted to talk to you in private without everyone staring at us." He appreciated the thought. "Thank you for what you said at the table today. That meant a lot, but especially to me and Mom. I don't know if I can fully forgive you yet, but I'm willing to try."

Still mostly dressed in her costume, she opened her arms, and Ben was more than willing to accept this olive branch.

"That means more than you can possibly imagine, Pauline. Thank you."

After they released from the hug, Ben pulled his phone out of his pocket and held it up. "Just so I have something better to remember us by?"

Pauline let out a small burst of laughter and nodded. She leaned into him, and he snapped a selfie.

"Send it to me?" she asked.

Ben tried not to channel his sister's exuberance as he typed Pauline's number.

"Whatever happens between you and Tracy," Pauline said, "you can put my name down as your reference for any job. I'll have to be honest about how you managed at the Peregrines, but I can also emphasize a lot of your wins, that you supported Austin, helped raise millions of dollars, and I can also say you've really changed and have done a wonderful job with this festival. And I'll be able to honestly say that I believe your efforts have come from the heart."

"Thank you." Ben tucked his hands into his pockets and stared at the floor. He'd actually made a friend. He couldn't wait to tell Susie.

Pauline turned her back to him. "Help me out of this?"

He was reaching for the zipper when Eric stormed in. "You are *not* taking my family from me!"

CHAPTER 34

"*E*ric! Stop it before you embarrass all of us!" Tracy followed close on Eric's heels and closed the family room door behind her. She was fiery mad.

But Eric's anger had taken over his reason. "I saw how you looked at each other at the parade, and how you held hands under the table. I'm done being lied to!" His face red, he whipped a finger in Ben's direction but glared at Tracy as he seethed. "Tell him to keep his hands off you!"

Pauline stepped forward, both hands raised. "Tracy, Eric, the kids can probably hear you. This old house isn't exactly soundproof."

But Eric ignored her. "Tell him, Tracy, or I'll make sure he understands."

"What happens between me and Ben is my business, not yours!"

Ben leaned over to Pauline. "I should leave," he whispered. "Then at least he'd calm down."

But Pauline held his wrist. "She needs you now. Don't desert her again."

Desert her again. Ben hadn't meant to desert her when he'd left for the hotel. He believed it had been the best for both of them.

"You want *his* hands on you? The hands of a homeless drunk?"

Ben closed his eyes and lowered his head. Who had told Eric? Ben had shared his story only with Pauline and Tracy, and from what he'd observed during his time in Kitchener, Pauline hadn't even told Todd. Had Tracy told him, maybe by accident?

Tracy's voice reached a fever pitch. "You did a full background check on him? That's illegal! He wasn't applying for the job!"

"I needed to know who was living with my wife and son since you wouldn't tell me!"

At least that answered Ben's question.

He'd never escape the assumptions his past came with. That Eric had easily found the information meant Ben's chances of a decent job were lower than when he'd first applied to the Peregrines.

"How can you have someone like that living with our son! How can you even find someone like that attractive?"

Ben's breathing quickened and his hands balled into fists. He was more than those years on the street, yet those years had contributed to who he had become. But his anger jumbled all the thoughts he wanted to express.

"How can you be so cruel, Eric? How can you have no compassion in your heart?"

"No compassion? I'm trying to protect our son and you let some loser off the street waltz into our house! I saw the photos from the committee Oktoberfest party online! I have to beg and plead for time with you while you spend it with some wino who's living in my house. He probably can't afford a place of his own. And where'd he get his car from? Did he steal it?"

"I'm right here," Ben mumbled as Pauline wrapped an arm around him. But did she do so out of compassion? Or pity?

Humiliated that his past had put Tracy in this position, Ben opened his mouth to defend her, but he and Pauline were invisible to Tracy and Eric.

"First off, Eric, he has a name, like everyone else who's unlucky enough to end up homeless because of uncaring people like you. It's Benjamin Landry. Second, he's one of the most caring, compassionate people I've ever met, and I was more than happy that he spent time with Austin. And third, I haven't just met him: we met in the summer! And I was so impressed by everything he'd done to *help others* that I kissed him, okay? *I kissed him in the summer!*"

Sugar had just hit the ceiling.

Eric's mouth fell open and he stepped back. But Tracy was locked in this marital argument, determined to win. Ben had seen this play out too often at the arena.

"So, no, I didn't just meet him! I didn't just let some random stranger into our house! In fact, he wanted me to work for him months ago. He offered me more than what I was earning at the tech company. And guess what? *I turned it down.* Now, Eric, why do you think that would be? Because of Austin. The son you claim I've been endangering by having a kind and helpful man living with us. I turned it down because it was in Austin's best interests to not uproot him. I put our son first so he could stay near family who loved him and stay in the community that supports him. I stayed because I put Austin *first!*"

Eric looked at Ben as though seeing him for the first time. When Eric finally spoke, his voice was almost a whisper. "You...you've known each other for months, then?"

Ben nodded, and Eric's humiliation scorched through Ben.

Ben dared glance at Pauline, and her shock at the full confession proved Tracy hadn't told her all the details either.

"But..." The confession had knocked all the fight completely out of Eric. "You said when I came over that first time that there was nothing between you."

~

Oh, fudge, what have I done?

All her suppressed anger toward Eric had exploded. She'd broken her unspoken agreement with Ben and had shared every detail about how their relationship had begun. She'd hurt her best friend again and betrayed and embarrassed Ben.

She also didn't want Eric believing she'd been leading him on this entire time. That simply wasn't true. She'd despised Ben at the beginning of his stay with her. But to say that in front of Ben would be cruel, too.

"She didn't like me at that time," Ben said, saving her. "I couldn't be fully honest at the dinner table because of the kids. But the truth is, Eric, I was an asshole to everyone around me. Tracy only let me stay at the house because the committee insisted I stay in town, and I needed the experience."

Eric crossed his arms. "I'm supposed to believe you?"

"You heard what I said at the table, you saw everyone's reactions. I was an arrogant son of a bitch, so much so—I might as well be totally honest—that I was so excited by the popularity of Austin's appearance at his school's anti-bullying rally that I wanted Pauline to find more kids like him for future rallies."

A sharp pain pierced Tracy's chest. She turned to Ben, stunned. "You...you were going to use the moment Austin risked being his most vulnerable as a marketing ploy for your own gain? By trying to entice other teens to do the same? You realize Austin got threatening messages, don't you?"

"I'm so sorry, Tracy. And Eric. I didn't know about those at the time. I swear, I didn't. It was just the initial numbers. But that's not who I am anymore. And I never went through with it. Pauline set me straight right—"

Tracy snapped her head around to face Pauline. "You knew about the plan to include 'more kids like Austin'?"

"I told him it was wrong as soon as he told—"

"So, yes?"

"Tracy, let me—"

"Answer me, Pauline! You talk about feeling betrayed because I didn't tell you about Ben, but you knew he was looking for vulnerable kids like my son." Tracy backed up from everyone. "Wow. I can't trust any of you."

"I'm the one who warned you about living with him," Eric said.

Tracy raised her eyebrows. "Excuse me? You engaged in an illegal background check of someone because you didn't trust me. I don't recall you once warning me about his exploiting our son. And where were you when Austin was dealing with the fallout from everything?"

Eric fiddled with his cuffs.

"Tracy," Pauline said, "everyone here has made mistakes."

"Because no one here has been as careful as I have. I'm clearly the only one who knows how to meet Austin's needs."

She straightened her hair, took a deep breath, and plastered a professional smile on her face before heading into the kitchen. "Everything's fine," she announced to anyone staring.

She'd just take Austin home. Where he'd be safe.

CHAPTER 35

*B*en held up his phone to show the bartender Tracy's angry text message from an hour before and gulped down some beer. It was just after three o'clock.

"I got fired from a volunteer position," Ben said.

"That takes effort," the bartender replied.

"Sad part is, I was enjoying it. Imagine that? Enjoying doing something for free." He took another gulp. The fermented sweetness tasted comforting.

Ben broke open a peanut and popped the two nuts into his mouth. He really was a despicable man, wasn't he? He remembered that conversation with Pauline clearly. *I want you to get me more kids like that.* What kind of jerk said that sort of thing?

"This kind of jerk," he mumbled to himself. He appreciated Pauline's attempt at trying to defend him to Tracy. He'd thank her someday.

That summer conversation replayed itself in Ben's memory. Truth was, as soon as Pauline had explained the extent of the bullying Austin had endured, Ben felt sick for even suggesting she recruit more kids to tell their stories. He had just seen it as another way to keep his job. But when Pauline had said that Austin couldn't look Tracy in the eyes out of shame, that Austin had opened up to Pauline about everything only after she was in full costume—where her eyes were covered—it reminded Ben of the sexual assault Susie had endured.

She'd been so ashamed, she couldn't report it, and the man was never apprehended. She only told Ben.

After he'd returned home.

It was the first time she'd never looked him in the eyes when something was wrong.

She'd finally begun to heal, but the criminal had gotten away with it because she didn't want to go through the whole ordeal again by telling the police, lawyers, and the jury. Not to mention being cross-examined and treated as if her story weren't true.

She had just wanted to leave the nightmare behind.

If Ben had been there, he would've tried to support her in laying charges, acting as her advocate, giving her whatever strength she needed, finding more strength if his own hadn't been enough.

But I was drinking.

He looked at the amber-coloured liquid in his glass. It was so nice to have the real stuff. He took another gulp and surveyed the bar. A few people played billiards. Some guys and girls were having fun. He could probably join in somewhere, but why bother? At some point, the alcohol would affect him, so he'd probably hurt someone with his words here, too. Maybe the good heart Susie believed he had was also a lie, a marketing ploy he'd used to convince her.

Maybe he truly was legal contracts and social media numbers.

He tipped the glass back again, the soothing flavour flowing through his body.

~

BY FOUR, Tracy and Austin had parked themselves in their pyjamas, *An American in Paris* playing on the TV.

"Think you'll be on Broadway someday?" Tracy was hoping to lighten the mood.

Austin answered, his speech slow as it had been since they'd arrived home. "I don't sing...and I can't lift women...so...no. And you still haven't told me what's...going on between you and everyone."

Austin had heard most of her argument with Eric, Ben, and Pauline. He knew Tracy had cancelled plans with Eric even though father and son had had fun over the weekend. Austin had argued with Tracy all the way home. It took all her concentration to drive safely. By the time they'd arrived, exhaustion had taken over, and she'd suggested a movie. Weakened from his own outburst, Austin had agreed, especially because the side effects from his medication were now stronger and he had difficulties speaking: the connections in his brain that thought of words were delayed.

"I've come to my senses, that's all," she said. "Nothing for you to be concerned about."

"Mom! Stop it wi—" He had a five-second seizure. "Stop it with that!" He tried to find his words. "Everyone could hear you...shouting in the house. Ben's gone...we're not at Dad's, and you and...crap, what's her name? You and the costume person stopped talking to each other after the fight."

"Pauline." This was the worst Tracy had seen him since the summer, and they had to wait another month before seeing the neurologist.

Austin stared into his bowl of popcorn. "Pauline. How stupid can I get?"

"It's not your fault."

"That doesn't make me smarter."

The best thing for Austin to do was to just relax. If he napped, it would mess with his sleep, then he'd for sure miss another morning of school.

"Why don't we just enjoy the movie? The distraction will do us both good."

"You still haven't answered me."

"Sweetie, we're both upset. The meds are slowing you down. We can talk about it later."

"You're trying to protect me. Stop it!"

Tracy dug into her microwave brownie and washed it down with a gulp of lukewarm tea.

"You don't know everything about Ben."

"Dad was really loud. Nice of him to…to tell Ben's personal story to everyone like that. So, what's the problem?"

"That's not the problem. It never was."

"Then tell me what is!"

Why did Austin always seek out the truth? Could he just for once leave it buried? Especially this time? Because this one hurt. Tracy had grown to trust Ben with all her heart. She couldn't bear to admit the truth, but the more she delayed, the more upset her son would become. "I can't be with someone who was willing to use my child like that."

Austin set his bowl of popcorn on the end table beside his armchair and wiped his hands. "He's done nothing different from almost every other business in town."

Tracy blinked. "What do you mean?"

"When it's…crap!" He whispered the months to himself, always stopping at May.

"June?" Tracy asked.

"When it's June, Pride Month, suddenly all these businesses show rainbow stuff on their social media. But the rest of the year, nothing. Or when companies hire people, a lot hire some people just to check off the…diversity checkbox. Your company does that, too, doesn't it?"

The question hit Tracy square in the chest. She knew the answer.

"Mom? Well?"

She nodded.

"And if Dad's the…whatever his job is…the main money guy…does that mean I'm not supposed to be around him anymore? Because he makes sure the company hires people in his department who check off the right boxes so it brings in more money?"

Tracy tried to suppress her I've-had-it-with-teen-logic sigh, but she couldn't. "He's your father."

"He walked out on us."

"Lots of places check off those boxes."

"And lots of places do what Ben wanted to do."

"That doesn't make it right. He wanted to use children."

"Like those charities that claim you're buying a goat for a family in Africa when you're really not? Or that you're sponsoring a child in South America, but when the charity leaves the village, they don't tell you? He wouldn't have been the first."

"He's not using my son for that."

"He never used me. Ben's not evil. He apologized to all of us. Why can't you see that?"

Because I'm your mother. She was tiring of Austin's holier-than-thou attitude. "A single apology from Ben doesn't cover that! He wanted to exploit marginalized kids, Austin! Nothing could hurt me—or you—more! With all the challenges, worries—"

"I've told you to lay off!"

"I can't lay off! I'm your mother! You can barely string two words together right now! How can I lay off?" Only after Tracy screamed did she realize how loud she'd become. "I'm sorry. I love you, Austin, and with everything that happened last year…"

But Austin had already picked up his phone. He'd begun shutting her out.

"Who are you calling?"

He didn't answer.

"Austin?"

A cold, hard stare was her only response until Austin held the phone to his ear. "I'm sick and tired of you speaking for me. I'm going to ask him. I want to know if his sorry was for me, too. If it was, I'll accept it. Because he's trying to make people around him feel better, and you're making it hard for him."

How could Austin not understand that she, too, had experienced pain throughout the past year, from watching his humiliation onstage as he came out of his seizure and was dumbstruck by the commotion around him, to having to accept that she'd failed him as a mother when she'd learned the extent of the bullying that had happened and realized she'd been unable to stop it?

Austin set his phone back on the table. "No answer."

"Probably because I told him to stay away from you."

Austin's glare pierced Tracy's heart. "Stop speaking for me!" He stormed off to his room and slammed his door shut. A minute later, *The Nutcracker Suite* was blasting from his stereo.

Tracy flicked off the television and called the only person she believed was still talking to her *and* who had children: her mother.

BEN'S PHONE rang and vibrated on the bar's surface. Austin's name showed up.

"One of your friends?" the bartender asked.

"Someone I'm supposed to be a mentor to." Ben held up his third pint. "Ain't happening." Good thing he'd eaten so much at the Robinsons'. He could hold a little more alcohol.

"Anyone I should call to get you home?"

Ben shook his head. "Home is in Toronto. Sister in New Hamburg. I'm staying at that hotel…what's it called? At King and Benton."

The bartender gave the hotel's current name. "Locals still call it the Valhalla."

"Yeah. She's a local. That's what she called it. But I'm not leaving yet. No one there to talk to."

The alcohol had already affected Ben's memory. He didn't recall having this much difficulty in his younger years. Not that thirty-five was old. Neither was forty-eight when you really thought about it. But twenty…twenty…*I guess it depends if I'm trying to figure out when I started, when I was really drinking, or when I stopped*, he thought. Regardless, he'd been younger.

But he hadn't had a drop in ten years. That much he could still remember.

CHAPTER 36

"They don't get it, Mom. He wanted to use my child to get to other children so he'd have higher social media ratings! I can't be with someone like that. And Pauline defended him, after all she's done to help kids like Austin. I'm in utter disbelief. She of all people should understand! But I guess Eric was right. You need to have kids to truly get it."

Where would Tracy be without her mom? Jan had patiently listened to her for...Tracy didn't know how long. She had rambled off all her frustrations, anger, and pain in one jumbled soliloquy.

"It's hard to parent a teen," Jan said.

Finally. Someone was listening to Tracy for the first time today.

"I sometimes wonder how your father and I survived three of you!"

"I guess I broke you in?"

"I guess you did. But parenting one child through difficult times is different from parenting twins. And you can imagine our surprise when the doctor told us he suspected twins!"

What does that have to do with my situation? She sighed. "That must've been quite the shock."

"Oh, it was. None of our friends had twins. We never thought to look for a support group for twins. We did find some useful advice in some library books, but the mother of one of our friends back then used to be a maternity ward nurse."

"Oh?"

"She wasn't exactly a mom of twins, but she could look after lots of babies at once. Even came to check in on us once in a while."

Tracy leaned back against the headboard of her bed. "This is a wonderful story, Mom, but—and I don't mean to be rude— what does this have to do with me?"

"You believe no one understands what your life is like because they're not parenting a gay, disabled teen boy on their own. And I'll be honest—once I met other parents of twins, I felt like I'd found people who really understood me. But if I'd refused advice from anyone until I'd met people in exactly our situation, I might not have made it. We're a large family, my sweet pea, including the Robinsons. Your siblings have children, but none of them are disabled and none, we think, are gay. But Ashley is the same age as Austin, so Thomas and Shannon could help there. And Dawn and Dean could talk to you about Destiny and what they've learned from parenting a child with diabetes. Or…just talk to Pauline, who's come across thousands of families, and she could share with you what she's learned."

Jan was right. Tracy was waiting for the perfect answer from the perfect person. "It's just that…it hurts to know Pauline supported Ben and not me."

"I can understand why his confession hurt you. But I have to admit, his apology at the dinner table today felt real to me."

Because it was.

"If you did something bad and were really sorry about it,

wouldn't you want those…" Jan paused. "Wouldn't you want those you love to forgive you?"

"I don't think Ben loves me."

"I saw the hurt in his eyes every time Eric put his arm around you. Not to mention the way he smiled anytime the two of you talked. It was love in his eyes when he looked to you for strength before he apologized. I think that's what angered Eric in the end."

Ben's hazel eyes appeared in Tracy's mind. Early on, they had been part of her physical attraction to him. Now they'd become part of how they communicated with one another.

"How did you feel about him before his confession this afternoon?" Jan asked.

"I guess I was falling in love with him, too."

"And would you still be falling in love if he hadn't told you the full truth this afternoon?"

"I can't ignore it, Mom! He was going to use more kids like Austin for his own gain!"

Jan's voice remained gentle. "His intent was selfish, but did he intend to hurt these children? Or was he just being naive?"

"But he's a communications professional. He understands context."

"His job was to protect and promote his employer's reputation. It doesn't make it all right and I'm not saying you shouldn't feel betrayed. But what was Ben feeling when he said those words to Pauline? What was Pauline feeling when she chose to hide that conversation from you? Were either of them feeling contempt toward Austin?"

It was just like her mother to reduce everything to feelings. Jan always found it difficult to consider *the facts* of a situation. "He was still trying to exploit him, and my best friend took away my right to know by not telling me! You're missing the point!"

Jan remained calm. "Then what you have is someone who already apologized for acting that way. He's trying to make amends with you and your family. And you have a best friend who made the wrong decision because she deeply cared for you. I've cut hair for thousands of people in my life. Please trust me when I say that not many people like them are out there."

Tracy had a nagging suspicion her mom was right. But the pain in Tracy's heart wouldn't dissipate. The only way to resolve this was to talk to them, but talking to anyone was the last thing Tracy wanted to do right now.

LOUD KNOCKING WOKE BEN UP.

"What the hell?!" he growled.

"Ben? Open up or the manager will. I need to get home. I have an early shift in the morning."

Ben rubbed his eyes. "Susie?" Or was he dreaming?

He stumbled out of bed. The red digits on the clock swam. He couldn't read the time. He opened the door.

Oh, shit. Pauline had come, too.

"I'll start packing." Pauline whisked past him.

"Oh my god, Ben. What happened?" Susie sniffed. "You absolutely reek of beer. How much did you drink?" Susie turned to the manager and passed her a folded bill before the woman left.

Ben's head felt like an orchestra of pots and pans being played by toddlers.

But then Susie wrapped her arms around him, and he responded in kind, never wanting to let go, only wanting to disappear with her to New Hamburg and never return to Kitchener.

"I fucked up so bad, Susie. So, so bad."

"We'll talk about it later, Big Ben. Austin texted Pauline after he tried calling you several times and didn't get an answer. Since you didn't pick up for her either she called me."

"I got your sister's number from Tracy Sunday night after you left," Pauline said. "Thank god for that."

"But Genny's parents…" Ben could barely form a sentence. He'd ruined his sister's perfect weekend with the people he'd hoped would be her future in-laws.

"I told them you'd had a bit too much fun at Oktoberfest. They don't need to know anything else. I also locked away all the alcohol after I got back from Quebec City because I assumed you'd be visiting me, anyway. They're driving back tomorrow, so all will be fine. Let's get you home."

Susie offered to take his suitcase and his laptop so Pauline could support Ben, who could barely walk.

Pauline's voice was gentle as she took his arm over her shoulders. "Lean on me, Ben. I've got you."

He avoided eye contact with her. She'd never seen him like this.

As they neared the door, he said again, "Susie, I'm so sorry."

Susie stood the suitcase on its wheels, grabbed his face in her small hands, and forced him to look down at her. "Big Ben, you're safe now, okay? I'll change the passwords on all your accounts once we get back to New Hamburg. And I have your wallet in my purse, so you won't waste any more money on booze. We'll get you a counsellor this week. You've been through a lot. But you're safe, and you've got more than just me looking after you."

They continued to the elevator. "One of the Belmont Village businesses is a career coach," Pauline added as they waited. "He knows nothing about this, of course, but he was impressed with all the work you've been doing. I'm sure he can help you get started again. And you can use the pullout couch at my place if you ever need to stay in town."

"You're not alone, Ben, got it?"

Ben lifted his arm away from Pauline and pulled his sister into him again. "I'm so lucky to have you." When he let go, he gathered the courage to look at Pauline. "And you. Thank you for everything."

Pauline smiled. "You're welcome, Ben."

"What did you tell Austin?"

"Only that we'd check on you," Pauline answered. "We'll talk about what you want me to say to him, okay?"

Without thinking, he asked, "How's Tracy?"

Pauline sighed. "I haven't talked to her since this afternoon."

Susie tilted the suitcase and pulled it onto the elevator. "Don't worry about her right now. Let's get you back to my place. The manager will have everything ready when we get downstairs, and Pauline will drive your car back to her apartment for safekeeping."

Despite his crushing headache, Ben realized one thing in the elevator. If Austin had contacted Pauline, and Pauline Susie, that meant Tracy had had nothing to do with Ben's rescue.

And *that* meant only one thing: she hated him.

CHAPTER 37

"How's Austin?" The CEO had called Tracy into his office as soon as she'd messaged him to say she'd returned.

"Not well. Yesterday was, well, Thanksgiving." She gave a weak smile, and he smiled back. It wasn't a genuine smile, though. "He wanted to go to school, because mid-terms are coming up and he's missed a lot already. I'm sorry about that. I should've told him to stay home. He can get caught up."

Tracy had only been at work for half an hour this morning before the school had called her to pick up Austin: he could barely answer questions when called upon, and his friends were concerned. In the car, he explained that the emotional upheaval from yesterday had kept him awake until well after two.

Now the CEO pulled out a folder, and Tracy's stomach dropped to her feet. "I'm sorry he's not doing well. I think this transfer will be for the best. It'll give you the flexibility you had before Eric came on board. One of the downsides of working for both of us, I'm afraid, is that we need you here every morning at eight-thirty."

Tracy nodded as she accepted the folder and opened it. *Job Title: Executive Assistant to the Chief Marketing Officer.*

"We've got someone lined up for Monday so you can use the rest of this week to finish up. Look at the bright side: no more quarter-end stress. Should be easier for raising Austin with all his difficulties."

As much as she wanted to appreciate the gesture, it was illegal for the CEO to consider her familial duties in his hiring decisions—she hadn't requested the permanent accommodation —and she was being judged for being a mother. He'd been accommodating for the past year, and she'd always made up her hours.

"I'd like to discuss the salary."

"That's what the position pays. But if you know of anyone who would be a good CMO, you could hire your boss. The head hunters have been useless in finding us someone. Anyone in your connections who could apply?"

Work for Ben now? She shook her head.

"Review the documents and have them signed and handed into HR by end of day. Any questions?"

Tracy shook her head and gave the only professional response she could. "Thank you for this opportunity."

He smiled as though he'd received a pat on the back. "You're welcome, Tracy. I think this will eliminate all the awkwardness that's accumulated in the office."

She nodded, her voice stuck in her throat, and left his office.

Ten thousand less. How would she afford Austin's dance lessons? What if he needed extra therapy? What if his seizures changed? Or his medication regimen and her drug benefits didn't cover all the costs? She hadn't even tried alternative therapies yet. They might help with the side effects. She checked her phone. Austin was still at home. If he kept missing school like this, she'd have to add a tutor to their budget. She had two options: take on a second job or ask Eric for more money.

She slumped into her chair, still staring at the new contract.

"Trace? You okay?"

She jumped at Eric's voice. "I-I-I got transferred."

He adjusted his cuffs. "I know. I came to apologize about that. But it's for the best."

It took her two seconds to process what Eric had just admitted. "Wait a minute. You knew about this yesterday? You'd already hired someone to take my position?"

"Isn't this what you want? To have a flexible schedule so you can take care of Austin?"

Tracy's blood reached its boiling point. "You wanted to come back into my life as my husband, Eric! How could you keep something like this from me!"

He kept his voice cool. "There were always going to be things I couldn't tell you."

Tracy's voice got louder by the word. "You know I need a job that will best let me help Austin! Or have you forgotten about him again?"

Eric closed the door. "I supported this with him in mind! With this job, you'll have a lot more flexibility. If it's about money, I can pay more towards his education, medical needs, dance training...whatever you want."

Tracy refused to hold back the sarcasm that was burning her tongue. "Because you've proven how reliable you can be."

"That's unfair. I've apologized for everything and am doing my best to make amends."

She came around her desk. "What's unfair is cornering me at every turn. When you get depressed, you leave me to raise your son. When you want me back, you take a job at my company without telling me. When you want to talk things over before we officially start working together, you show up unannounced.

When things don't work out, you shove me out of your way. You always have the upper hand. The risk is being your wife. There's no risk in being my husband. *That's* unfair."

Eric sat down calmly as though he'd anticipated this conversation. "Contrary to what you might believe, I love him, too. But it's clear you and I can't work together."

"Then why do *I* have to leave?"

He answered her question as though stating that the world was round. "There's only one CFO, but there are multiple EAs."

Tracy slammed her hands on the desk. "*You* chose to accept this position *after* I was working here. You knew I worked here. And you find it completely acceptable that you're kicking me out of a job I need? All because you wanted to get back together? Did you think about the risk to *me*?" She marched past him and opened the door. "You make me sick, Eric."

He stood up. "Tracy, that was never my intention."

Tracy's eyes were slits, her voice low. "You know how corporations work. You chose the option with the least risk to yourself with little consideration for me. If things didn't work out between us, at least you would have a high-paying job." She opened the door wider. "Get out of my office."

Tracy closed the door behind him, leaned against it, and squeezed back tears. How was she going to survive this week with her pride in check? Ben had said once that when a door closed, a window opened somewhere else.

But right now, she felt trapped in a basement cellar with the door locked and Austin upstairs, crying for help.

TWO DAYS LATER, Ben took the bus into Kitchener and picked up his car from Pauline. He'd thanked her again for her help. She hugged him and said, "Of course I'm going to help you."

After how he'd treated her for three years, she had still found it within her to support his recovery.

Ben drove by Tracy's work, and regret pulled at his heart. Her last text to him had told him to stay away from her family. He had to respect that.

But was it possible to recover from that? Could she forgive him?

He continued to downtown Kitchener and parked in a parking garage. A few minutes later, he found himself at the entrance to the shelter that had housed him over a decade before, the one from which he'd been hiding his identity as he helped coordinate donation efforts for the festival.

A woman exited the building, leaned against the wall, and lit a cigarette. Ben could see the signs that she was someone who was living rough. He reached into his wallet, pulled out a twenty, and gave it to her. She promptly tossed it to the ground. Realizing she had wrongly assumed he wanted sex, he picked it up and handed it to her again.

"I didn't mean it like that. Use it for supper, or another pack, or whatever. I've got a meeting with the volunteer coordinator."

Whatever her situation, she would need cash, and he hoped to relieve that need for her for one evening, no matter what she used the money for. He also hoped someone wouldn't steal it from her. One reason he'd lived on the streets for so long was that most shelters didn't have anywhere safe to keep belongings. On more than one occasion when he'd slept in a shelter, he'd woken up in the morning to find valuables stolen: whatever he'd collected the day before, his pants, even his glasses. He'd spent at least a year having difficulties seeing. When his parents had booked him his bus ride home from Montreal, he couldn't pick up his ticket because he had no ID. His family drove to Montreal together—no one could wait to see him—to pick him up.

He recalled the shock and pity in their eyes at his appearance. His mother had cried.

Ben entered the building and stopped in the foyer, studying the pamphlets on the board.

His father had found a hotel for the night and even bought alcohol so Ben could satiate his cravings until he started an addiction program at home. Nothing had humiliated Ben more in his life than needing to drink in front of his family.

He must have spent an hour that afternoon under the shower in the Montreal hotel. When Susie had unpacked old clothes she'd brought along, they sagged on his bone-thin frame, so she bought new ones. Susie had also brought an old pair of glasses. Better an old prescription than none. His mother had booked him a haircut, and at Ben's request, a full shave. When the hair stylist removed the smock, exposing his new clothes with his hair and face, Ben didn't recognize himself in the mirror.

Ben had silently cried himself to sleep that night in the hotel.

The family ate in a restaurant every couple of hours on the drive home so Ben could order a beer—open alcohol in the car was illegal in both provinces. No, he wasn't going to "hide" the bottle in a paper bag. Ben didn't want his father to be pulled over for an alcohol-related offence on his account.

Holy sugar. How had he not seen it? Tracy's reaction at Thanksgiving—severing ties with people close to her—was another trauma response. Ben had avoided his family for two years because of his trauma, and he'd seen it often enough on the streets. She was doing the same. He needed to keep this appointment, but he'd call Pauline afterward and ask her to talk to Tracy. She needed to get help before she drove Austin away, too.

Ben entered the office and found a young woman, cleanly and casually dressed, sitting behind the desk. He first made a one-hundred-dollar donation. He'd have donated more, but Susie had only given him enough cash for his bus ticket, food, gas, and donations.

The receptionist asked him to fill out a donor form.

"I'm here to see Sebastian. It's Benjamin from Belmont Village." Pauline had said it would be fine to complete this task on behalf of the committee.

The receptionist thanked him for the donation and left to get Sebastian.

Ben surveyed the reception area. Old fluorescent lights flickered in the ceiling. *Not even enough money to change to LEDs*, he thought. An old man passed him, smelling like gasoline and counting to himself. The mental health issues among the homeless were so complex. Ben's situation had been relatively simple compared to that of others. It was another reason he hesitated telling people about his past: they'd assume everyone's situation was like his and expect all the homeless to just "change their minds," go back to family, and enter the workforce again.

Hard to do if you were Austin's age, a member of the LGBTQ community, and shunned by your entire family. Or you were so poor you couldn't afford any kind of dwelling. Or when your mental health disorder had you convinced that everyone was your enemy. Or when your parents introduced you to addictive substances in childhood because they had yet to heal from their own traumas. Or when you needed to pay off a heavy debt before you qualified for subsidized housing, but you required an address to land a job. Or when you came from a marginalized group who'd had no choice but to pass on trauma from one generation to the next with few resources to aid healing.

Or...

Solutions existed for all these problems, but they needed more than hundred-dollar donations.

A Black man entered from the hallway behind the reception desk. Ben recognized Sebastian immediately: half his hair was now grey and he had a little more girth around the middle, but he still had the same warm, friendly smile Ben remembered.

"Benjamin, nice to finally meet..." He studied Ben for a moment. "I'm sorry, but have we met before?"

Ben reached out his hand. "We have, actually. You found me sheltering in a bank twelve years ago on King Street. You were volunteering for Out of the Cold and you helped me get a spot here. I eventually left with a group for Montreal. Ben Landry."

Sebastian's hand flew to his chest. Neither said a word and then both men embraced.

"Oh, my good lord," Sebastian said, not letting go. *"Ben Landry.* That's the Benjamin I've been emailing with this whole time?"

A treasure chest of memories of Sebastian's kindness opened inside Ben in that embrace, enveloping him in comfort. When the men stepped back, both laughed as they wiped away tears.

"I almost never get to see someone after..." Sebastian clasped his hands and looked Ben up and down again. "You look phenomenal."

"Thanks. And you look about the same." Ben smiled. "Just with a few more greys."

"Happens when you pass the fifty mark. I'll get you those brochures."

"Actually, can we talk? I'm not doing well. I..." Ben took a deep breath. His skin burned in anticipation of his confession. "I relapsed Monday."

"Oh, Ben, I'm so sorry. Did you want help getting connected with a counsellor? Or a recovery group?"

"I'm good there, thank you. I have a sister who's a nurse practitioner. She's helping me find someone. I'm staying with her right now." But there was one thing he still needed to discuss with Sebastian. Something he'd never talked to anyone about before, not even Susie. It was the only obstacle holding Ben back from fully reconciling this part of his life.

"I need help understanding something about me back then, and you're the only person I'm still in touch with who knew my darkest self. I was hoping you could help."

Sebastian nodded. "That was a long time ago, but I'll certainly try."

Trying was all Ben needed.

CHAPTER 38

*I*t was her last day in this position — Friday the thirteenth — and she could barely keep her eyes open. Nightmares about Austin needing her had interrupted her sleep the past few nights. In real life, he constantly asked about Ben. When she had picked Austin up from the tea shop Wednesday, she had waited in the car, too afraid to enter and see Pauline.

And because windows apparently weren't opening for her despite all the closed doors, a massive storm front was guaranteed to hit Kitchener that weekend, its torrential downpours and severe thunderstorms making any possibility of the festival unsafe. The committee had been forced to cancel.

"It's just as well," she muttered. "Now I've got the weekend to feel sorry for myself."

While she waited, she messaged the committee to spread the word as fast as possible, scheduled social media posts for immediate release, and informed local media outlets. She'd fired Ben and she didn't regret it but even now that the festival was cancelled, it had added more work to her load.

She crossed her arms on her desk and lay her head on top.

A gentle knock on the door moments later made her look up. "You've seen the weather?" Eric said.

"Festival's been cancelled." Tracy choked back tears. "Everything I've gone through these past few weeks...all for nothing." Without a festival to plan, she wouldn't have needed Ben's help, would've only had to deal with Eric's advances — maybe she would have even fallen for him again — been able to pay more attention to Austin, and probably kept this job.

"I'm sorry, Trace." Eric paused. "Have you heard from him?"

Ever since their public argument at the Robinsons' Monday, followed by Tracy's blowout in the office Tuesday, Eric had taken several steps back. Although he had never outright apologized, Tracy heard regret in his voice and noticed it in his demeanour.

"I made it pretty clear I didn't want him near my family again."

He wiped his hand over his face and sighed. "I guess I got a little out of hand Monday."

Tracy huffed. "A little? You ruined Claire and Richard's last Thanksgiving in their family home. But it made it clear to me we need to start working on a custody arrangement."

Might as well finish the week with a bang.

"So you want a divorce?"

"I absolutely want a divorce. You're the last person I want to be married to."

Eric stared at his feet. "I didn't know how else to try to keep the woman I love, Trace."

"Showing up and immediately trying to invade my life was your way of showing you loved me?" Tracy let out a dry laugh. "Or was publicly humiliating another human being your way of showing your love? Or is your way of courting me so subtle I missed it? Because all that's happened from your return is that

I've lost my job and the man I actually fell in love with. And Austin's lost more school time." Tears trickled down her face. "You miss work? No problem. I miss work? I get transferred and lose pay. Did you think about how much guilt your son's going to carry with him because of this? Or did you only worry about how awkward it would be working together after I rejected you?" She huffed again. "Save your breath. I know the answer."

Eric closed the door and pointed to a chair. "May I?"

Tracy was surprised he'd ask permission. She nodded.

"I was so certain I'd be able to win you back, and so certain you'd be hyperfocused on Austin when I moved back to town that I didn't factor in another man."

I hadn't "factored in" Ben, either.

"But did you 'factor in' your son's epilepsy?"

Eric shook his head. "I'm sorry I was selfish, Trace."

Tracy wanted to accept his apology and tell him she forgave him. But she couldn't. She nodded to show she'd heard him, but that was all she could manage. His jealousy had ruined what would've become a beautiful relationship, and his inability to acknowledge that his son was disabled had caused harm.

"Do you think Austin will mind still spending time with me?"

As angry as Tracy was with Eric, she needed to set that aside for Austin. Austin had said it himself: away from Tracy and Ben, Eric had proven he could indeed be the father he had been. Even though the events of the past week had distressed Austin, Austin had also experienced happiness again with Eric. And Eric had admitted to having been in the wrong and was now sitting here, again asking for forgiveness and the chance to try yet again.

He wasn't running away.

"We can start with you driving him to dance during the

week. If Austin's okay with that." She'd miss that time with him, but Austin needed his father back in his life. His excitement when he'd returned from the trip to Toronto had been more than just exuberance from seeing ballets. He'd been genuinely happy to have spent time with his dad. Tracy was certain the two were close to healing their rift. This week had widened it again, but not beyond repair.

She indicated her computer. "I've got some things to finish up before the company movers get here, and then some of the teams want to say goodbye before we all leave for the weekend." The pressure of needing to be Eric's wife a second time dissolved. "We have a lot to iron out, but we can make it work. We don't have to be together for you to be Austin's father."

Eric stood up and walked to the door. "It'll take me some time to get used to that."

As soon as he left, her phone dinged that special ding she'd reserved for Pauline's texts. Her hand raced to her phone before she could even deliberate if she wanted to pick it up. She hoped a text from Pauline meant her best friend had stopped hating her.

Can you come by the shop after work? I'll have comfort tea waiting for you.

Relief washed over Tracy. Her son was right. She needed friendships, people besides her mother, because Tracy couldn't handle everything life threw at her alone.

Yes! I'll text you when I'm on my way.

Two hours later, Tracy knocked on the back of Claire's Tea Shop; the store closed at six on Fridays.

Pauline, a gentle smile on her face, welcomed Tracy in.

"I honestly thought you'd never talk to me again after what I said to you Monday," Tracy said. "That's why I didn't come in Wednesday when I picked up Austin."

Pauline locked the door behind her. "I was really hurt. I

honestly thought I was doing what was best for you. You were going through so much. I didn't think you needed to hear about one more of Ben's jerky episodes because I didn't expect the two of you, well, together." She smiled and shrugged. "And you had a lot to do with the festival. I didn't want to interfere. But now that it's cancelled..." She let the sentence hang as she held her arms open, and Tracy fell into her best friend's embrace.

"I'm sorry, Pauline."

"So am I."

When they let go, Pauline led Tracy out to the lounge area, where she already had tea waiting. Tracy sank into the plush sofa and Pauline into the armchair. With the lights off at the front of the shop and those above them dimmed, the calming atmosphere relaxed Tracy.

She envied the freedom all this space gave Pauline. She and Austin had certainly benefited from it, too.

"Listen," Pauline said. "I've been talking to Ben these past few days—"

Tracy's heart skipped several beats, and she immediately broke in. "How's he doing?"

"He's concerned about you. He mentioned something that I didn't recognize, maybe because I'm too close to you. We need to talk about trauma, Tracy."

The room spun. She held on tightly to her tea so she wouldn't drop it. "Why's that?" She breathed in deeply to settle the physical sensations while she waited for Pauline to speak. She'd been hoping for more of a fireside chat with her best friend this evening, not a deep dive into a distressing topic. Then she thought about her mother's advice. Maybe this would be good.

Pauline spoke again. "Have you ever gone for counselling for yourself after Austin's accident and diagnosis?"

Anticipation and dread released themselves in a nervous

laugh. "Of course not. People are traumatized in war zones and abusive relationships. Not when their son has—"

"A life-altering diagnosis that's followed by your spouse walking out on you? All of that can lead to trauma, Tracy. Absolutely."

"I'm fine." Pauline was a good friend. Ben was a good man. However, the more they talked about Tracy being traumatized, the sillier it sounded. Tracy needed to relax a bit around Austin, certainly. But traumatized? That wasn't her.

When Pauline continued, her voice expressed no judgment. "Ben told me about visiting a farm where a child fell down. He said your reaction was a lot stronger than he would've expected."

"So I overreacted. I've been going through a lot. But that doesn't mean Austin's fall traumatized me. And let me guess: he said the falling peregrine reminded me of my 'trauma,' too, right? Ben's a creative type. They find meaning in everything."

Pauline remained calm. "It's the full picture, not just individual incidents. The situation with the girl tipped him off. You're hypervigilant with Austin, have very few friends—"

"Neither do you." Tracy wasn't going to take this amateur diagnosis lying down. Austin had epilepsy. *Any mother with a disabled child keeps an eye out on them, and when you work almost fifty hours a week, volunteer, help your mother out, drive your son to dance lessons and his own part-time job, when do you have time for friends?*

Pauline's voice stayed warm as she kept talking. "I eventually had no friends because Ben worked me like a dog. Which he's apologized for. And since returning to Kitchener, I've been too busy with the shop. But I've actually gotten to know some people through Oktoberfest and my book fair work. We'll see where that goes."

Tracy didn't admit to the twinge of jealousy at the thought of having to share Pauline with others. She was too special. As

Tracy took a sip of her tea, she recognized how much tension had built up inside her just from this brief conversation. But that was what happened when someone criticized your parenting abilities.

Pauline continued. "You're always on guard for Austin — and I understand you have to watch out for him, but it's become unhealthy for both of you."

"Look, Pauline, if we're here just so you can psychoanalyze me —"

"Have you been having nightmares about him?"

How did she know? "Ever since getting transferred at work."

"What?"

Tracy realized she hadn't told Pauline any of this. She recounted the story.

Every shade of anger and indignation played across Pauline's face. "Oh my god, Tracy. No wonder you've been having nightmares. Your worries for Austin were already high, and now you're terrified you won't be able to provide for him."

Hearing her fears articulated so clearly hit something inside. Maybe Pauline was right.

"So how will we deal with your CEO and Eric? What kind of monster do you want me to dress up as?" Pauline asked. "Or if you'd rather, I can hunt down a head-to-toe garbage collector costume and show up with a trash can."

Tracy had to set her tea down on the coffee table before she spilled it from laughing so hard. "Apart from the security issues, Eric would put two and two together pretty quickly."

Laughing together felt so wonderful. Tracy couldn't remember the last time it had happened. Pauline wasn't criticizing her; she truly supported her and was trying to help. Beating around the bush was simply not Pauline's way of communicating.

If everyone was saying Tracy worried too much about Austin, were they right? No one was saying to *never* worry about Austin, just to worry less. Austin was saying it the loudest of all. The more Tracy thought about it, the more she realized that each argument about his autonomy had increasingly distressed him.

Was that what she wanted? Mental stress not only exacerbated the side effects of his medication, it also brought on more seizures. They had only begun part two of this medication a few months before. The first time—after moving back to Kitchener—had proved such a disaster that Austin had rejected medication altogether. She wanted to avoid that.

"A truffle for your thoughts?" Pauline's gentle smile returned.

Tracy sighed. If her actions were harming Austin, she needed to hear all of it, no matter how painful. This was about helping Austin, right? "Is that everything?"

"Actually, no. What confirmed it for Ben was how you avoid the topic of your trauma."

Tracy let out a nervous laugh. "Well, no one likes to talk about something that makes them uncomfortable."

"For sure. But our reactions are stronger when our pain runs really deep. That's why Ben lived on the streets for two years: he was avoiding telling his family about losing his job. But the longer he avoided that talk, the more he drank, and the more he drank, the more disgusted he became with himself, and the more disgusted he was, the scarier that moment of honesty became. It was a vicious circle. Being fired might not drive you or me to such extreme behaviour. But in his mind, there was nothing more shameful than that. That he told us without drinking was a huge step for him."

Tracy hadn't thought about that.

Pauline set her tea on the coffee table and joined Tracy on

the sofa. She wrapped an arm around her, comforting her like she had the day Tracy had come into the shop after the car accident. Pauline's voice was almost a whisper. "What about you? What are you too ashamed to say? What makes you believe we won't love you anymore?"

Tracy's chest ached at the truth that wanted to remain buried. Her throat closed, and her mind darted in a million directions to escape the truth.

Ben and Pauline were right.

Tracy thought back to Austin's health since Thanksgiving at the Robinsons', when she'd taken the most drastic steps possible to protect him—by removing some of the most important people in his life. What had happened? His neurological health had plummeted overnight.

Tracy reminded herself that no one was telling her not to worry. But how would she know when to stop?

Pauline rubbed her back. "I will never leave you again, Tracy. We're best friends. But you need to talk to someone about this. You can't go through this alone. At least start with me."

Tracy's chest shuddered as the truth came out. "There's nothing more shameful...than a mother who can't protect her child."

As the belief that she'd failed Austin that evening at the ballet school's theatre came out of her mouth, sobs wracked her body. Pauline pulled her into a tight embrace while Tracy let everything out: her choice to not listen to Eric's warnings, his ensuing accusations, her feelings of failure and inadequacy as a mother, her regrets about the decisions she'd made these past few months about Austin's care, her fears about not knowing when enough care was enough...all of it. Her only indication of how much time had passed when she finally stopped crying was the pile of nine or ten crumpled serviettes on the table.

"I guess I had a lot in me."

Pauline squeezed her shoulder. "You still need to see a professional to help you, but this was a good first step. You can talk to me about anything. You know that, right?"

"Man, do I ever." *Speaking of men...* "I miss him."

"Then call him."

Tracy shook her head. "After what I said to him, he won't want to talk to me again. Besides, if these past few weeks have proven anything, it's that I don't have time for a man. I need to get the divorce settled with Eric, and then I need to get my life in order with Austin."

A coy smile curled its way onto Pauline's lips. "You're doing it again."

"Doing what?"

"Planning your life like you tackle a box of chocolates: looking at the truffle guide so you can avoid the cherry truffle. But look what happened when you let the cherry truffle walk into your life."

Pauline had a point.

Then something inside Tracy clicked. "A box of chocolates..."

The idea was so wild, so unlike her, it frightened her.

But it was also the answer.

She pulled out the pad of paper she kept in her purse and began scribbling down ideas.

Tracy was about to take control of her life in a way she'd never before dared.

CHAPTER 39

*B*uckets of rain poured down from the heavens on the day of the festival.

Nobody would've faulted Tracy for burrowing under blankets in her bed, surrounded by a wall of chocolate bars and supported by a picnic thermos of hot chocolate and can of whipped cream.

But instead, her hands were shaking with joy. She'd just gotten off the phone and was going to explode with incredible news if she didn't tell the first person who came in the front door.

Which would be Eric and Austin.

They were just pulling into the driveway. Dang it. Not that she was expecting anyone else, but she now remembered today's plan: that Tracy and Eric—*together*—were going to explain to Austin the new arrangement and let Austin voice his opinions. He was sixteen. Both parents had agreed he deserved a say.

She opened the front door so they could dart inside.

After they towelled themselves off from the rain, Tracy

brought out a box of truffles from David's and invited Austin and Eric to join her in the family room.

"So, you're talking to each other again?" Austin asked.

"I apologized to him over lunch," Eric explained to Tracy. "It's not like me to lose my cool like that." He unbuttoned his cuffs and rolled up his sleeves. "I'm embarrassed to imagine what the Parsons think of me. At least everyone else knows I lost my mind and hopefully understands I've found it again."

"I'm sorry, too, Austin, for the way I've handled things lately," Tracy said. "Transitions are hard and these past few weeks have been full of them. It's been painful and embarrassing, to say the least."

Austin nodded in acknowledgement.

Now for the major news: "Your father and I are not getting back together."

"Saw that coming a mile away."

Excellent. Teenage snark. But Austin being himself again was comforting. Austin leaned back in his armchair, one leg crossed over the other, his eyes focused on them instead of looking toward the basement door. He was relaxed with his parents, and a quick exchange of glances between her and Eric told her they were on the same wavelength.

"We wanted to talk to you about what happens next," Eric said.

"Sure."

"Because we want your input," he added. "When I said at lunch that what you say matters to me, I meant it. I missed a year in your life, and you've changed so much. I wasn't prepared for that." He cleared his throat. "Among many other changes. I tried to plan for every possibility, and I need to pivot and stop doing that with my family."

Tracy and Eric exchanged smiles, and Austin almost seemed confused.

"You're probably not used to us getting along," Tracy said. "The plan is that—if you're okay with it—this house will still be your home base. Your father will give you a key to his condo. However, you do need to let us know where you're going to be. You're still our child."

"And you don't want me walking in on you when you're having sex with someone."

Tracy's cheeks turned red and Eric shifted his position.

"You're going to date other people. I get it," Austin said with a shrug.

Eric scratched the back of his neck. "That doesn't bother you?"

"If it means I can avoid all this drama, I'm all for it. Just please choose decent people. If I don't approve of them, they go."

Apparently, the world had moved along faster than either Tracy or Eric had thought. Eric had wanted Tracy back, and Tracy had assumed rekindling their marriage was best for Austin. Sure, they both knew lots of divorced couples, but it didn't mean they believed divorce could work for them if a healed marriage was possible.

"Your father will join us several times a week for family meals and drive you at least once a week to dance."

Austin mulled over everything, but not once did he glance to either his bedroom or the basement door. Tracy also didn't detect a single seizure.

Then came the tough question. "And Ben?"

Eric bit his lip and Tracy held her breath, but Eric ended the awkward silence moments later. "Your mother's free to date whoever she wants. I promise I won't interfere like that again. If I see him again, I will apologize. I may need time to adjust, but I won't stand in her way."

Tracy appreciated his answer. She just wasn't sure if she was ready to call Ben.

Austin nodded. "Is that it, then?"

"Actually," Tracy said, "I have something else to tell you both. It's big news, but I need you both to keep it quiet for now." She took a deep breath. "There's a good chance I might soon be the owner of the Belmont Village Chocolate House." The words sounded almost implausible spoken out loud.

Austin looked like a stage light had hit him, and that face of caution that drove her nuts in her marriage showed on Eric's face.

Not exactly the reactions I was hoping for.

"You were concerned about your drop in income with the transfer," Eric said. "How will this work out financially?"

Since this decision would affect them, she had to explain everything.

"I had an honest conversation with David this morning, and we discussed everything, including finances. I think I can make it work. Plus, you said you'd contribute more, so I'm taking you up on that. I know how to run a business, and I know about risk, but I didn't realize how long I've had the idea of owning a business in the back of my mind. It became more real, more conscious this fall, and it started screaming at me these past few weeks." She looked in Austin's direction.

Austin rolled his eyes. "I'm fine, Mom."

"I know. But I'd feel better if I could decide my schedule so I could be available to help you if it's ever needed. And to be honest, I enjoyed meeting more Belmont Village business owners. I can really picture myself working as part of this community. All the building blocks were in place for that phone call."

"You do love chocolate," Eric said.

Tracy flapped a hand in his direction. "That has *nothing* to do with it."

Austin sat forward. "But Mom, Pauline and Todd tell me all the time about weird things that happen to them every day. You love predictable. I don't think owning your own business is very predictable."

"You mean unpredictable like this?" She popped a random truffle in her mouth and immediately regretted the decision. Her face scrunched up in disgust.

Eric and Austin doubled over in laughter.

"That was cherry, wasn't it?" Eric asked.

Tracy nodded as she chewed and swallowed. "But I'm still buying David's shop. Switching the icing on cherry truffles to pink will be my first executive decision."

To completely get rid of the cherry flavour, she popped another truffle in her mouth. Almond flavoured. Much better.

"After I change the decorations on cherry truffles, I'm going to ensure we don't have any performative hiring practices."

Austin positively beamed.

"What do you mean?" Eric asked.

Austin explained the term to his dad. Tracy soaked in father and son engaging with each other in the warm way she'd been dreaming of these past weeks. She didn't need to love Eric for him to be Austin's father. She'd never been more positive about that until this moment.

But Tracy's heart was begging for the man it had grown to love. Pauline and Tracy had forgiven each other but their friendship had a long history. Tracy and Ben had only known each other a few months. Plus, the way he'd seen Austin and "kids like him" still gnawed at her.

But if she loved him, and he'd tried so hard to seek forgiveness for his mistakes, it was time she talked to him.

CHAPTER 40

*H*e winced. The tea was so bad, Ben felt a terrible poem surfacing in his mind. Maybe helping Austin with his homework had awakened some latent skills. Or it was his copywriting skills masquerading as poetry. Even worse.

Bitter till the last drop, bagged tea makes life really pop.

Yeah. No. Just because something rhymed didn't make it poetry. And no company would hire him for making up a ditty that highlighted the negatives of the product.

Quick into water, quick out, bagged tea will make you shout.

Ben closed his eyes. *No one's going to hire me if that's all I can come up with.*

"You okay?"

Ben smiled. "Sorry. I'm lamenting at my inability to create slogans about bagged tea. It's making me more unemployable."

Susie laughed and shook her head. "You know, you never told me about your meeting at the shelter."

The talk with Sebastian earlier in the week had unburied pain so deep, Ben had wanted to escape. But he needed to heal the deepest pain to finally move forward without fear chasing him.

He set the tea down. "Walking into the foyer of the shelter was like being left unprotected, with the best hockey players in the league ready to bodycheck me and send me flying into the boards." His voice caught. "But seeing Sebastian? It was like I had my goalie in front of me, protecting me." He swallowed and then laughed wryly. "That probably sounds stupid."

"Not at all. I know what you mean when someone comes to the rescue like that."

"I didn't mean to compare it—"

"You know our agreement."

They'd promised long ago to never compare each other's traumas. It'd been a while since they'd spoken about her sexual assault. But that agreement had built the foundation of their trust and their support for one another.

"When Sebastian realized he'd helped me in the past and that I'd made a future for myself? Suse, it was pure joy on his face. You know how happy I got when I'd raised all that money? This was a thousand times better. He said that knowing I'd found shelter and a job has given him energy to help others for another twelve years, because if I overcame it, it means he's making a difference. All because I showed up to talk to him."

Susie glowed.

"I didn't want to die and my family welcomed me back. Not everyone's so lucky." Ben wiped his eyes. "We talked for a good hour. He helped me understand that failing once doesn't automatically mean I'm going to land on the streets again. I know how to ask for help now."

"And now you have friends who care enough about you to help. *And* you accepted that help. Ben, those are big changes!"

Ben stared at his hands but a smile tugged at the corner of his mouth. "It's hard to accept, but you're right."

Susie bounced on the couch. "So? When are you going to call Tracy? I want a happy ending!"

"I went too far, Suse. She made it clear she didn't want to see me again."

"You have to fight for her!" She punched the air.

Ben snorted. "Like some jousting match? These aren't medieval times. When a woman says no, you stay away. Besides, I make everyone angry."

Susie rolled her eyes. "Oh, my freakin' lord, Benjamin." She yanked him by the wrist and dragged him outside into the pouring rain before he had a chance to protest.

Ben pulled his shoulders up to his ears in that useless human reflex used to protect yourself from the rain.

"This is what it's like to be around people like you who only put themselves down!" Susie called over the rain.

"Can we go back inside? I don't need the analogy!"

Susie wouldn't let go of his wrist. "Yes, you do! Your self-esteem is like this weather. But your heart is like your car, powerful, fast, ready to manoeuvre in any direction to protect someone, just like you tried to manoeuvre out of the way so you wouldn't hit Tracy."

"I was more concerned about protecting my car."

"Why can't you admit you care for others, even when you're being a jerk?"

Ben squeezed his eyes shut. "Because I'm fantastic at hurting them, dammit! Look at what I did to Mom and Dad when I disappeared! And right when they were diagnosed! You dealt with all that yourself. Your sexual assault happened while I was drinking like a fish. Then anyone I managed at the Peregrines…"

She let go of his wrist and held his wet face in her hands. "The only reason you replaced alcohol with your willful igno-rance at the Peregrines was because you're still holding all that regret inside about your time on the streets." She looked up and Ben couldn't tell her tears from the rain streaming down her face. "I was so terrified for your safety those two years. I tried to be strong for Mom and Dad. On-campus counselling helped me get through it."

"I'm so sorry, Suse."

Rain pounded the ceramic coating of Ben's Porsche, trying to penetrate its shell. But it slid right off. All Ben had to do was get his key fob, slide into the driver's side, close the door, and he'd be protected.

Like he was protected inside his heart from all that hurt.

"If I don't at least ask her if I can talk to her, I'm going to make a big mistake, aren't I?"

The hope on Susie's face said it all.

He rushed back inside to the bathroom to dry off. After he put on fresh clothes, he grabbed his phone and dialled, but it rang once and went straight to voicemail.

"See? She doesn't want to talk to me."

Susie, standing wet in the foyer, threw her arms in the air. "For crying out loud! She could be on a call or in the middle of an important conversation, or paying for cherry truffles at the checkout..." She winked at Ben. "I can't believe this is the same man who brought the fandom of the worst hockey team in Canada to such a fever pitch *before* the cup win! Call again and leave a message! Or text her!"

"You don't text important things to Gen X. Marketing Strategy 101."

"But what's the slogan from all those late-night infomercials? 'Don't delay! Call today!'"

Ben dialled again while Susie changed her wet clothes.

CHAPTER 41

"*P*ick it up," Austin said.

The phone rang a second time.

"I can't."

"Mother." Austin grabbed Tracy's phone. "Actually, no, you're not going to just talk to him." He swiped away the call.

"What are you doing?"

Austin handed her phone back. "Unlock it. You're doing a video call."

Tracy tightened her jaw and shook her head. "I'm not wearing any makeup, and my hair's not done."

"Listen to Austin," Eric said, "before I buy you a box of cherry truffles and sit here until you eat all of them. I've sat through long AGMs—and no offence to our incredibly talented son here and what he may choreograph in the future—and long, boring, experimental performances. Trust me. I have the patience."

Austin snickered.

Eric gazed at her with the expression of someone who'd known her for almost half her life. "He's seen you as yourself,

Trace." His smile was both comforting and sad. "And you're beautiful, with or without makeup."

"I can't do this. After everything I did."

Austin pulled up Ben's number, opened a video call, dialled, and handed the phone to her. Father and son headed out in the rain again, leaving Tracy alone in the house, heart hammering in her chest.

Ben answered, and she thought her heart would burst out of her body.

"I was certain you wouldn't take my calls anymore," Ben said. "Susie was going to steal my car if I didn't try a third time."

Tracy had to smile. "The first time was my nerves. The second was my family. Eric and Austin insisted I video call you instead."

Ben raised his eyebrows.

"We're signing divorce papers, and we've told Austin we're going to be dating other people."

The glow in his eyes brightened. They stared at each other for another minute, as though neither could believe they were actually talking after what had happened.

Ben broke the silence. "But how are you doing? I mean, with the festival being cancelled and everything?"

"Disappointed. Sad. Like everything that's happened these past three weeks has been for nothing." She'd hold off telling her good news for now. She wanted to see where this conversation led. "I'm sorry I reacted as I did and fired you, Ben."

He waved her apology away. "You had the right to do that. But I'm going to go out on a limb: the past three weeks haven't been for nothing." He looked straight into his phone's camera. "I got to work alongside an amazing, formidable, resilient woman. And I'm hoping she'll take me back." Tracy opened her mouth to respond, but before she could utter a sound, he continued. "But I need to be completely honest with you about something first, Tracy. Are you somewhere private?"

Tracy's heart sank. Could there be anything worse than what she'd already dealt with? "I'm alone in the house. Is everything okay?"

Ben paused. "I asked Pauline to not tell you this because I promised I would if we talked again. So, please don't be angry at her."

"Okay..."

He looked down and let out a nervous laugh. "I thought I'd left all this behind, but it's become abundantly clear I haven't."

Tracy remained silent.

He pressed his lips together and swallowed. "I got drunk Monday afternoon. Austin had tried to get hold of me several times. When he couldn't, he called Pauline."

Tracy's hand flew to her heart. Austin hadn't said a word. *I was probably too angry.*

"Pauline and Susie came to pick me up. Susie helped me find a psychotherapist who specializes in addictions. My first appointment is next week. And I had a long talk with Sebastian at the shelter Wednesday. I'll tell you more about that later, in person." He took a breath. "But before we continue—if you want to continue—you need to know that I relapsed."

Ben was doing his best to atone. How long was she going to hold on to her own hurts? Weeks? Months? Years? Grudges injured only the person holding the grudge. On her screen was a man who was truly kind. For a long time, he hadn't known how to deal with his own pain. He did now and was doing so.

"The day I said what I did about kids like Austin? I can promise you that Pauline set me straight within seconds," Ben said. "I assumed she'd told you. And I hoped that letting her use the Peregrine accounts to help Austin might have helped show that I was sorry." Ben averted his eyes from his phone as though scared to see Tracy's reaction.

"I've always been grateful that you allowed Pauline to help out that way," Tracy said. "I didn't know it was an apology. I accept."

Ben had been trying to make amends for months. It would've been better if he'd come out and apologized right away, but now that Tracy knew his whole story, she understood the depth of his fears.

Ben's voice was barely a whisper. "Thank you." His chest rose and fell in an apparent attempt to calm himself.

Maybe it was time she shared her story.

"Pauline talked to me about what you said. About me being traumatized by Austin's accident. And Eric's leaving. I just wasn't ready to hear it last weekend when you brought it up." She sighed. "I think I'd hardened myself so much against the world I eventually believed I was invincible. Maybe we're on similar journeys? I don't want to suggest that my worrying about Austin is the same as your—"

Ben looked back into his camera. "Stop right there, Tracy. That's one of the big reasons I don't tell people my history: because everyone will give me some version of, 'oh, your life was so much worse than mine.' I don't want to hear that. You're struggling with your demons while raising a child on your own." He smiled. "To avoid using an old cliché, it's like comparing a Yaris to a Panamera."

Tracy had missed Ben's ability to make her laugh.

Ben continued. "Can we promise each other right here, right now, that we're not going to compare traumas?"

"I promise."

As they continued to talk, she recognized the whole man she was falling in love with, from her physical attraction to his hazel eyes and triple-fudge-worthy kisses, to the soft heart that had been encased in pain so protective it had pushed everyone away. But the drive that had at first been focused solely on his career was now intent on healing his pain and seeking forgiveness.

"But I've got some good news to tell you, Ben."

"Oh?"

"I'm going to be the new owner of the Belmont Village Chocolate House."

Ben's look of happiness came through her phone and into her heart.

"Would you have time to talk about it early next week?" she asked. "I'd love to hear some of your marketing ideas."

"I'd love to. And… Could we see each other again? For real this time? I've fallen in love with you, Tracy Tschirhart."

The words didn't hesitate to come out of Tracy's mouth. "And I'm falling in love with you, Benjamin Landry." She blushed. "So…yes."

Seeing the light of happiness in Ben's hazel eyes was one of the best things that had happened to her all week.

NO SOONER HAD Ben hung up than a wonderful marketing idea popped into his head.

"You okay?" Susie asked as Ben emerged from his guest room. "You look like you just got run over by a Nash Rambler: happy, because you've finally seen your favourite classic in action, but also kind of in pain, because you got hurt."

Ben laughed at the reference to his favourite song. Susie didn't know it now stood for Tracy's Yaris. He had indeed been run over by love. And sometimes that hurt, no matter how excited you were. "I just set myself up for the biggest risk in my life, and I have two weeks to prepare."

He told Susie his idea, and the longer he talked, the more

she squealed. After the excitement died down, though, he became serious.

"Which means I'm going to need access to my accounts again."

"Let's wait one more week, okay? Emotional highs are the worst time to free things up."

He sighed but accepted her decision. Part of him was embarrassed that he needed supervision like this, but another part was grateful he could trust her to help him.

Because his life was no longer about just himself.

For that reason, the next morning, he stood outside Tracy's door, two small boxes in hand, willing his body to stop sweating.

The temperature had jumped again after the storm, which wasn't helping.

Tracy opened the door.

Ben held his breath for a moment. "It's good to see you," he said.

She stepped back and invited him in.

Austin stood at the back of the foyer. "Hey, Ben."

"Hey." He handed each of them a box.

Tracy opened hers.

"From a chocolatier in Stratford," he said. "I'd heard they were good. And no cherry truffles."

Tracy immediately popped a truffle in her mouth.

Austin's eyes popped out when he opened his box. "Did you do this?" He held the box of artistically cut crudités toward his mother so she could see.

"I learned how on nights when the Peregrines were away."

Austin studied a radish that had been sliced into layers. "I feel bad for eating this: it's beautiful."

"If you don't eat it, the worms in the green bin will."

"Well, if you put it that way. But first..." Before Tracy could even react, Austin stole one of her truffles. "These also look too good to pass up."

Tracy rolled her eyes. "I just made some iced tea. Anyone want a drink?"

"I can help," Ben said.

"This time, you're my guest."

While Tracy was in the kitchen, Ben spoke to Austin. He needed to right his wrongs. "Listen. First off, thank you for coming to my rescue on Monday. I...this is really hard for me to say...I relapsed, which is why I didn't answer. I didn't want you to hear me at my worst."

Ben summarized his entire past to Austin. At sixteen, Austin was old enough for the full truth. If Ben was going to date his mother, Austin needed to know everything about the man standing before him. Austin didn't bat an eyelash.

"I can kind of get a brain that's not listening to you," Austin said after Ben finished.

If only everyone understood how addiction worked on the brain, the world would be a better place. "Thanks, Austin. And..." This was the hardest part. "I'm sorry for..." His stomach tightened. "I'm sorry for wanting to use your rally video to recruit more teens going through difficult times. The alcohol was still talking, and I didn't realize it. I thought being ten years sober meant I was cured. They told me in treatment that once an alcoholic, always an alcoholic, but I didn't think alcoholism spoke that way. I still take full responsibility, of course, but I'm sorry I got you involved."

Tracy stood in the doorway between the dining room and the family room. Austin had his back to her.

"It hurts to be used."

"Again, I'm really sorry. I spent my ten years at the Peregrines scared every day that I'd lose my job and that the entire cycle—getting fired, then drinking, and then being back on the streets—would start again. When that video went viral, I just saw another way to not lose my job. I'm sorry, Austin."

Austin shook his head in sorrow. "They teach you in school about how addiction ruins your life, but they don't tell you these kinds of details. At least you never followed through with it. And you're trying to make up for it, which is more than most corporations do. I believed your apology on Monday, and I do now, too."

Ben held out his hand, and Austin accepted it.

Tracy entered and set the drinks on the table: iced tea for her and Ben, and water for Austin, since he couldn't have caffeine.

A glint of Austin's impish personality flashed across his face. "No stammering this time, Ben. Pretty good."

Oh, fudge.

"Stammering?" Tracy asked, confused.

Double fudge.

A grin covered Austin's face. "Mom, you should've seen him the other week. He was practising apologizing."

Tracy snickered. "Really?"

Ben sighed but smiled. "Keep going. I deserve it."

"He just couldn't get it. He'd keep saying, 'I'm s-s-s...'"

The most beautiful smile appeared on Tracy's face. "Okay, that's cute."

"Yeah, yeah, I found apologizing hard," Ben said dryly. "Chalk it up to the hard shell around my cherry-truffle heart."

"The Fonz stammered like that when he first tried apologizing. I remember my family laughing so hard."

The what? Or who? Ben made eye contact with Austin, who shrugged.

"Seriously?" Tracy asked Ben. "You have no idea who Fonzie is? A pop culture icon of the seventies and eighties?"

"I was born in 1982. I have to keep on top of *current* pop culture. Not old stuff." He winked at Austin, who laughed.

Tracy's mouth gaped. "You are so going to get it!"

Austin covered his peripheral vision with his hands. "I'm taking the bus to Dad's so I don't have to hear or see you two. I have newfound freedom, Ben! I'm going to exercise it."

Austin texted on his phone, presumably to Eric, and two minutes later, he was out the door.

Ben was surprised. "You're good with that?"

"I thought more about what you and Pauline said. I've found a few therapists experienced in helping parents of disabled children. I'm going to make some calls tomorrow. But in the meantime, I can take one step and let him bus to his dad's without me checking my phone."

"We're both taking it one step at a time, aren't we?"

Tracy tossed the pillows aside, and Ben pulled her down on top of him.

"You realize," she said, her voice low and sexy, "that my being older makes me more experienced. Men sometimes get weirded out by that."

Ben laughed. "How many younger men have you been with?"

Tracy turned beet red. "That's...not what I meant. Men just like being the ones with...more experience."

Ben chuckled. "The important thing for me that June night was meeting this sexy woman who could outsmart me. I had to get to know her, even if kissing the best friend of my employee was going to be the biggest mistake of my life."

Tracy drew finger down his neck. "Was it a mistake?"

Ben pulled her face toward his. "Fudge, no."

The warmth of her lips on his held the promise that everything would turn out fine. When Tracy lifted her head, he asked, "Why don't you swear, actually?"

"It's just easier to not do it at all than to watch my language. It's not appropriate at work, and Austin can get suspended for using it at school and his dance studio." She suddenly turned serious. "There is something important I'd like to ask you. I find you…all of you…incredibly sexy. But you're a fitness nut. I'm not and never will be. Is that a deal breaker?"

Ben tucked her hair behind her ears. "I'm attracted to you as you are now, Tracy. I want you to feel good about who you are, inside and out. I would never expect you to change your body for me."

She stood up.

"Did I say something wrong? I mean it. I love you as you are, and I want you to be happy as you are."

Tracy reached for his hand and pulled him up. "I was just thinking that with Austin's newfound freedom and my phone in my purse by the front door, I don't know when he'll be back. So…bedroom?"

Ben kissed Tracy on the nose. "Not sure I can wait that long." He kissed her on the neck. "I seem unable…" He kissed her on the ear. "To keep my lips off you." He kissed her on the mouth.

They eventually made it to her bedroom. It took a little time, though.

CHAPTER 42

He was wearing a brand new suit because he wanted a suit that stood the test of time.

Benjamin Landry was staying for the long haul.

But it was a really expensive suit.

"I don't think I can do this." He turned his application, tucked away in an envelope, over and over in his hand.

Pauline, for once dressed in a costume that showed her face and hands so she could serve customers—the Mad Hatter— smiled at him. "Your idea to turn the autumn festival into a Halloween one so the committee's work wouldn't be in vain made Tracy cry. No matter what happens next, Ben, you've already proven yourself."

Susie patted him on the back. "I told you: show people your good heart, Big Ben."

Pauline giggled. "Big Ben? Like the clock tower in London?"

Ben shot his sister a look. "You need to stop calling me that in public."

"Why did I never think of that?" Pauline said. "Would've made my years at the Peregrines so much easier. I could've just started chiming to let out my frustrations." She bumped Ben with her shoulder and he bumped her back.

"Does that mean I'm forgiven?"

Pauline nodded. "It does."

Susie and Pauline returned to the work at hand: ensuring Ben looked like the perfect job applicant for when he surprised Tracy, who was standing by the door of Claire's Tea Shop spreading the word that she was the new owner of the Belmont Village Chocolate House. The chocolate store had temporarily closed, as planned. But it would allow her time to learn the business, make her first improvements, and settle the divorce.

"I'm still flabbergasted by the price," Ben said.

"Flabbergasted?" Susie smoothed out his lapels. "Does anyone still use that word?"

"I do when I pay for an expensive suit."

"I don't follow," Pauline said. "You have lots of suits."

For once in his life, Ben answered without shame. "Most of my clothing is second-hand. Including my suits. My goal for the past ten years has been to save as much as possible to reduce my chances of ending up in financial oblivion in case I started drinking again."

Pauline's jaw dropped. "All those suits…?"

"Were mostly from the Salvation Army."

Pauline blinked. "Wow. I made so many assumptions about you."

"I had lots of reasons for not wanting to tell people, and I'm sure we can both agree I was not the most likeable person. It's okay."

Susie stood back and studied Ben, and Pauline stepped in line with her. Both women nodded in unison.

"And?" Ben asked.

Susie turned him around to face the mirror. "What do you think? Is this how you pictured yourself dressing up for a job interview?"

He raised his eyes. His breath caught. The reflection no longer showed a man whose pain had caused him to hurt others. The disgust that had turned his stomach that day a few weeks before had disappeared.

He'd forgiven himself.

Now, he saw the Benjamin Landry from long ago, the one who could again be trusted to care for others, the one who would do everything possible to never hurt anyone.

"Even better," he said.

Pauline offered her arm, and Ben took it. "Then let me lead you to the most important job interview of your life." A hint of mischief sparkled in her eye. "Big Ben."

Even if the absolute worst happened—if Tracy refused his offer—Ben at least had friends, had found his heart again, and perhaps most important of all...

Ben was no longer a cherry truffle.

AUSTIN CAME over to the counter to pick up a tray of tea and food. Seeing him in one of Todd's old costumes gave Tracy hope that Austin still had a professional career ahead of him. The side effects of the medication had subsided somewhat, but whether that was the passage of time or the lack of emotional upheaval— or both—she didn't know. He was still having seizures, so they weren't done with their medication journey. But they were seeing improvement. Plus, throughout this ordeal, Tracy had forgotten one important point: Austin hadn't had a single seizure while dancing.

There was definitely reason to continue hoping.

"You look stunning, Mom."

Tracy wore a rose tea dress from the 1920s, with a square neckline, three-quarter length sleeves, a pleated bust, Empire waist, tiered tulle skirt, sheer overlay, and fancy embroidery. She had rented it from a local costume store. Jan, delighted to have been asked to style her daughter's hair, had rolled it up to the nape of her neck, secured it with hairpins, and added in some faux pearls.

"Thank you. So do you."

Austin whispered, "I'm in a Todd Parson's costume for the second time this year!" He performed an *entrechat quatre*, a ballet jump that involved keeping his legs straight underneath him while he switched his feet back and forth. Tracy would not attempt to copy him, not if she wanted to retain her dignity.

Austin carried the tea and food to the customers.

Each store and restaurant in Belmont Village was open today, the Saturday before Halloween, and all owners had dressed up in a theme that suited their business. Claire's Tea Shop's theme, naturally, was a tea party. Ben had paid each student in Austin's ballet class an honorarium to play a prince or princess, with no pressure to play any romantic role.

Tracy had been enjoying the past two weeks with Ben—he'd driven in from New Hamburg and continued meeting with the committee to alter the plans as required. They went on dates, and she felt giddy each time. The joy of fresh love!

When he told her he was going to spend the day with Susie, though, she had to admit she was disappointed.

"We haven't had our family Thanksgiving yet," he'd said. "I've missed it every year since I started working for the Peregrines."

She understood. It was just too bad that he couldn't see the fruits of his labour: families having a wonderful time, and attendance for the postponed festival at an all-time high.

When there was a break in the foot traffic of customers enjoying the festival, Tracy looked around. Todd was talking with Austin and some of the other teens, but where was Pauline?

Tracy glimpsed her best friend, but then something as delicious as several triple-fudge chocolate truffles caught her eye instead.

Holy sugar.

Dressed in a perfectly tailored navy suit, crisp white shirt, paisley tie, and those polished brown shoes, Ben looked bold and stunning.

"Ms. Tschirhart," Pauline, as the Mad Hatter, said formally. "Your next applicant, Mr. Landry." Pauline bowed and stepped away.

Before Tracy could react, Ben wrapped his arms around her and pulled her in. His warm breath sent shivers down her spine as he whispered in her ear. "You look gorgeous. But I think that dirndl was easier to take off."

Tracy blushed.

Ben stepped back and scratched the back of his neck before handing her the envelope. He actually *was* an applicant as Pauline had said.

She opened the envelope and pulled out the pages inside. The first few words of the cover letter made her heart flutter.

Dear Tracy,

I love you. I know some of my past actions have left the taste of cherry truffles on your palate, but I hope this past month has, overall, shown you the triple-fudge truffle I truly am, even if I have a few remnants of cherry left. (Looks like the chocolatier forgot to clean the bowl when he made me.)

Despite my bits of cherry, I hope you will allow me to remain in your life. However, I do not wish to be just a man who loves you and wishes to be loved by you. This note is more than a love letter; it is also my business proposal.

I have loved hearing about your new business venture, and I hope by now you know I fully support your vision. Would you accept me as an investor? Aside from my marketing experience, DIY skills, and newfound knowledge of Belmont Village, I am well acquainted with cherry truffles and, I hope, triple-fudge truffles.

Literally and metaphorically.

(I actually quite enjoy your microwave brownies, too. We could call them Oh, What the Fudge. *Like an ice cream bar, only…a microwave brownie bar. We could offer different liquid bases, like concentrated tea, hazelnut milk, full-fat cream, because OWTF, right? No swearing needed. But I digress.)*

My offer to invest is not an attempt at purchasing a job. It is a demonstration of how strongly I believe in your vision. Extra money coupled with my experience can help you achieve it faster. I would, of course, work in the shop, too.

Another benefit I would bring to your company: I have been told I make wonderful kisses. Interpret that however you please.

My resume is attached. I am free all night to talk. I understand your amazing, talented, funny, compassionate son will be staying with his father for the night. That suggests your schedule is therefore open. If so, I look forward to being interviewed by you at your house. I have no known allergies to kisses. Chocolate or otherwise.

Love,

Benjamin Landry

Tracy fought to keep a straight face.

She looked up and saw Pauline and Susie watching her eagerly. So, they'd known about Ben's plan. Tracy really had special friends in her life.

She gazed into Ben's hazel eyes and envisioned what this particular "interview" might look like. "This is rather short notice, you understand. I was planning to spend the evening watching two movies by myself. But I could squeeze you in."

"I'm very confident in my abilities to satisfy your needs."

Tracy and Ben tried to retain their composure.

She moved the cover letter to the back and read the résumé. Her hand flew to her lips when she read one particular entry.

May 2005 — Feb 2007, In Need of Shelter, various locations between Toronto, Ontario, and Montreal, Quebec

- *Spent most of this period addicted to alcohol*
- *Unable to protect my sister when she was in trouble at university*
- *Unable to help my parents when they received life-changing diagnoses*
- *Unable to help my friends when they needed support for any reason*
- *Witnessed the woman I loved die after she received no support for her addiction*
- *Committed to turning my life around due to the above events*

Ben's eyes had already welled up by the time Tracy's gaze met his. "Your 'friend' who died of an overdose was…was your girlfriend?"

He blinked his tears away. "She was the last woman I loved before you. I only ever called her 'a friend' because to say anything closer to the truth would have hurt too much."

Any words Tracy wanted to say escaped from her voice, and the hand holding Ben's papers trembled.

Ben clasped her hand in his to still it. "Sebastian helped me see that she was the real reason I kept pushing everyone away from me, no matter the cost: to ensure I would never allow myself to be that vulnerable again."

He lay his application on the counter and lifted both her

hands to his heart. "He helped me realize I was already following my instincts by stopping here where I knew people, to help me avoid drinking. That was already a sign that my life wasn't going to repeat itself. He said that my one afternoon of drinking was precisely because I'd cut myself off from every-one...especially one I'd come to love."

The kind, gentle smile Tracy cherished appeared on his lips, and he kissed Tracy's hands. Beautiful butterflies fluttered in her stomach.

Ben's face became serious. "I had to revisit my darkest self with someone who knew me back then to understand that. I have a therapist now to help me." Ben lowered their hands and took a step back. "I have to be honest: I don't know for sure it won't happen again. I just know that I'm committed to doing my best. Will you be okay that?"

Part of Tracy wanted to ditch her duties, jump into her Yaris with Ben—or his Porsche—and disappear to her house now. She loved him with all her heart. But she also understood what he was asking: could she love him if he relapsed again?

She didn't know. Tracy had been so full of anger that she hadn't gone to help Ben when he needed it.

She was broken, too.

But Pauline had stood by his side. So had Susie. They still stood by his side now. Well, metaphorically speaking. They were attempting to give Tracy and Ben privacy in the crowded café by standing maybe twenty feet away, but they were watching closely.

Tracy had her own demons to deal with. How had she reacted when everyone had tried to help her? By pushing them away. Including Ben. And here he was, ready to make a more formal commitment to her. What if Austin's diagnosis wors-ened? Could Tracy guarantee she wouldn't react the same way again? Her new therapist said she exhibited classic signs of post-traumatic stress disorder. Tracy was committed to healing herself, but she also couldn't guarantee she wouldn't relapse in her own way, either.

Ben was taking a risk on her. Was she ready to take a risk on him?

"We both carry deep pain inside ourselves," she said. "I don't know if it's possible to ever fully heal that. You're obviously ready to support me if my pain comes out." She squeezed his hand. "I'm ready to support you if yours does, too."

Ben's eyes shone like glistening hazel-milk chocolate. He reached for her face and pulled it up to his. Tracy hoped for a deep, long kiss, but it didn't last long: Pauline and Susie were whooping and hollering.

Ben shot them both a look. "I guess I can't get back at Pauline in her place of business but maybe I could get Susie."

"Or wait till we're in business," Tracy added.

Ben pecked her on the cheek. "You. I'm just an investor." He tucked his hands into his pockets, the playful bravado completely evaporated. "I hope what I'm about to say isn't intrusive. But I asked David to let me tour the chocolate shop, too. I think we can renovate the back so we can have a small room with a cot for Austin. I also have lots of marketing ideas that will help you—even though I'm sure you already have lots of your own." He smiled and pointed to Pauline, who raised her hands to ask "What?" "She thinks I can still sell bar soap for men. Imagine what I could do for chocolate for women."

Tracy laughed. "So, I'm supposed to kiss you, accept your money, and then loan you out via online videos to other women?"

Ben shrugged. "Yes?"

Tracy wrapped her arms around him. "Let's start with the kiss, Mr. Landry. And then I'm going to have to ask you to continue the interview at my house."

Ben pulled her in, his hazel eyes warm as he smiled. "That's a fair offer."

Tracy ignored the noisy jamboree that seemed to include most of the store, led by her best friend and new friend, as she enjoyed the most amazing triple-fudge-chocolate truffle kiss with the most remarkable triple-fudge truffle kind of man.

EPILOGUE

S tanding in the alleyway behind the Belmont Village
Chocolate House in July, Tracy lifted Ben's
sunglasses off his face. "Have I ever told you that your hazel
eyes were the second thing that attracted me to you?"

"I don't think you have."

She brushed her lips against his, and Ben pulled her in for a
kiss before they opened the store for the day.

"And that your kiss was the third thing?" Tracy asked.

Ben shook his head. "What was the first thing?"

Tracy smiled and unlocked the back door without
answering.

Tracy loved few things more than making Ben squirm.

It was really no surprise. She'd already told him before, just
not in this context.

And, as Ben had told her countless times, context in
messaging was everything.

She flicked on the lights to the store. She still couldn't
believe she was standing in her own business. After she'd taken

over in October, Tracy and Ben had done initial renovations over the first two weeks of November, updating the tables, chairs, and floors, while David introduced Tracy and Ben to chocolate-making. They reopened in time for Christmas shopping.

Of course, chocolate-making wasn't something you learned in two weeks, and Tracy retained all of David's employees. But she wanted to understand how everything worked so she understood her employees' jobs. David also continued to work four half days a week.

"I can't leave my love," he'd said to her, with his wife by his side. Cecilia had laughed.

They closed for another three weeks in January to complete renovations before opening in time for Valentine's purchases. Those renovations included the OWTF Bar, complete with a bank of small microwaves for baking microwave brownies in a mug from scratch.

Tracy leaned on Ben's shoulder and admired their work.

"We make a great team, don't we?"

He reached around her waist and kissed the top of her head. "We do. And I love you with all my heart. But I have a hard time believing that a year ago you knew we'd end up together. What was the first thing? If you don't tell me, I'm not going to let you go."

Tracy extended her arm around his hips. "That's a very enticing reason to stay quiet."

They'd kept the wooden shelving across the back walls for boxed truffles and other packaged delights. They replaced the massive, aging, brass-outlined display cases with smaller, modern domes that would let them add smaller batches of beautifully decorated truffles more frequently without looking like stock was running on empty. Perennial favourites were now in both pre-packaged boxes of varying sizes and stored in bins between two groups of the new domes.

After looking at David's financials, Tracy had suspected societal shifts had plagued him as they had Claire over the decades: mass production, with its lower prices, had stolen many of his customers. The difference was that Claire had adjusted without leaving her brand—serving only loose-leaf tea. David, by contrast, had relied solely on customer loyalty and the ingenuity of a handful of new products.

Now thanks to Ben's investment and marketing skills, and Tracy's business skills and knowledge of chocolate and her target markets, Tracy had a solid business plan and enough collateral to make the necessary changes for a strong start out of the gate.

However, a business partner with a lot of drive would be helpful and would ensure the community had a chocolate shop should anything ever happen to her. Tracy was in good health, Austin was heading into his last year of high school, and she was with the man of her dreams.

But if she'd learned anything in the past two years, it was that the perfect box of chocolates could be overturned in an instant.

Austin would never take over the shop. His dreams lay elsewhere, and the perfect person to take over should something happen to Tracy was standing right next to her. Besides, they'd already discussed moving in together. They'd simply chosen to move slowly on Austin's account.

What she wanted to propose was happy middle ground.

"I loved your idea for softer lighting." She turned around to face him. "I didn't realize that I'd spent so much time in corporate offices that harsh blue had become normal for me."

Ben's face relaxed into that gorgeous smile she got to see every day at work and sometimes at home. They also didn't live together because he'd insisted on staying in his own apartment to give the Tschirharts their privacy for any time Eric came over. His support of her original family had touched her so deeply in those early days when she'd discovered his attraction to her.

The hard part about working with Ben Landry was the difficulty in working side by side while keeping their hands off each other. But since their relationship had begun as pure, intense physical attraction, could they expect any less?

"But you still haven't told me number one. As your investor, I'm certain there's a law out there somewhere about access to information."

Tracy smiled. "I'm certain there is. So, I should probably obey that law, shouldn't I?"

"I would highly recommend it."

Tracy pulled a legal-sized envelope out of her purse.

"Uh-oh," Ben said.

Tracy stroked his arm and opened the envelope. "Ben Landry, the first thing that attracted me to you was your drive and determination. In a single night, you raised millions of dollars for research into childhood diseases —"

He quickly interrupted her. "I had lots of help, though, Tracy. You know that." Another aspect of him that had changed: he always credited others now.

"But you spearheaded the project from the Peregrines side and worked with the hospital."

"Who knew me through my mother. I could've raised more had I listened to their advice. And Pauline's."

She gave him her "you're doing it again" look, the one that said he was beating himself up. It was one thing to acknowledge your mistakes and learn from them. It was another to act like you still deserved to be punished.

"As I was saying, the first thing that attracted me to you was your drive and determination because you had *contributed consid-erably* to helping raise millions of dollars. I'd participated in a few of those fundraisers myself a couple of times, so I knew that was no easy feat. I was intrigued."

"But not enough to say yes when I asked you to work with me."

"But enough that you never left my mind." She pulled out a contract and took a breath. If he said no, it could make things awkward between them. But she also couldn't imagine a life without him in it.

She pressed it against her chest so he couldn't see its cover page.

"Ben, I love you. You have taken my son under your wing, have miraculously smoothed things out with my ex-husband, and have worked your magic on my store." Ben blushed. "We've talked a few times about moving past dating, so…I thought I'd take the first step." She presented the contract. "Would you be the co-owner of the Belmont Village Chocolate House?"

Ben's mouth gaped. His hand slowly reached for the contract. "Tracy…I don't know what to say."

"I'm hoping 'yes'…?"

He flipped through the contract. "I should probably read this carefully. You know, make sure there's no clause that says 'must submit to mascot-level jokes every Thursday,' or something like that."

"Take your time. Definitely have a lawyer look it over. I want you to feel good about this. But David had no one to pass this store on to, and if anything happens to me, I want this store left to someone I can trust with all my heart and who cares about this community. You already act like my partner. I'd like to make it official. What do you think? About the idea, at least?"

Ben wrapped his arms around her tight.

"I love it, but not as much as I love you, Tracy Tschirhart."

"And I love you, Benjamin Landry."

Tracy took all the time in the world to enjoy a triple-fudge-chocolate kiss with the cherry truffle who'd melted her heart.

SETTING THE RECORD STRAIGHT

Love on Belmont mixes real locations and situations with fictional ones. Here are some of the facts.

HOMELESSNESS

Homelessness has *many* causes. For information on homelessness in Canada, visit www.homelesshub.ca.

Although the shelter Ben stayed at is fictional, the Out of the Cold program did exist. It was a volunteer-run program that offered homeless people in Kitchener-Waterloo overnight shelter in the winter, usually in churches, from 1999-2015. You'll find information at https://wwwkwootcca.github.io/dev/, though the website was last updated in 2017 at time of printing.

(All characters in the novel are fictional.)

TRAUMA AND PARENTING

Tracy's story, though fictional, was inspired by my own experience with trauma. I was diagnosed with partial previa during my first pregnancy, which necessitated five weeks in the hospital, a C-section birth, and a short NICU stay for my baby. My trauma expressed itself differently, but I didn't seek out the help I needed in part because I believed I didn't need therapy. After all, I was a woman, biologically made and programmed to give birth. I could handle all this, right?

Wrong.

I've observed all too often that we normalize trauma around birth and parenting as part of our lived experience. Don't be afraid to access mental health resources for yourself the same way you do physical health resources. Let's start making mental health check-ups normal.

EPILEPSY

Austin's form of epilepsy is similar to my own, but my eyes flicker and my seizures last only a few seconds. Other than that, our journeys are very different. For example, I was eleven when I was diagnosed. I wasn't even aware I was having seizures; my parents noticed my symptoms and thankfully had them investigated before I was old enough to drive. In those days the Internet didn't exist, so only in high school did I meet my first friends with epilepsy.

I had to create Austin's medication journey a little after mine, though, to give me something real to work from. My neurologist said five medications apply to my situation. I'm on the fourth. The third has a tendency to produce a rash, and since I'd reacted with a rash to one of the first two, he refused to let me try the third one: he'd lost three patients in his decades-long career to rash.

As of this writing, I have partial control of my seizures, and I won't lie: it's been nice. (Out of my forty-plus years, I've only been on medication for a total of maybe three years over two periods.) But the difficulties with memory that Austin experiences are real not only for me but for millions of people with epilepsy who need these medications to control their seizures. If you meet people who seem forgetful, bear in mind they may be on medication they don't wish to tell you about. One of my most recent embarrassing moments came when I had to count plants into groups of six in front of a cashier and I suddenly couldn't do it.

For more information about epilepsy, visit epilepsy.ca or epilepsy.com. If you'd like to learn more about the lived experiences of people with epilepsy and you're on Twitter, follow #EpilepsyAwareness. If you listen to podcasts, *Brain Ablaze* is an excellent one. For more general neurological research, look up a podcast by the Krembil Institute, which is part of the University Health Network out of Toronto.

Austin will eventually get his own young adult series that will explore the backstory to his diagnosis. I plan for the first book in this series to be published in 2024. Email me (author@loriwolfheffner.com) if you'd like to be added to an email list for updates.

PEREGRINE FALCONS ON A TV STATION?

Kitchener has indeed had a peregrine family living atop the TV station on King Street in the past. I don't know if it's still there, but the peregrine family lived at CTV Kitchener in 2017, the time this novel takes place.

BEEP BEEP

"Beep Beep" was written by Carl Cicchetti and Donald Claps and sung by the Playmates. It was released in 1958. I've loved it since I was a teenager (in the nineties, not the fifties!).

If you've never heard it, I won't spoil it here. But it is about a Nash Rambler, which was marketed as a family vehicle, and a stylish Cadillac getting into a bit of an unintended race. It's a fun song. Look up "the Beep Beep song" on YouTube and have a listen.

You can also read more about the Nash Rambler and the song here: https://www.blog.ontariocars.ca/beep-beep-the-story-of-the-nash-rambler/.

A co-op student who worked for me in early 2022, Savina Rueffer, researched and wrote the article.

MEASURING LIKE A CANADIAN

In the 1970s, Canada moved over to the metric system. For some reason, though, many measurements colloquially remained imperial. For example, I buy my apples in 5-lb bags, but it's about 100 km to Toronto.

Because this series takes place in Canada, I've retained our colloquial use of measurements. You'll find a more detailed explanation here: https://www.clivemaxfield.com/coolbeans/how-to-measure-things-like-a-canadian/.

BELMONT VILLAGE

Belmont Village is real and is a wonderful, quaint shopping and eating strip on Belmont Avenue in Kitchener, Ontario, Canada. You can learn more about it at TheBelmontVillage.ca.

Although the stores and businesses I use in *Love on Belmont* are fictional, if there's overlap with a real store, I speak with the owner(s) first to ensure they're comfortable with me moving forward with my idea. Claire's Tea Shop is partially inspired by All Things Tea, owned and run by George Broughton. Their website is AllThingsTea.ca. They can ship their delicious teas anywhere Canada Post can ship.

The Belmont Village Chocolate House is completely fictional. Instead, I tasted chocolate from these fine chocolatiers in Canada to better understand the flavours of chocolate: Hummingbird Chocolate in Almonte, Ontario; Qantu in Montreal, Quebec; SOMA Chocolatemaker in Toronto, Ontario; and AURA-LA Pasteries + Provisions in Kitchener, Ontario.

If you ever find yourself in Kitchener, Ontario, Canada, drop by Belmont Village for a bite to eat, a package of tea, a lovely gift, or just to see where Tracy and Ben may have had that fateful second chance.

STAY IN TOUCH

Did you enjoy the book? You can stay in touch with Lori by visiting LoveOnBelmont.com and signing up for Lori's newsletter. She writes each one herself, so it's her words to you. You'll receive updates on *Love on Belmont* and other books, be the first to hear about specials, and get deleted scenes. Plus, if you haven't read the short story prequels to *Tea Shop for Two*, you can download them for free by subscribing.

ENJOY ALL THE LOVE ON BELMONT BOOKS

Join Tracy, Ben, and all your other friends on Belmont Avenue, where love and tea create a magical blend 🩶.

THE LOVE ON BELMONT PREQUEL SHORT STORIES

1. Claire's Tea Shop
2. Trick or Tea
3. Oh, Christmas Tea

THE LOVE ON BELMONT NOVELS

1. Tea Shop for Two
2. Oh, What the Fudge
3. Tentative release date November 2023. Sign up to Lori's newsletter for updates!

Visit LoveOnBelmont.com to buy your next book!

ACKNOWLEDGEMENTS

Part of the inspiration for this book came from a time in my life when things looked pretty bleak. I'd first like to thank the team at Grand River Hospital NICU in the late 2000s for looking after our first child. Thank you, too, to Nasrin, our midwife, for supporting us through the birth of both our children; to the obstetricians who delivered them; and to the different therapists I've worked with over the years who have helped with my psychological well-being.

Sometimes psychotherapy isn't the right path for me, so thank you, also, to Conrad Grebel University College's certificate program in conflict management. When I have to take a back road to good mental health, working through some of their workshops has really helped.

Thank you to my friends and extended family for all your emotional support, visits, and offers to babysit. Our family survived because of you, and detailing all your help would require another novel. Know Corey and I couldn't have done it without you.

But most importantly, I can't thank my husband enough for sticking by me during perhaps the most turbulent time in my life. PTSD, even if self-diagnosed (I was too scared an official diagnosis would require me to stop breastfeeding, the only lifeline I believed I had at the time), is extremely hard on a marriage. We survived thanks to you.

Once our second child was born, things became easier, and

I'm happy to report that we're all doing well. It really does take a village to raise a family.

Research for Ben's story was conducted predominantly through articles in *The Waterloo Region Record* and *The Toronto Star*. With permission, local activists shared social media stories of those living in encampments. I've also learned much about alcoholism over the years, and conducted fresh research to ensure my knowledge was still current.

Thank you to *Brain Ablaze* for the incredible online community you've built. And thank you to Epilepsy Southcentral Ontario, EpLink (the epilepsy research program of the Ontario Brain Institute), the Epilepsy Foundation, and the University Health Network for all the information. If you want to learn more about epilepsy, following these organizations on social media is a great place to start.

But there's also a practical side to writing a book. So I'd like to thank my writing team:

- Heather Wright, consulting editor and mentor;
- ali macgee, consulting editor and mentor;
- Susan Fish, editor;
- Jennifer Dinsmore, proofreader;
- Michelle Fairbanks, book cover designer;
- ZG Stories, marketing consultant;
- Anita Woodard, virtual administrator and bookkeeper;
- Savina Rueffer, co-op student at Lori Straus Communications; and
- Phoebe Wolfe, communications specialist at Lori Straus Communications.

My family also provides a lot of support. Thank you to Mom and Dad for enrolling me in dance; to Kristin for answering some of my dance questions; and to Corey, Khristopher, and Jonnathan for being patient with my work hours.

And last, but never least, thank you to my dance teachers: to Deardra King-Leslie for teaching me tap and jazz for over fifteen years; to my ballet teachers, Beth Krug and Sharon Laramie, for supporting me during my RAD exams in my youth; to April March for supporting my competitive dance career later on; and to Rosemarie Harris and Julia Allan for reintroducing me to ballet as an adult.

ABOUT LORI

Lori's first memory of Belmont neighbourhood is of her falling out of her bed at her grandparents' home when she was perhaps three. Opa, her grandfather, sadly passed away in his mid-60s, but that didn't stop Oma, her grandmother, from creating many, many happy memories in her home for her family.

Across the tracks and up a set of cement stairs was Belmont Village, a quaint shopping strip. Oma always bought her lottery tickets there and often took Lori and her sister to the convenience store to buy them a sugary treat.

But at the time, Lori had no idea Belmont neighbourhood and Belmont Village would be the source of the most wonderful romance in her life: her future husband.

When she met her future in-laws about 20 years later, they learned they had already met: Lori's in-laws had run that small convenience store until the mid-80s. Moreover, their paths had crossed often with those of Lori's mom's family before Lori was even a thought.

Happy memories, shared fates, love…
And shopping.

How could Belmont Village *not* be the perfect place to set a sweet romance series about different couples in different stages of a relationship?

Lori lives in Waterloo, Ontario, with her husband and two sons and visits Belmont Village whenever she can.

facebook.com/loriwolfheffner

twitter.com/LoriWolfHeffner

instagram.com/loriwolfheffner

goodreads.com/lori_wolf-heffner

bookbub.com/author/lori-wolf-heffner

pinterest.com/loriwolfheffner

amazon.com/author/loriwolfheffner

CPSIA information can be obtained
at www.ICGtesting.com
Printed in the USA
BVHW080620091122
651119BV00001B/2